# STORMS:

THEIR

## NATURE, CLASSIFICATION AND LAWS.

WITH

THE MEANS OF PREDICTING THEM BY THEIR EMBODIMENTS

## THE CLOUDS.

BY WILLIAM BLASIUS,

FORMERLY PROFESSOR OF THE NATURAL SCIENCES IN THE LYCEUM OF HANOVER.

---

PHILADELPHIA:

PORTER & COATES,

822 CHESTNUT STREET.

WESTCOTT & THOMSON,
*Stereotypers and Electrotypers, Phila.*

SHERMAN & CO.,
*Printers, Phila.*

TO THE

MEMORY OF MY BROTHER,

PROFESSOR J. H. BLASIUS,

AND OF MY FRIEND,

PROFESSOR LOUIS AGASSIZ,

TO THE FORMER OF WHOM I OWE MY ENTIRE EDUCATION AND TRAINING, AND TO THE LATTER MANY ACTS OF FRIENDSHIP, AND THE INTEREST AND ENCOURAGEMENT WHICH INDUCED ME TO PERSEVERE IN THE INVESTIGATION OF METEOROLOGY,

THIS VOLUME IS

GRATEFULLY DEDICATED.

# INDEX TO PLATES.



# INDEX TO FIGURES.

# PREFACE.

In presenting in the following pages the results of my investigations and studies, I fulfil a long-cherished desire, and one which has received additional strength as often as accounts have reached me of the terrible disasters at sea taking place almost daily, and which can be to a great extent avoided by knowing the true nature of storms. I am convinced that the existing theories of the nature and laws of changes of weather are intrinsically erroneous, and that at least a much nearer approximation to the truth will be found in this volume.

I have not until now published the conclusions to which I had arrived principally because I found it necessary to corroborate them by other witness than my own. Twenty years ago I in vain exhausted every effort to obtain a hearing for what I believe to be the truth, and I have patiently awaited the development of the science and the formation of those investigating corps by whose observations I most hoped my views would be confirmed. When, a few years since, these institutions, for which I had labored so many years ago, became at last a realized fact, another difficulty presented itself in the method of investigation pursued; observations are made only at fixed periods of the day, which I am thoroughly convinced will never lead to definite results, since it necessitates averages, while I have aimed at a knowledge of individual phenomena by continuous observation. The consequence of the method of observation generally pursued is that an area of barometric depression is considered the storm itself, and the *cause* of the movement of air-currents, while I am certain that the storm is the conflict of air-currents of different temperatures, and the barometric depression the *effect* of their movement. And, in addition, the most important elements in the life of storms—heat, their originator, and the clouds, their embodiments—are those to which least attention has been paid.

In endeavoring to reach results from tangible facts, I have been compelled to discard much of the theoretical terminology at present in use—such as the terms "cyclone," "anti-cyclone," "dangerous semi-circle," "manageable semi-circle," "centre," "gradient," etc.—and to substitute such as grew out of the development of the subject.

Some familiar terms—as for example "stratus," "cumulo-stratus," "equatorial and polar currents," etc.—I have preserved, although in some cases with a slightly altered significance; their use, however, will be readily understood. Instead of the modern invention of the "barometric gradient," from which so much has been hoped and so little realized, I have introduced the *plane of meeting* (for which in the German language I would propose the name *Begegnungs-fläche*). It is defined in its position to the storm by the clouds, and has a meaning and an intimacy with the life of storms which make it more comprehensible and useful than the gradient; and it is besides much older, having been explained in my lectures twenty-two years ago.

I have found it necessary to represent the circulation of the atmosphere somewhat differently from the common acceptation, in order to explain the regions of calm (the "horse-latitudes"), the increased atmospheric pressure at the tropics, and the frequent existence of lower temperature there than in higher latitudes (see Blodget's *Climatology of the United States*), as well as some other phenomena. It would appear that Lieut. Maury has been credited as the author of the explanation of the calms at the tropics, but in a letter to me of Nov. 29, 1852, in acknowledging the receipt of my article in the New York *Times* (Appendix A), he says: "You have classed me in the storm-field, I observe, but I have not entered it either as a theorist or as an advocate of any theory. I am holding back for my facts yet." However, even if Lieut. Maury had conceived and published his explanation of the tropical calms before he received the New York *Times* article, his theory in truth neither explains the calms nor is in accord with the dynamics of aërial currents.

In conclusion, I trust that scientists will excuse in the following pages the positiveness of statement which is born of conviction, and the introduction of many explanations with which they are already familiar, but which may be unknown to the general reader. The Introductory, although of necessity personal in its tone, is important to a thorough understanding of the subject, and I should therefore wish it read. The chapter on "Corroborative Evidence" will be found to contain in great measure the practical application of my principles.

I cannot close these remarks without expressing to Joseph H. Coates, Esq., my heartiest thanks for the valuable assistance he has given me in preparing this work.

WILLIAM BLASIUS.

PHILADELPHIA, May 10, 1875.

# CONTENTS.

## CHAPTER I.

### INTRODUCTORY.



## CHAPTER II.

### THE SITUATION OF THE SCIENCE OF METEOROLOGY.



## CHAPTER III.

### AËRIAL CURRENTS, THEIR CAUSAL CONNECTION WITH THE VARIOUS CLOUD-FORMATIONS, AND THE CLASSIFICATION OF STORMS.



## CHAPTER IV.

### LOCAL STORMS AND THE PRIMARY ORIGIN OF ATMOSPHERIC DISTURBANCE.

## CHAPTER V.

PROGRESSIVE STORMS.—EQUATORIAL OR NORTH-EAST STORMS.—WINTER STORMS.



## CHAPTER VI.

PROGRESSIVE STORMS.—POLAR, OR SOUTH-EAST AND SOUTH-WEST STORMS.—SUMMER STORMS.



## CHAPTER VII.

LOCO-PROGRESSIVE STORMS.—TORNADOES.—HAIL-STORMS.—DUST-STORMS.—WATER-SPOUTS.

## CHAPTER VIII.

STORMS OF THE TORRID ZONE, AND THEIR PROBABLE INTIMATE CONNECTION WITH THOSE OF THE TEMPERATE ZONE.



## CHAPTER IX.

CORROBORATIVE EVIDENCE FROM OTHER SOURCES.



## CHAPTER X.

WEATHER PROGNOSTICS FROM THE CLOUDS, WITH SPECIAL HINTS FOR NAVIGATORS.



## CHAPTER XI.

METEOROLOGICAL OBSERVATION.

## APPENDIX.

# STORMS:

THEIR

# NATURE, CLASSIFICATION AND LAWS.

## CHAPTER I.

*INTRODUCTORY.*

TO assist in a more ready comprehension of the system of storms which it is the object of this volume to promulgate, I have thought it well to give here a brief account of the manner in which my principal conclusions have been reached. This at the same time will explain why, having, as I firmly believe, been enabled to establish facts of much importance to science, I have for so long neglected to urge them on public attention.

Coming to America from Germany in 1850, the greater part of the first two or three years of my residence here was spent in Cambridge, near Boston, with Prof. Agassiz, to whom I had been introduced by a letter from my brother, Prof. J. H. Blasius of Brunswick.

In the afternoon of August 22, 1851, in company with Mr. Stimpson, then an assistant of Prof. Agassiz, and afterward director of the Academy of Natural Science in Chicago, I was engaged in fishing for new species—or, as Agassiz expressed it in his humorous mood, "collecting intellectual food"—in a meadow at West Cambridge.

All at once our attention was attracted by a long, continuous rolling of thunder from the north-west, in front of us, where there appeared a very heavy black bank of cloud rising slowly above the horizon. It stretched from west-south-west to east-north-east.

The air was calm, sultry and oppressive. Not the slightest breeze was blowing, not a leaf moving. A death-like stillness prevailed around us in nature. The clouds had such a threatening appearance, particularly to me, who had never seen anything like it in Europe, that we thought of running immediately to shelter. But seeing that the cloud advanced very slowly, and at last seemed to cease moving entirely, we continued our work, and became so much interested in it that we forgot all about the approaching storm. About two hours after the first appearance of the cloud we returned to Old Cambridge, thinking no more about it.

The next morning, however, we learned from the newspapers that an extremely violent and destructive tornado had passed over West Cambridge, and from the account we found that about ten minutes after we had left it must have passed near the place where we had been fishing.

My first thought brought the tornado into some connection with the dark, heavy cloud which had attracted my attention. Mr. Stimpson and I started at once for the scene of destruction at West Cambridge. The road was literally covered with the curious from Boston and its neighborhood, attracted to the scene of destruction like ourselves; and the sight was worth the trouble to any one, but made a particularly forcible impression on my mind, as I had never before seen any spectacle approaching it.

I could scarcely trust my eyes. Large orchards were completely destroyed, oaks and maple trees two or two and a half feet in diameter broken, others twisted like a rope at an angle of 180° and more, still others uprooted and carried in a mutilated state forty or fifty paces distant. A great number of houses in West Cambridge and Medford were unroofed and the débris carried from fifty to a hundred paces away. A two-story brick house had been entirely demolished and carried away, so that scarcely a trace of it was left. Railroad cars had been blown from the track a great distance. A man and a horse had been lifted, whirled around and set down about a hundred yards off. Everything had been thrown into great confusion.

My interest in this mysterious phenomenon grew, and the desire to get light on its strange doings became so strong that I induced Mr. Stimpson to assist me in making a survey of the destruction, in order to discover, from the position in which the destroyed objects lay, the manner and direction in which the destructive force had acted.

Intuitively and without much reflection, I selected the portion where the destruction was very severe and evenly distributed over the whole width of the area. The question whether such a portion would be the most suitable for our purpose seemed to me quite affirmatively answered by the argument that the law governing the destructive *force* would be most perceptible where the destruction was the most general and severe.

This argument is so natural that I was not surprised in finding, by studying afterward the investigations of others, that they also had acted upon the same principle.

Redfield gives in the "American Journal of Science and Art" for October, 1841, p. 77, direct advice as to how investigations should be made. He says: "In order to make a just and satisfactory investigation of the effects of a tornado, it appears necessary to select portions of the track where the extension of wood or single trees on each side is found sufficient to mark clearly the exterior limits of the prostrating power, and where the effects on both sides of the axis are clearly developed."

I had adopted and followed the very rule and mode of investigation prescribed by Mr. Redfield, without at that time knowing it. But however wise this rule at first sight seems, I must declare it not only totally wrong, but even mischievous.

The section I had selected would have gone to prove to me that Redfield's theory of storms was the true one, while another section farther on in the track would have evidenced the truth of *Espy's* theory, which is entirely contradictory of Redfield's. Fortunately, I was then unacquainted with either of these two theories, and came therefore to no satisfactory results at the time.

The mode of investigation is always most important as to the results. But nowhere can it be exhibited more strikingly than here by showing the errors which I committed in my first survey, and which others have committed before me.

It will be seen from this how from the facts of one and the same phenomenon such contradictory results may be obtained as exist between Redfield's and Espy's—the Rotary and the Inblowing theory—by partial or disconnected observations. A section of a tornado twenty-five rods in length, which Mr. Redfield, in another paper, thinks is sufficient, will give us as little an idea of the law of this destructive phenomenon as a section of the middle of a fish can give us a just idea of the whole fish. It is absolutely necessary that we should have the *whole* of the phenomenon.

Without knowing Mr. Redfield's advice, Mr. Stimpson and I surveyed a section of about six times the size recommended by him. I then made a plan of the relative position and direction of the destroyed objects, and tried to arrive at the law of the direction of the destroying force by studying my plan, but without any definite conclusions. Thinking that we had not taken a long enough section to show the continuity of the destroying force, we continued the survey at each end, but without success. Prof. Agassiz, perceiving, probably, from our discussion on the subject, that we had no knowledge of the investigations of Redfield and Espy, tried to assist us by demonstrating on the black-

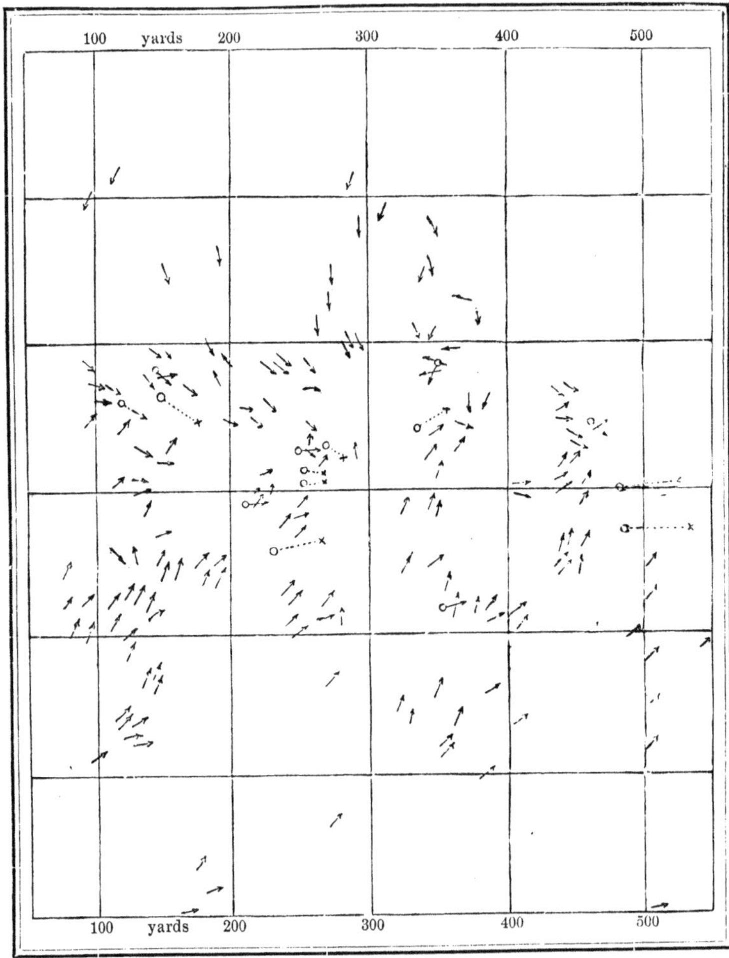


PLATE II.—MIDDLE SECTION OF THE WEST CAMBRIDGE TORNADO.

The arrows indicate fallen trees. Where two arrows cross, the one with a circle attached indicates the tree lying uppermost. Where a circle is connected with a cross by dots, it indicates the distance and direction that an object has been carried by the wind.

board what he had learned from the stormy discussions between the adherents of both theories on occasions of the yearly scientific meetings, but we were not satisfied.

The general results were as follows, and can be seen on the map of our survey. (*Plate II.*) The width of the destroyed area averaged from five hundred to six hundred paces. The general direction of the destroyed trees on the right side was inward, with an inclination forward; that of the left was inward, with a slight inclination backward, especially at the outer limit.

The right side of the destruction extended over about two-thirds of the whole width, and that of the left side over one-third. The line which is supposed to divide these two arrangements has been called the axis of the tornado. Over more than half of the whole width of the track on both sides of this axis the destroyed trees were found in all possible directions and positions, and in some parts there seemed to be particular confusion, trees crossing each other in every direction.

A rotary motion of the destroying force was very visible, but it did not seem to extend to the outer limits of the track of the tornado. Trees pointing forward or backward, and at the same time parallel to the axis, could not be found on the outer limits, as we should expect from the Rotary theory, the rotary motion being, however, quite evident in the middle of the track. There was also an upward motion exhibited just as clearly, for I found large trees torn out of the ground and carried far away. If I had stopped here, however, I should probably have become an adherent of the Rotary theory; but following the track toward the end, beyond Medford, I found in a cursory examination the appearance of the destruction changed. Here the rotary motion seemed less visible, and instead of it the in-blowing motion became more plainly exhibited, which might have led me to become an adherent of the In-blowing theory of Espy. But my experience in the West Cambridge section made Espy's theory as untenable as the Medford section made Redfield's. I felt quite discouraged at my inability to arrive at any definite and satisfactory results.

Seeing the use Prof. Agassiz made of Embryology, or the study of the phases of a living being from its earliest and simplest form to its complete development, and the progress he was making in Zoology by applying this method of investigation, the idea struck me that a similar course might be taken with my subject. Storms, I began to argue, have also a beginning, a duration and an end; they have in certain respects a life; they cannot remain in the same state during their existence, but must change in every moment of their life; like other living beings, they must develop themselves.

As all living beings appear first in the simple cellular form and assume in their growth more and more complications, passing through the principal types of lower organizations until they arrive at their own individual type, so I hoped to find an analogy in this tornado. I began to think that its actions must be more simple in its *beginning*, and more easily to be understood, than when it had developed itself to its greatest fury and caused the greatest destruction.

Animated by this hope, I started from the section I had surveyed in West Cambridge and walked about six miles toward the origin of the storm, always following back the track of destruction, until I came to the first destruction beyond Waltham. After having certainly ascertained that no traces were to be found west of this, I turned and walked along the right margin, which is indicated by the line *CD* (*Plate I., Fig.* 1), in the direction the tornado had taken, and noted by the compass the direction in which the destroyed trees or objects pointed.

Thus I found east of the Lexington road the first trees in the direction of the arrow 17. As I went farther the trees I met made a greater angle with the direction of the course of the track, as indicated by the arrow 18. Going farther, I found some trees broken in the direction of the arrow 19, and the broken top blown away at a still greater angle with the course of the track.

Continuing my walk, and always noting the direction of the destroyed trees, I found, at the arrow 20, trees corresponding in direction to those at 17. Farther on they made again larger angles with the course of the track, till at 21 I found them corresponding to those at 19. Between 20 and 21 was a meadow with few trees, but enough could be found to indicate plainly the direction of the destroying force. It appeared to me singular that no trees crossed each other as at West Cambridge, and it also struck me that I found a similarity in the arrangement of the trees over two sections. As I went farther on I found again trees in the direction of the arrow 22, corresponding to 20 and 17. Then they again turned gradually as I went on, always making larger angles with the course of the track, till they assumed at 24 a direction almost at right angles to it.

Finding a repetition of the same phenomenon a third time, I anticipated a *law*. So I stopped my onward march at the arrow 24; and following the trees lying in the same direction as those of 24, I crossed the track, walking along the line *c″b″*, and was led over a gentle slope up the hill into a dense wood to the point *b″*.

Here I felt a joy as never before, and as only those will comprehend who also have been guided by Nature through a labyrinth of complications to a point where simplicity begins to emerge from apparent confusion. In this wood all prostrated trees pointed to the point *b″*.

From this point *b″* I was able to overlook the whole width of the track of destruction, which I had found to measure about four hundred paces. When I placed myself at this point and looked down the hill toward the line *CD*, I became at once aware that the last series of trees on my walk over the line *a″c″*, and in fact *all prostrated trees in the triangle a″b″c″*, *were point-*

2

*ing to* $b''$, and indicated a force acting in one and the same direction.

This discovery was the first and most important letter in the story the tornado had written on the surface of the earth. It was marked so distinctly that its meaning could scarcely be mistaken. It appeared as if a wedge with its base at $a''c''$ had been driven in from the south and destroyed the trees over this area. The limits were marked with almost mathematical precision, particularly toward the apex $b''$ of the triangle. This triangle, it must be remembered, was pushed into a thick wood, yet none of the trees outside of its lines were at all injured, while inside, particularly near the apex, where the trees were thickest, they were all prostrated. The lines were drawn with astonishing distinctness. I felt that this discovery was of great significance, although I did not yet see its exact meaning.

I now turned back along the line *CD*, which marks the right edge of the track, and from $c'$ followed the trees and destroyed objects which pointed with the arrow 21 across the track, along the line $c'b'$, and was led to $b'$ analogous to $b''$. Although the triangle $a'b'c'$ was less developed than $a''b''c''$, the destruction was visible on the ground by other objects enough to be characteristic.

I then started from the point *c*, following the trees in the direction of *cb* on the steep hill, and from the point *b* near Mr. Lyman's house, three hundred and fifty paces from the point *c*, I was able to overlook the whole area of *abc*, and observed as distinctly as before all prostrated trees pointing to me at *b*. About ten paces from the house, south-west of it, around the point *b*, there was a slight indication of a rotary destructive force.

Observing thus the destructive force active only in one direction, from the south-west, and assuming that there ought to be found a balancing force from the opposite side to account for the limitation of destruction, I looked for similar destruction beyond $b, b'$ and $b''$, coming from the north, but found none. Although the plateau north of the left margin of the track was covered with trees, not a leaf was injured.

It became evident to my mind that neither Redfield's Rotary nor Espy's Inblowing theory could explain these new facts, and that there must be found something different and on a broader platform to account for the undeniable and distinctly expressed phenomena. I became determined to find this something, if possible, by surveying the first portion of the tornado and by studying its embryology.

For such a survey I was now much better prepared than at West Cambridge. I had discovered whole areas in the track which had been left *uninjured*, and concluded that they must be of fully as much importance in determining the direction of the destroying force as those areas over which destruction had taken place. I therefore paid them as much attention as the others, and thus corrected a gross mistake made in my first survey, and which I found afterward others had committed.

The deficiency of surveys so made has grown out of the mistaken idea that tornadoes come ready made to the surface, do not change during their existence and appear the same at each point. A small section is thought sufficient to exhibit the law governing the whole. Portions which are not equally developed are thought accidental and not belonging to the character of the fully-developed phenomenon, and the investigator naturally goes to those points which seem to prove his own preconceived theory. Such surveys are for the discovery of true laws utterly useless.

In addition to this great mistake in the method of investigation, I soon became aware of another point, equally if not more important, to which I had paid no attention in my first survey, and I found later that this had also been overlooked by my predecessors.

A few trees showed exceptions to the general arrangement in

their positions relative to the points $b$, $b'$ and $b''$. This fact at first presented some difficulty, but led me afterward to the true explanation of the tornado by bringing the configuration of the ground into the consideration.

Examining closely the circumstances connected with these apparent exceptions, I found invariably that the trees were prevented from falling in the general direction—in some cases by rocks or other obstructions, against which the destructive wind had rebounded and thrown the tree backward in the opposite direction to that in which I should have expected it; in others by the roots of a tree being unsymmetrically arranged around it, the tree naturally falling to the side where the support was weakest.

These exceptions directed my attention to the influence which the configuration of the ground had in connection with the wind on the direction and kind of destruction, and I was thus gradually led to see the influence of Prospect Hill on the *origin* of the tornado, which is the most important point in the whole investigation. After Nature herself had thus kindly taught me where and how to investigate these phenomena, I commenced a survey of the track from the earliest beginning at Prospect Hill over two and a half miles to Wellington Hill.

The instruments at my disposal were only my legs and a pocket compass; but as I made a conscientious use of them, they served my purpose to determine fully the relative position and direction of things destroyed and things left uninjured in the track. I spent about five weeks in this survey and the collection of facts regarding the storm. I then with my map and notes studied the track from beginning to end with particular reference to the configuration of the ground.

During this time and afterward I made inquiries as to the state of the atmosphere before, during and after the tornado, not only in its direct course, but also north and south of it. In thus making inquiries I became acquainted with ex-President

Hill of Harvard College, who lived at that time in Waltham, close to the right margin of the tornado. As this was the second storm of the kind which had passed almost over his house (the first being the tornado of 1835, which passed over New Brunswick, N. J., where he then lived), he took a special interest in my studies. He went several times with me over the track, satisfied himself of the facts as I had found them, and thought the views I had formed more satisfactory than those of Redfield or Espy in their bearing on the origin and nature of tornadoes in general. He rendered me much assistance in procuring through his extensive acquaintance facts as to the temperature and other conditions of the atmosphere before the tornado and to the north of it, in the States of Vermont and New Hampshire.

The facts I gathered in the course of my investigation are arranged in Appendix B.

I had found the existence of two opposing currents of air of different temperature, coming respectively from north-west and from south-west, acting suddenly against each other after a sultry calm of some duration, and shortly a third gyratory force making its appearance between them, traveling in their diagonal, growing to such magnitude as to obliterate all traces of the straight line forces of the opposing currents, and finally abruptly disappearing. The two currents must have been during the period of sultry calm in a state of equilibrium, since the clouds were observed to remain for some time almost stationary. South of the tornado's track the south-west wind prevailed until the beginning of the tornado, and from information obtained for me by ex-President Hill it appeared that a storm had traveled from north-west to south-east over the States of New Hampshire and Vermont, and that during its progress a south-west wind was replaced by a north-west wind. I was thus led to conclude that the storm announced that afternoon by the black bank of cloud consisted in the conflict of two aërial currents of different temperature—that the colder northern current displaced the warmer southern current in the direction from north-west to south-east, gradually decreasing in velocity until, north of Waltham, West Cambridge and Medford, it came to a perfect standstill, producing the sultry calm felt before the tornado.

Here the two currents, being in equilibrio, exerted a great compressive force against each other. The equilibrium was disturbed by the uneven configuration of the earth around Prospect Hill. This disturbance produced the tornado, which traveled, not in the direction of the storm toward the south-east, but in the diagonal of the two opposing currents over the region of calm at their line of meeting, and in and underneath the black bank of clouds stretched out from west to east which must have marked this line of meeting.

I came thus to two distinct phenomena, the tornado and the storm in the ordinary sense of the word, both different in their origin, nature, direction, progress and appearance, and governed by entirely different laws. It would therefore be an error to base theories regarding the laws of storms in general upon the tornado as a type, which Redfield and Espy have done.

In order to witness, if possible, the phenomenon from beginning to end, I repaired during the same autumn and the succeeding year to Prospect Hill as often as I saw indications in the clouds of the approach of another tornado. I thus obtained many valuable experiences which confirmed me in my views, but I had not the pleasure of witnessing a tornado, because the state of the atmosphere was never entirely in the proper condition.

The clouds were in these studies my principal guides. Toward the winter I found that they changed their usual form and came from a different quarter; the storms also changed in direction and nature.

I became thus exclusively engrossed in these observations for about three years. Finding that the phenomena repeated themselves in regular order during this time, I became satisfied that storms in the temperate zone at least, and over the United States, are the *effect* of the conflict of opposing aërial currents of different temperatures, and not the *cause* of these currents and temperatures, as seems to be assumed by some cyclonists.

The question naturally arose: Where do these currents and their conflicts originate? and I was led to find the answer in disturbances of the general circulation of the atmosphere, and in the cause of these—the origin of all life and power and motion—the sun acting in combination with local circumstances.

In the mean time, however, after the completion of my investigation of the tornado, I had arrived at the following general results:

1. This tornado was in intimate connection with the storm I had seen approaching, but was not the storm itself.

2. The origin, mode of progress and appearance of both are totally different.

3. The storm consisted in the conflict of two opposing aërial currents of different temperature and pressure.

4. This conflict commenced at some point to the north, and shifted its place, the northern, cooler current in its course from north-west to south-east displacing the southern, warmer current.

5. This conflict was accompanied along the region of meeting of the two currents with copious rain.

6. The wind blew in straight lines from the north-west and from the south-west toward the region of meeting.

7. The long black bank of clouds had a defined relation to this region of meeting: it was parallel to it.

8. The region of conflict must have slackened its progress, as was evident by the black bank of clouds becoming almost stationary, which fact I had observed while fishing, before I knew of the tornado.

9. The tension between these two currents must have been

at this time at its maximum, the opposing currents balancing each other.

10. When, in this critical condition of the state of the atmosphere, a disturbance occurred which made the colder, heavier current rush suddenly forward, or made it sink at one point, the other more elastic, warmer current rushed over that portion of the colder current upward, producing an eddy or whirl which traveled in the diagonal of the forces of the two currents along the line of meeting or underneath the black bank of cloud which indicates it.

11. This disturbance was produced by Prospect Hill, the highest elevation near Boston, and by the valley east of it.

12. The coincidence of a certain condition of the atmosphere with the peculiar configuration of the ground will not only explain the origin of the tornado, but also its gradual development and its final dissolution.

Toward the end of the year 1851 I communicated these results, with the facts on which they were based, to the Academy of Science in Boston, being introduced by Prof. Agassiz, who took a deep interest in my discoveries, seeing at once their importance scientifically and practically. He proposed that my investigations should be published at the expense of the academy; but a statement being made by a member that he too was making a survey of the tornado, and had not found such a law, his impression being that "the whole was a confused mass," it was resolved to defer the publication of my investigations until the completion of this gentleman's survey. As, however, he unfortunately did not begin it until the destruction was two weeks old, when the débris had been largely removed and the position of fallen objects in most cases changed, there was little hope that he should find anything but "a confused mass," especially as he had also fallen into my original error of beginning in the middle.

I never again offered the results I had reached for publication, with the exception of an article which appeared in the New York *Daily Times* of November 18, 1852, and which is reprinted in the appendix to this volume.

Having found during my investigations that tornadoes and other storms are different phenomena, and that they follow different laws, I endeavored to investigate storms in general by the same method I had used with the tornado.

My researches were not made by filling out the ordinary meteorological formulæ from observations made three or four times daily, as is the custom. I had learned that no storm will be accommodating enough to develop itself just at the specified periods for observing; and I do not believe that this method will ever lead to any definite results.

It is like a zoologist who, desiring to study different kinds of fishes so large as to require separate observations of their parts, goes to the stream at seven o'clock in the morning and takes notes of the head of the first fish that passes him. He then goes away, and returning at noon punctually notes the tail of a fish swimming off, which is all he sees; in the evening he comes again, and notes the middle of fish number one, which this time is swimming past in the opposite direction. Putting together the three parts he has noted, he constructs a fish; but what kind of one if perchance it happens that number two is of a different species? Yet this is the method pursued in meteorology, and we can expect to arrive at no better results as to the nature of storms by averaging observations made always at fixed hours of the day, without reference to the changing character of the phenomena to be observed.

A storm must be treated as an individual which is subject to development. This is difficult, on account of the nature of the subject, but it is possible and essential. We must take the storm at its earliest appearance, and not lose sight of it for one moment until we know it throughout its whole extent, in all its parts, from beginning to end.

In my first endeavors to investigate storms in my own way, I felt the want of assistance in other parts of the country, and conceived the idea of inducing gentlemen of leisure and scientific inclinations to make voluntary observations whenever a storm passed. I desired to have them in telegraphic communication, so that when a region of low barometer formed in the south notice should at once be given to observers in the north, so that the clouds forming in advance and other phenomena should be noted. My principal aim at the time was to establish definitely the connection between the first cloud—the herald of the storm—and the line of lowest barometer, or the main storm.

Ex-President Hill, to whom first I communicated this idea, with the practical intelligence of an American suggested that such a corps of observers as I proposed organizing might also be used to signal the approach of storms from stations on the coast, so that shipping might be warned in time to avoid danger.* The U. S. Signal Service Bureau has realized with much more completeness than I could have hoped to attain the plan for which I labored and the principles announced in my lectures more than twenty years ago. It devotes more attention to predicting and signalling than I should have advocated, perhaps, since investigation and the establishment of laws is of so much greater importance.

My New York *Times* article contained the principles by which, with a corps of observers, the areas of rain and sunshine can be determined with little trouble at least a day in advance, but it also contained the principles by which every one may predict the weather for his own locality from the forms of the clouds.

* After I had abandoned the enterprise, ex-President Hill, through the press, urged very vigorously on public attention the subject of systematic storm signalling, and it is probable that his writings are the origin of our present effective Signal Service. In fact, he said to me a couple of years ago, "I have no doubt that this institution is the offspring of the seed we have sown, but I doubt very much whether we shall ever have any credit for it."

To carry my plan for a corps of meteorological observers into practical effect, and at the same time as a means of livelihood, I gave popular lectures on the subject, at first in Boston and the small towns in its vicinity, and afterward in New York, in New Brunswick and Trenton, New Jersey, and in Philadelphia, where I delivered a course at the Polytechnic College, then lately instituted.

I found several gentlemen willing and able to undertake the task of observation, but had great difficulty in interesting the general public in the subject, principally because any one who, at that time, maintained that the phenomena of weather are governed by strict law, was popularly looked upon as an empiric or an enthusiast. I was finally compelled to abandon my project for the lack of means to carry it on.

As a last effort, I addressed myself to Prof. Henry and Lieut. Maury, at Washington, requesting that I might have the opportunity of lecturing on the subject at the Smithsonian Institute; I sent to each a copy of the New York *Times* containing the *résumé* of the results of my investigations. I received answers acknowledging their receipt, but refusing my request.

With deep regret I was now forced to enter into commercial pursuits, but with the hope that at some future time I might be enabled to take up the subject again and with the firm purpose to do so. I did not abandon, however, my investigations; for the observatory of a meteorologist is open to all, and at all times and places, and does not require elaborate preparations. The chief results of my labors I have embodied in this volume.

## CHAPTER II.

### *THE SITUATION OF THE SCIENCE OF METEOROLOGY.*

METEOROLOGY, at the present time, appears to be in a state of transition. The theories that have been established, and have had their various adherents, seem now to be acknowledged as insufficient, although there has been nothing better to take their place.

The cause of the state of uncertainty that exists is not difficult to discover. Clement Ley says: "The solution of the most important problems in Meteorology has not hitherto been accomplished, on account of the abstruse character of the inquiries involved and the almost interminable complexity of conditions that influence the motion of the atmosphere;" but it should be added, *principally* because the wrong method of investigation has been pursued, and because scientists have been too apt to mistake *effect* for *cause.* Prior to 1812 dew was believed to be the cause of cold; Wells reversed the proposition, and the problem was solved. And so, in our day, the storm has been thought to bring heat from tropical regions into the temperate zone, whereas, in truth, it is heat that brings the storm.

So it happens that the commonest phenomena of weather are still involved in mystery, and that, notwithstanding the most powerful and eminent minds have devoted to the subject their assiduous labors, the most ingenious instruments invented and thousands of observers in different parts of the globe are making daily observations, the science has been almost at a standstill for the last quarter of a century.

It is true that the genius of Humboldt, Dove and others by

creating the science of climatology, has contributed greatly to the means for a final solution of the problems of meteorology, but the nature, laws, and even classification, of storms have remained an unpenetrated mystery.

Hundreds of volumes have been written and an infinity of facts collected, but the navigator is sent to sea with the same confessedly unreliable rules as twenty years ago.

That there is something amiss in the method of investigation that has been pursued has been freely recognized by the most eminent men.

M. Biot, to whom is in great part due the development of Inductive science, after counting up what the different nations have done in establishing observatories, asks: "What will come of it? Nothing; and nothing will ever come of it: no single branch of science has ever been fruitfully explored in this way."

Sir W. Herschel says: "In endeavoring to interpret the weather, we are in the position of a man who hears at intervals a few fragments of a long history related in a prosy, unmethodical manner. A host of circumstances omitted or forgotten, and the want of connection between the parts, prevent the hearer from obtaining possession of the entire story."

G. Airy, of England, Royal Astronomer, speaking of the increase of meteorological observatories, says: "Whether the effect of this movement will be that millions of useless observations will be added to the millions that already exist, or whether something may be expected to result which will lead to a meteorological theory, I cannot hazard a conjecture."

Proctor says: "At vast expense millions of records of heat, rainfall, winds, clouds, barometric pressure, and so on, have been secured, but hitherto no law has been recognized in the variations thus recorded—no law, at least, from which any constant system of prediction for long periods in advance can be deduced."

Prof. De Morgan says: "There is an attempt at induction going on which has yielded little or no fruit—the observations made in meteorological observatories. This attempt is carried on in a manner which would have made Bacon dance for joy."

The helplessness of Meteorology at this day cannot better be shown than by reproducing here the six questions propounded to the principal meteorologists of the world by direction of the Leipzig Conference of 1872, and extracts from the answers that were received. These questions are as follows:

1. Of what opinion are you in regard to the usefulness of storm-signals hitherto in use either from your own experience or from examination of the American, English and French bulletins?

2. Are you of opinion that, besides communicating the direction and strength of the wind, the "gradients"* of the barometer should be included in order to indicate the coming wind?

To what shall these "gradients" be referred—(*a*) to the difference between the observations at the different stations; (*b*) to the level of the sea; or (*c*) to the mean standard of the barometer at each place?

3. In what way should we take into consideration the temperature, humidity, etc.?

4. If we assume that each director in his district or country makes suitable arrangements, what would you recommend as a minimum of communication which one director should make to the director of another district or should receive in exchange from another?

5. Are you of opinion that the present state of our knowledge of the weather justifies giving definite prophecies or predictions instead of the telegraphic communication of facts, or shall we limit ourselves to intimations upon the state of the

* Mohn in substance defines a gradient as the gradual decrease of atmospheric pressure between places in a line at right angles to the isobars, or lines of equal pressure.

atmosphere in the surrounding countries from which the receivers of the communications may deduce their own rules? And in the latter case, shall we give in quite a simple way, by signals visible from a distance, the general condition, with the addition at each place of detailed communications from other places?

6. How can we arrange so that by semaphores or signals from lighthouses the state of the weather should be made visible to vessels sailing by?

These questions were drawn up and sent out by a committee composed of Buys-Ballot, Scott and Neumayer, who laid the answers received before the Vienna Meteorological Congress of 1873. The congress appointed a "committee on weather-telegraphy and storm-signalling" to examine and report on these answers; and the report, made through Dr. Neumayer, together with the original documents, was directed to be published,* since they were found "to contain such valuable material for gaining a more exact idea of the present state of weather-telegraphy and storm-warnings"—*i. e.*, of the *practical* part of Meteorology, which is a meter of the condition of the whole science.

The committee deduce in substance the following results (the figures refer to the questions):

1. All the respondents are satisfied of the importance of signals for practical purposes.

2. As to the first part of the question, all agree that the gradient must be given; as to the second part, some are in favor of *b*, some of *c*.

3. In regard to temperature, humidity, clouds, general appearance of the sky, the state of the sea, tides, the precipitations,

* "Bericht über Wetter-Telegraphie und Sturmwarnungen, abgestattet an den Meteorologischen Congress in Wien von dem dafür auf der Leipziger Conferenz ernannten Comité." Edited by Dr. G. v. Boguslawski. Berlin, 1874.

etc., most of the answers recommend these for consideration; but no one says in what way they should be considered, and the committee is of the opinion that the question has not been answered, and recommends it to the attention of those scientists who occupy themselves specially with the investigation of the causes of storms. It also recommends particularly in this connection the works of Dove, Mohn, Clement Ley, Peslin, Buchan and Reye.

4. In regard to this question, the opinion is that for theoretical purposes all elements are to be considered, while for practical purposes each director must accommodate himself to the necessity of his district.

5. All answers disfavor "prophecies" or "predictions," but are in favor of giving only opinions or "probabilities."

6. Give only warnings when the most severe storms are indicated by the "gradients." A general rule as to this cannot be given, as the gradient is frequently of a local nature; each director must be guided by his own experience, and for this reason a director should not promulgate "probabilities" immediately after the establishment of a system of signalling.

In his reply to the questions, Mr. F. Gaster, of the London Meteorological Office, says: "Besides the general extensive depressions, local storms of great strength are frequent along a considerable extent of our coast, as, for instance, the storm of February 12, 1871. At present, I believe, we are not capable of predicting them; but a careful investigation will doubtless show that they too follow a law or several laws, and that they also may be predicted. I am of the opinion that in storm-warnings, besides the strength of the winds, something else must be given. Gradients may be useful, but just the greatest gradients accompany rather than precede the storms; so that in telegraphing storm-warnings the state of the weather may have essentially changed before the warnings have reached their destination. On the other hand, the place of a depression may accidentally be so situated that the greatest gradient cannot show itself at two selected stations."

Prof. H. Mohn, of Christiania, Norway, says: "The chief problem in Meteorology is the law of the variation of atmospheric pressure. At this time we may consider ourselves only on the threshold of a knowledge of it. It is true we can give several causes which, acting together, increase or diminish the atmospheric pressure, but a quantitative treatment belongs still quite to the unsolved problems. We are, therefore, not able to find by calculation how the atmospheric pressure varies at every place, and how it may be determined; how the gradient varies at each place in direction and strength. We can just as little calculate the direction and strength of the coming wind as the character of the weather to be expected."

Prof. Prestel, of Emden, says: "The physical laws in accordance with which the movements in the aërial sea take place are at present not known exactly enough to determine beforehand the path that a storm will take which has appeared at a certain locality on the earth's surface; most of our predictions prove, therefore, failures."

Rev. Francis Redford, of Silloth, Cumberland, England, says: "After much reflection I cannot understand in what way ships on sea should receive from the coast communications of dangerous winds so that the communications could be of any benefit to them. The atmosphere at such times is generally so foggy that a vessel on a lee shore would shipwreck without being able to see a semaphore or other signal."

The Meteorological Society of Scotland, Edinburgh, says: "The present state of the science does not justify us in giving definite prophecies of future weather."

Mr. R. Strachan, of the London Meteorological Office, says: "Temperature, in regard to its normal value at the time, must be taken into consideration in the prediction of the weather, the same as rain, humidity, etc.; but if we are asked how this shall be done, a prize subject is made; because this subject is not ripe enough to be treated in the right way. Such meteorological elements might give more information to those on land than on sea." "It is said that good measurements of the tide are better indications of the change of atmospheric pressure than the barometer. This subject should draw to it the attention of official meteorologists."

Prof. Buys-Ballot, of Utrecht, Holland, says: "No 'prophecies,' if we do not want to bring this matter into discredit. It is impossible for the director to say in which part of the coast the wind will blow first, and be the strongest, if he does not await the beginning of the storm at a place at some distance, and then it is too late. For as I said, at repeated times, well-marked gusts appeared only five hours later in Vlyssingen or Helder than in Greenwich, and we cannot indicate the direction of storms which do not yet blow so exactly as to be able to say, to the north or the south of The Hague the storm will be fearful. Such a prophecy is besides considered as an official announcement. The state of the weather may be given. Every one may have the fixed rules by which, from this state, he may deduce his own results. He may, if it interest him, inquire and see from the barometer, at the place where he is, whether this state has become better or worse. Every one of us hopes to be able some of these days to determine the weather beforehand, but that time has not arrived yet. Even Dove himself says that he has predicted many storms, but also many he has not. To this is to be added that he who shall predict the weather, if he does it conscientiously and with inclination, will have no quiet life any more, and runs great risk of becoming crazy from nervousness."

The uncertainty that exists could scarcely be more strikingly illustrated than in the foregoing utterances of some of the most able and eminent meteorologists in the world. They find themselves groping in the dark. Some progress has been made and a few rules established, notably by Buys-Ballot; but the only comprehensive theories of the nature of storms that have received any general support are, although of long standing, not yet made adequate or serviceable. The two theories upon which almost all investigation has been based are the Rotary or Cyclone and the Inblowing or Centripetal; and before entering further on our subject, it may be well briefly to set them forth.

The Rotary theory has had by far the most support, and most of the rules established of late years have been made by its adherents and in accordance with its principles. It is held by the greater number of meteorologists, and is in part correct; although, in its main principles, it is farther from the truth than the Inblowing theory.

The Rotary theory asserts, according to Redfield, its most able advocate in this country, that a storm consists of a column of air of unknown height and varying in diameter from a few hundred feet to one or two thousand miles, revolving around an axis perpendicular or somewhat inclined, and moving onward, its base being the surface of the earth.

According to the Nautical Rules issued by the U. S. Hydrographic Office, "The movement of translation (*Fig.* 1) is upon a parabolic curve, the apex of which is always turned toward the W., and the branches throw themselves out to the E. The apex of this curve is tangent to the meridian about the latitude of 30° in the northern hemisphere and about that of 26° in the southern hemisphere—that is to say, nearly at the polar limits of the trade-winds. The hurricane moves on this curve in departing from the equator; in other words, the point of departure of the hurricane is at the eastern extremity of the curve of its path nearest approaching the equator, and in a latitude nearly equal to the declination of the sun; from thence the hurricane, in the first half of its course, is directed toward the apex of the curve, or toward the W., then it follows this apex as tangent to the meridian, bending afterward to the E. in the portion of the curve of its path the farthest removed from the Equator.

"The velocity of the translation is in proportion to the violence of the tempest. In the mildest hurricanes observed it has not been less than ten miles an hour, and in the most violent it has not exceeded thirty miles.

"Nearly all authors on this subject, observes M. Lefebvre,

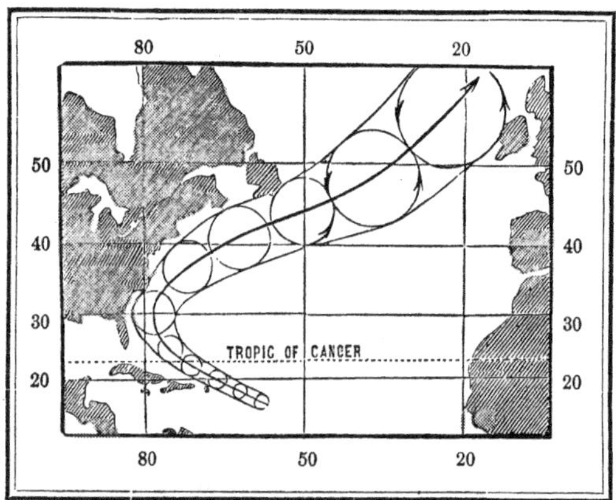


Fig 1.

have sought to measure the diameter of the vortex, and, this diameter being known, to determine from the force of the wind and the falling of the barometer at what distance the observer was from the centre. They have succeeded but indifferently; the diameter of the vortex of hurricanes is very variable. M. Keller states that the initial diameter of the gyratory movement is from 3° to 4° of the terrestrial arc, and that it increases progressively as it advances, until it attains 8° or 9° at the extremity of the curve of its path.

"DANGEROUS SEMI-CIRCLE.

"In the northern hemisphere the vessels placed on the edge of the right parallel to the path of the centre, and in the southern hemisphere those placed on the edge of the left, are those most injured." (*Fig.* 3.)

"If the wind hauls by the compass to the right, as in accordance with the movement of the hands of a watch, you are in the dangerous semi-circle of the tempest; and whatever may be the latitude, you should heave-to on the starboard tack, or, if the force of the wind is not too great, stand on close-hauled on the starboard tack. If, on the contrary, the wind hauls by the compass to the left, or in an opposite direction to the movement of the hands of the watch, you are in the manageable semi-circle of the tempest; and if the sea is not too heavy, you should run with the wind on the starboard quarter, or, if the sea is too heavy, heave-to on the port tack."

The Rotary theory, first indicated by Col. Capper in the beginning of this century, has been developed by Piddington, Thom, Col. Reid, Redfield, Dove and others, Piddington proposing the name *Cyclone.* Prof. Dove of Berlin, who has done so much toward the solution of meteorological problems, has also endeavored to explain how the rotation of a column of air may originate. His explanation is here given:

"The cause of this phenomenon—viz., the rotary motion—seems to be as follows: Suppose *a b* (*Fig.* 2) to be a row of particles of air parallel with the equator which by some impulse have been set in motion in the direction of *a c* towards the north.

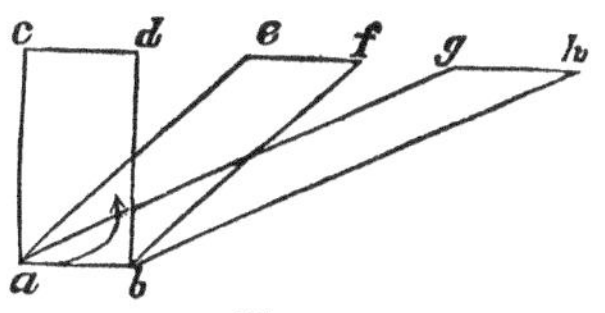

Fig. 2.

These particles would move to *g h* if the space *d b h* were empty, because they move from larger parallel circles to smaller ones. Were this space *d b h*, however, filled with air at rest, the air at *b* would meet, on its way toward *d*, little particles of air of less velocity of rotation than they have; their velocity toward the east will, therefore, be diminished. The air at *b* will move, therefore, to *f* instead of to *h*.

"Between the particles *a* and *b* lie particles of air which have originally the same velocity of rotation. They will move, therefore, precisely as if in an empty space—viz., to *g*.

"If, therefore, *a c* be a mass of air pressed from south to north, the direction of a storm on its east side will be much more to the south of it than on the west side, where it will be more west, and thus a tendency to a whirl originates in the direction S. E. N. W.

"This tendency to a whirl would not exist if there were no opposing matter in the space *d b h*. This tendency will therefore grow in proportion as this opposition hinders the storm in its deflection toward the west. The more the storm keeps, therefore, its original course, the more violently must it rotate.

"In the zone of the trade-winds this space is filled with air, which flows from north-east to south-west. The opposition will therefore be the greatest in this zone. The air at *b* can therefore be hindered so much in its tendency to the west that it preserves its direction to *d*, while *a* has a tendency to go to *g*.

"The storm will therefore rotate here the most violently, but progress with an unchanged breadth.

"But as soon as the storm enters the temperate zone it finds air in the space *d b h*, which is already in motion from south-west to north-east. The opposition which the particles at *b* hitherto found will suddenly be diminished or entirely vanish—that is, the direction *b d* changes suddenly in the direction *b h*.

"The storm bends around, therefore, suddenly almost at a right angle, and grows in breadth at the same time; for the difference in the motion between the points *a* and *b* does not exist any more. The phenomena in the southern hemisphere are explained in the same way. The whirl takes place, however, in the opposite direction."

To quote again from the publication of the U. S. Hydrographic Office: "A ship surprised by a hurricane perceives successively every direction of the rotary movement of the air on a secant parallel to the path of the centre of the meteor; these changes of direction never make the tour of the compass. When the secant traverses the centre of the meteor, the wind changes sixteen points at the centre perpendicularly to the line of translation, and after an interval of calm."

According to the theory, a point over which the centre of such a whirl passes will experience during the first half of its passage the wind blowing with increased violence as the parts of the whirl from the outside circle to the centre move over it. Then comes a dead calm, lasting about a half hour, after which the storm breaks loose with renewed violence from the opposite quarter.

In a place which lies to the right or left of the line on which the centre of the whirl moves onward, the wind will be seen to veer around. The angle through which the wind veers will grow smaller as the place lies farther away from the line toward the outside circle of the whirl, where it remains always from the same direction. This will be seen by moving the lines *AA*, *BB*, *CC* and *D* (*Fig.* 3), over the points *A*, *B*, *C* and *D* in the direction of their arrows.

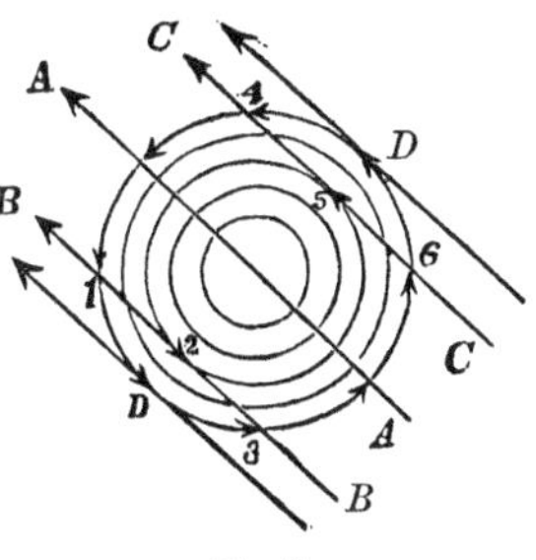

Fig. 3.

The Inblowing or Centripetal theory was principally advocated and developed by Espy, and contains more of the germs of truth than the cyclone. It is in fact true so far as it goes, and is in the position of a *part* of the truth seeking to take the place of the *whole* truth. It sets forth that the air in every storm blows from all quarters toward a common centre if the storm is round, and toward a common line if the storm is oblong. It attributes this motion to the rushing upward of a current above this centre or line on the surface, which of course causes the rushing in of air to take its place.

The adherents of this theory are divided as to the first cause of the air's rushing upward. Peltier, Hare and others ascribe it to a "convective discharge of electricity;" Brandes and Espy attribute it to heat. It seems to be universally admitted now that, as not all storms exhibit electrical phenomena, electricity cannot be the first cause, and that *heat* therefore must be.

Espy's exposition of the Inblowing theory is as follows: "When the air in any locality acquires a higher temperature or a higher dew-point than that of the surrounding regions, it is specifically lighter, and will ascend. In ascending, it comes under less pressure and expands; in expanding from diminished pressure, it grows colder about 1¼° F. for every hundred yards of ascent. In cooling as low as the dew-point (which it will do when it rises as many hundred yards as the dew-point at the time is below the temperature of the air in degrees of Fahrenheit), it will begin to condense its vapor into water or cloud. In condensing its vapor, it will evolve latent caloric; this evolution of latent caloric will prevent the air from cooling so fast in its farther ascent as it did in ascending below the base of the cloud now forming; the current of air, however, will continue to ascend and grow colder about half as much as it would do if it had no vapor in it to condense; and when it has risen high enough to have condensed by the cold of expansion from diminished pressure one-hundredth of its weight of vapor, it will be about 48° less cold than it would have been if it had had no vapor to condense nor latent caloric to give out—that is, it will be about 48° warmer than the surrounding air at the same height; it will therefore (without making any allowance for the higher dew-point of the ascending current) be about one-tenth lighter than the surrounding colder air, and of course it will continue to ascend to the top of the atmosphere, spreading out in all directions above as it ascends, overlapping the air in all the surrounding regions in the vicinity of the storm, and fall still more under the storm-cloud by the outspreading of air above, thus leaving less ponderable matter near the centre of the up-moving column to press on the barometer below.

"The barometer thus standing below the mean under the cloud in the central region and above the mean on the outside of the cloud, the air will blow on all sides from without inward under the cloud. The air, on coming under the cloud, being subjected to less pressure, will ascend and carry up the vapor it contains with it, and as it ascends will become colder by expansion from constantly diminished pressure, and will begin to condense its vapor into the cloud at the height indicated before, and thus the process of cloud-forming will go on.

"Now, it is known that the upper current of air in the United States moves constantly, from a known cause, toward the eastward—probably a little to the south of east; and as the upward-moving column containing the cloud is chiefly in this upper current of air, it follows that the storm-cloud must move in the same direction. And over whatever region the storm-cloud appears, to that region will the wind blow below; thus the wind must set in with a storm from some eastern direction, and as the storm-cloud passes, the wind must change to some western direction and blow from that quarter till the end of the storm."

Both the Rotary and the Inblowing theories are based on and proved principally by facts found in the destruction caused by tornadoes. Tornadoes are selected for this purpose because their effects are more visible and extend over a comparatively small space, and they can more easily be examined than other storms. The supporters of the Inblowing theory lay stress on the fact that houses are unroofed and other objects carried upward through the air, trees lifted out of the ground, and so on, and say that this proves an upward current. They show that the trees and all destroyed objects do not cross each other, but lie with their heads toward one point when the storm is round, and toward one line when the storm is oblong, and say this proves the inblowing current on the surface.

The adherents of the Rotary theory show in the destruction, and, strange to say, in the very same tornadoes cited by the others, that the destroyed objects lie not only inward and forward, but also backward, especially on the left side, and, as a whole, just as a rotating mass of air, which moves at the same time onward, would prostrate them. They lay particular stress on those cases of trees that are twisted.

The New Brunswick tornado is referred to especially by Redfield, but also by Espy, each one holding that it proves his own theory. Now, the same phenomenon cannot prove both of two such contradictions; and the probability, therefore, when two such able men as Redfield and Espy are concerned, is that they were both partially right, having most likely observed different parts of the storm and where the effect is different. Really, the error of both lay in taking a part as representative of the whole, thinking that the action of a storm was of the same nature at its beginning and throughout its whole duration.

# CHAPTER III.

*AËRIAL CURRENTS: THEIR CAUSAL CONNECTION WITH THE VARIOUS CLOUD-FORMATIONS AND THE CLASSIFICATION OF STORMS.*

THE first inquiry in the consideration of our subject is, What is a storm?

I understand by a storm in general *the movement of the air caused by its tendency to re-establish an equilibrium which has in some manner been disturbed*, and we may call all such movements storms, whether they are gentle breezes or furious hurricanes, whether they are accompanied by more or less condensation of moisture or clouds, or even by none at all. In general, the laws of the motion and changes of the wind in re-establishing an equilibrium must be the same, whether the action takes place in a greater or less degree.

We know from common experience that disturbances of the air are caused by differences of temperature and moisture in different places, but there may possibly also be astronomical causes; and I have little doubt that similar influences to those which produce the tide of the sea have a corresponding effect upon the atmosphere. It is well known that tides are produced by the combined action of the attraction of the moon and the sun on the water. Should these forces not have a greater influence on the aërial sea, which is a more elastic fluid, and more exposed to their action?

Such an influence is, however, denied by many on the ground that at such times as these forces act in combination we do not find as great a change in the barometer as we should perhaps expect from the pressure of the increased mass of air brought to one spot by such attraction; but may the increased weight of this mass of air to the earth or the pressure on the barometer not be neutralized by the increased attraction in the opposite direction of the sun and moon due to their position? In this case we may have no particular change in the barometric pressure, and yet the lunar aërial tides may take place and produce motions. That calculations of the weather based on these assumptions have mostly failed does not necessarily prove that this influence has no existence.

It is a matter of common knowledge that there are various influences of the moon little understood, but whose existence is undoubted. Such, for instance, is the lunar influence sometimes found to exist in brain affections, a perfectly authenticated case of which has come under my own observation. The derivation of the term *lunatic* from a very ancient recognition of this influence is of course familiar.

The same influence, it is maintained by physicians who have given the subject their attention, exists in other disorders than those of the brain; and Dr. Foster most interestingly connects these lunar influences with the direction of the wind. In a letter to Prof. Arago he says: "L'influence exercée par la nouvelle lune ainsi que par la plaine lune sur l'atmosphère et sur certaines maladies, reste encore un mystère, quoique les faits sont matière d'histoire. J'ai vu beaucoup de malades qui éprouvent de fortes migraines précisement à la nouvelle lune; et d'autres qui deviennent toujours malades *par le vent d'est.*"*

The whole subject is one of great interest, and probably of practical importance; but as concerns the attraction of our atmosphere by celestial bodies, all that we can now say is that

* "The influence exerted on the atmosphere and certain diseases, as well by the new as by the full moon, remains still a mystery, although the facts are historical. I have seen many sick persons who improved of acute megrims at the time of the new moon, and others who always grew sick with a west wind."

if there exists such attraction it is not sufficiently strong relatively to the influence of the sun's heat to be taken into the account at present.

We may, then, only take into the consideration the influence of *heat* on the air; for the formation of clouds will, in most cases at least go on by whatever power the currents be set in motion. We consider, therefore, a difference in temperature at different points the main cause of motion in the air.

If we observe the motion of the little particles of dust above and around a fire in the open air, we see them rise immediately above the fire, while they descend at some distance from it and are drawn over the ground from all sides toward it. Those particles of dust show the direction of the air's motion in this case.

In cold weather, if a window of a heated room be opened and a lighted candle be lowered from the top of the opening, we shall find the flame bent outward at the upper part, straight at the middle, and bent inward at the lower part. This shows that the warmer air of the room flows outward in the upper part of the opening, while in the lower part a cold current flows inward. This is Dr. Franklin's familiar experiment, and it illustrates the principle which must not once be lost sight of in the consideration of our subject—that when two currents of air of different temperatures flow horizontally in opposite directions, the warmer current, being lighter, will *always* be uppermost. Between these two currents there is a region where the particles of the air flowing in opposing directions neutralize each other's motion and produce a calm, so to speak.

We see thus an exchange of air between two places of different temperatures. The warm air flows toward the cold place, and the cold air flows underneath in an opposite direction toward the warm place.

The greater the difference in temperature between the two

places, the greater is the velocity of the currents of air in the interchange.

From the peculiar position of the earth to the sun and the effects of the sun's heat on our atmosphere, we find in the aërial sea which surrounds us the temperature distributed unequally in two directions:

1. *It decreases as we ascend perpendicularly upward from the surface.*

2. *It decreases as we go from the equator toward the poles.*

We must, therefore, find disturbances and restorations of equilibrium in currents in these two directions:

First. *Currents caused by a tendency to re-establish in a perpendicular direction from the surface, both upward and downward, an equilibrium which has been disturbed;* and

Second. *Currents caused by a tendency to re-establish in a horizontal direction, from the equator to the poles and from the poles to the equator, an equilibrium which has been disturbed.*

We now pass on to the causal relations between these currents and the clouds and their forms.

It is well known that air at a certain temperature can hold only a certain amount of invisible aqueous vapor; and when its capacity to do this is exerted to the utmost, we call it saturated and its temperature then the dew-point. With increase of temperature its capacity increases, and with decrease it diminishes. If, therefore, air at the dew-point either receives an accession of moisture or is cooled, part of its vapor becomes visible in cloud.

Whenever a warm current of air moves to a colder region, either perpendicularly upward or horizontally toward the poles, it becomes cooled by contact with the colder air, and also by expansion from diminished pressure in case it ascends. It then loses its capacity to contain all the aqueous vapor which it held in an invisible state when at a higher temperature; and that portion it can no longer contain condenses, and appears in the form of clouds or fogs.

PLATE III.—CUMULUS AND ITS MODIFICATION.

When a cool current moves into warmer air which is saturated with moisture, clouds are also formed. But when a cool current moves to a warmer region where the air has just discharged its moisture in rain or snow, that part of its condensed moisture which still floats as clouds in the air will dissolve as the cool current advances, and the clouds will disappear; for the cool current becoming warmer as it advances to warmer regions, its capacity to contain aqueous vapor in an invisible state increases.

Now, it is thus that, although we cannot see the aërial currents themselves in motion, their movements are betrayed by the appearance or disappearance of their constant companion—cloud; and we are thus afforded the means to determine whether currents are flowing around and above us, and in what direction.

Whenever in a clear sky a cloud appears, it tells us that a warm current is moving or flowing to a cooler region, or that a cool current is moving into warmer air which is saturated with moisture. Whenever clouds disappear, we may know that the cool current above which they are moves to a warmer region the air of which has been previously deprived of its moisture to some extent.

Thus the clouds will tell us by their appearance or disappearance whether the air is moving, and in which condition the air is as to moisture. They tell us still more. A vertical current moves upward in a column-like mass, rolling up in billows, so that its upper surface is similar in form to the unevenness of the surface of boiling water. The moisture in the tops of these billows of course condenses first, and shows itself in the small, rounded, detached clouds known as *cumuli*, and in this commencement of condensation the cumuli, seen from below, present the appearance commonly known as "a mackerel sky." (*Plate III., Fig.* 1.) If still further condensation takes place, these little cloud-spots grow larger, unite and form gradually into one round, mountain-like cloud called *cumulus*. (*Plate III., Fig.* 2.) On a warm, calm summer day one has abundant opportunity to see these clouds form over valleys, hills, woods and rivers. The sky is at such a time a picture of the surface beneath it; and it is said the Indians, who are good observers of Nature, judge from the clouds the nature of the ground at great distances. Thus the cumulus—round, mountain-like cloud—is characteristic of a vertically rising current.

Horizontal currents of different temperatures moving in opposing directions overlap each other. The warmer, rising obliquely over the cooler current, moves to the cooler region, while the cooler current flows over the surface of the earth beneath the warmer current to the warmer region, in the same way as the two currents flow over each other through the open window from and to a heated room in Dr. Franklin's experiment, which has been cited before. They overlap each other like two wedges: the warmer current has the thin end of the wedge upward, pointing toward the cool region; the cool current has its thin end on the ground, pointing toward the warm region, and the plane of the region of meeting of the two currents is therefore inclined to the surface of the earth.

When the warm current begins its motion over the cooler current, it begins first in the upper region. Its thin end flows upward and forward in waves. The tops of the first wave being thus pressed or drawn upward into higher and colder regions, the little vapor it contains condenses at that height, and forms a very thin, hazy, almost transparent stripe of cloud. The second wave makes a second stripe almost parallel to the first, and so on. (*Plate VI.*) These waves, moving principally in one direction, must appear at great heights as parallel stripes converging toward the horizon.

These elongated, narrow, hazy stripes or bands of cloud form themselves in the highest and coldest cloud-regions—according to Howard, at a height of about six and a quarter miles—and consist probably of little needles of ice, at least those which form first, because the condensed particles of vapor will congeal at that elevation. Their height, however, should vary somewhat, as indeed is true of all clouds.

Whenever the first stripe of a cloud forms, the latent heat in the vapor is of course liberated by the condensation. The air in which it floats, being thus heated, rises, allowing the air from lower regions to follow in greater quantities and higher waves. This causes the stripes to become thicker and more visible as they follow each other more closely, at last uniting to form a uniform screen over the sky. The appearance of the first of such stripes over the horizon is a sure indication that a warm current is moving obliquely over a cooler one to a colder region. Howard and other meteorologists have called these stripes cirro-stratus; I would propose the single name *stratus*, for I consider this the second elementary form of clouds, the first being cumulus.

We have thus two elementary forms of clouds—the *cumulus*, or rounded, mountain-like cloud, characteristic of a vertically upward warm current, and the *stratus*, elongated cloud in straight lines, characteristic of a horizontally moving warm current. All other clouds are modifications and combinations of these two forms, the round and the straight line.

Air may be cooled from below as well as from above; and when a current at or near the dew-point is thus cooled by passing over a surface at a lower temperature, the cloud-formation called *fog* is produced. This mostly occurs in winter; or in summer over places more cooled than the surrounding country, as rivers, swamps, meadows or forests, and at sea where the water has been cooled by icebergs. Patches of fog alternating with clear areas are very frequent on the banks of Newfoundland, where the icebergs drifting south are apt to strand.

When a warm current of air moves obliquely up over a cool current, this sort of cloud-formation from below often takes place in the region where the two currents meet and mingle; and it happens sometimes that the veil of mist thus formed above us is sufficient to shut out from view the upper clouds.

In the movement of a warm current to cooler regions it may happen, when the stratus is thus concealed by the mist-cloud of the plane of meeting, that the cool current becomes sufficiently heated to dissolve the mists from below, and the stratified appearance of the upper clouds will then suddenly become visible.

The movement of a cool current to warmer regions may be either horizontal or vertically downward.

In the first case, where the cool current moves horizontally, it shifts over the ground like a wedge, with its lower edge foremost. The warm air is thus lifted or forced up, and flows over the cool current as in the other case, but with different results.

If the warm current is saturated and its capacity is increased by its temperature's being higher than usual, when it is forced or lifted up its moisture will condense in the form of the cumulus, and these round clouds will arrange themselves along the higher, thicker end of the wedge of the cool current, forming a long black bank of cloud. This is a combination of the *cumulus* and the *stratus*. It is the cumulus arranged along a straight line, or the real *cumulo-stratus*. (*Plate VIII.*) Whenever such a cumulo-stratus is seen to rise above the horizon, it is a sure indication that a cool current moves underneath a warmer one more saturated with moisture to a warmer region than the one from whence it comes.

But when a cool current moves toward warmer regions underneath a warmer current that has just been partially deprived of its moisture, the clouds which may be floating in the plane of meeting or above it will dissolve and vanish as the cool current becomes more heated and its capacity for holding invisible aqueous vapor is consequently increased, or as the

PLATE IV.—STRATUS AND ITS MODIFICATIONS.

clouds themselves are shifted bodily into warmer regions. This dissolving will take place from below upward—first of the mist in the plane of meeting near the surface. The cool current by its contact with the ground which has just been covered by the warm current becomes heated first at its foremost edge, which is of little depth; but as it progresses farther into the region of the warm current it is heated through greater depths and dissolves higher masses of mist-cloud, until it reaches the stratus clouds above, which then become revealed. As the operation proceeds to still greater heights, and the stratus clouds themselves begin to be dissolved, the most northerly will be finally seen to be altogether dissolved, except the uneven tops, which will appear as lines of cumuli. (*Plate IV., Fig.* 1.) If the cool current, as is often the case, comes at an angle to the direction of the warm current, the most northerly clouds will thus appear as lines of cumuli, and next to them, at an angle to the line of the stripes of the main cloud, short stripes (*Fig.* 2), which are the stratus less dissolved, owing their arrangement to the *waves* of the cool current. Farther south will be the stratus not yet at all dissolved. (*Fig.* 3.) These three formations may frequently be seen together, although, of course, they are not absolute in all cases, but, as with all other cloud-formations, are subject to more or less modification. I have frequently seen together these three forms of the most northerly margin of a sheet of stratus-clouds which is being dissolved by an advancing cool current, and have seen the clouds of *Fig.* 3 change into those of *Fig.* 2, and then into those of *Fig.* 1.

Stratus, then, of the form of *Plate VI.*, indicates the advance of a warm current to the north, but stratus of the form of *Plate IV., Figs.* 1 and 2, indicates the retirement of a warm current to the south before an advancing dissolving cool current.

Sometimes similar effects may be produced with the mist-cloud of the plane of meeting if it is of sufficient density, and then we may have these formations below the true stratus clouds, which they appear to cross. If the warm current has still a high dew-point, the advance of the cool current may, instead of dissolving the stratus, form cumulus underneath or in combination with it.

The movement of a cool current to warmer regions vertically downward should occur chiefly at the tropics, and I have had little opportunity to study it; but it seems probable that it is the cause of one form of the fibrous, hair-like clouds called technically *cirrus*, and popularly "mares'-tails," "cats'-tails," etc. (*Plate IV., Fig.* 4.) All forms of these clouds I take to be merely the hazy stripes of the stratus drifted into these shapes by currents of a somewhat different direction to the one in which they are formed.

Howard, who ascribes the formation of clouds to electricity, in his "Modifications of Clouds," says: "The upward direction of the fibres or tufts of this cloud is found to be a decided indication of the decomposition of vapor preceding rain; the downward as decidedly indicates evaporation or fair weather." If this statement is correct, it would seem to indicate that the cirrus with the fibres pointed upward is caused by the upward motion of an advancing warm current, which will bring rain with it; and that when the fibres point downward the cause is the descending cool current which brings no rain, but on the contrary is a dissolving current as it gets into the warmer regions near the surface.

The different modifications of the two elementary forms of cloud, the stratus and the cumulus, are of course as numerous and varied as the movements of so flexible and elastic a fluid as the air, but some of the forms hitherto given seem to be nothing more than different views of the same forms, and to owe their apparent differences to the relative standpoints from which they are observed.

From the consideration of the movements of aërial currents

and their effects, the following classification of storms and their characteristic clouds is educed:

1. **Local** or **Vertical Storms.**

Stationary. Centripetal. Produced by a tendency of the atmosphere to re-establish in a vertical direction an equilibrium that has been disturbed.

*Characteristic cloud*—CUMULUS.

2. **Progressive** or **Lateral Storms.**

Travelling. Produced by a tendency of the atmosphere to re-establish in a lateral direction an equilibrium that has been disturbed. They are of two kinds:

(*a*) **Equatorial** or **North-east Storms.**

Winter storms. Produced by a warm current displacing a cool one to supply a deficiency toward the poles. Temperature changing from cool to warm. Direction to the north-eastern quadrant.

*Characteristic cloud*—STRATUS.

(*b*) **Polar** or **South-east** and **South-west Storms.**

Summer storms. Produced by a cool current displacing a warm one to supply a deficiency toward the equator. Temperature changing from warm to cool. Direction to the southern semicircle.

*Characteristic cloud*—CUMULO-STRATUS.

3. **Loco-progressive** or **Diagonal Storms.**

Travelling locally. Rotary (tornadoes, hail-storms, sand-storms, water-spouts, etc.). Produced by a tendency of the atmosphere to re-establish the equilibrium of a *polar storm* which has been disturbed in the plane of meeting by a peculiar configuration of the ground. Direction the diagonal of the forces of the two opposing currents transversely through the polar storm.

*Characteristic cloud*—CONUS.

Certain of the elements of the foregoing classification will develop as we proceed in the consideration of storms in detail. The tornado-cloud I have called *conus* for the sake of uniformity of nomenclature; it has hitherto been without a distinctive name, and its form, that of an inverted cone, justifies the title I have given it.

# CHAPTER IV.

## *LOCAL STORMS, AND THE PRIMARY ORIGIN OF ATMOSPHERIC DISTURBANCE.*

THE Local or Centripetal storms, although not the type of all storms, as they were considered by Espy to be, are in reality their most simple form. Their characteristic cloud is the *cumulus.* (*Plate III.*)

Whenever, from its geographical position or other physical causes, the surface of the earth at a given point becomes more heated than the surrounding locality, the air above this point is also correspondingly more heated than the air around it. It therefore expands, becomes lighter and begins to rise. In rising, the pressure upon it being diminished, it continues to expand, and consequently cools. If it cools to the dew-point, the invisible aqueous vapor it contains begins to condense and to form clouds.

Air cools about 1° F. for every hundred yards it rises above the surface before it can form a cloud; therefore it must rise as many hundred yards as the number of degrees the dew-point lies below the temperature of the surface. The height of the clouds may thus be approximately estimated.

By the condensation heat is set free, which retards to some extent the cooling and promotes the ascent of the air column. The rising air will be replaced at the surface by air from the surrounding locality flowing in from all sides, and the inflowing air, coming under less pressure, will also rise.

In this way a storm may be produced on the surface of the earth by the air blowing from the surrounding locality to that point which is most heated.

This process, which Espy has well described, may go on as long as the cause that produced it lasts. It can develop itself, however, only in places where the upward current is protected from outside lateral currents, or where these are not strong enough to overcome the upward motion. It occurs, therefore, frequently in valleys that are surrounded on all sides by mountains, as for instance at Lake Como and Lake Maggiore.

But as soon as a stronger outside horizontal current comes these storms are decapitated. Configliachi observed that during fourteen days storms which formed themselves in the afternoons in the valley of Molina ceased as soon as a stronger wind from Intelvio brought another storm.

At the equator and near it this kind of an upward current takes place all around the globe in the most gigantic manner. The sun, which throws its rays perpendicularly over a region of about 6°, never moves far enough away to allow of any cooling. This upward current, *A* (*Plate V.*), spreads out like a mushroom in the upper regions, and divides into two currents, *a* and *a'*. They come down between 25° and 35°, north and south latitude, in a similar manner to the currents shown by the particles of dust above and around a fire. For if particles of air rise at the equator, they will be replaced by the particles next to them at *the surface*, and these will be replaced not only by those next at the surface, but also by those next *above*, because the temperature decreases in both directions, upward as well as toward the poles. This process, if continued, must bring the equatorial currents *a* and *a'* down to the surface at the tropics; and these currents *a* and *a'*, having arrived at the surface, will flow partially in the currents *b* and *b'* toward the equator to supply the uprushing air. These currents *b* and *b'* form the trade-winds.

The current *b* on the northern hemisphere would be a true north wind, and the current *b'* on the southern hemisphere a true south wind, if the earth were a cylinder or if it did not revolve on its axis. But as the earth is a globe and revolves on its axis from west to east, each point on the earth, and the air above it, must describe a circle corresponding to its parallel of latitude in each twenty-four hours. These circles or parallels of course grow larger from the poles to the equator.

| | | |
|---|---|---|
| At 90° lat. the circle will be | 0 | geographical miles. |
| " 70° " " " | 1847 | " " |
| " 60° " " " | 2700 | " " |
| " 45° " " " | 3818 | " " |
| " 20° " " " | 5074 | " " |
| At the equator " " | 5400 | " " |

The air at the poles has therefore less velocity* than the air at points nearer the equator. If air from the poles moves toward the equator, it will come, on its way, to points which have a greater velocity than it has. If air from the poles or near them could be brought suddenly over us, we would be revolving much faster than this air, and the effect would be as if it were blowing against us—that is, as if it came from the east, toward which we are moving. We feel the same effect in travelling rapidly in a railroad car on a calm day—the air appears to come toward us—which phenomenon is of course familiar to every one.

As the air from the poles is not brought suddenly but gradually over us, it will assume a westerly direction gradually, and appear thus to come from the north-east in the northern hemisphere and from the south-east in the southern hemisphere. The farther from the north it comes, the more easterly will it appear to us. If such a current, however, flows against a high mountain range, as the Rocky Mountains, it will be deflected and come to us as a north-western or western current. Or if it flow along the western margin of a heated continent, it also may be deflected from its course, and will then flow over the continent as a north-west current. Hence currents from arctic regions may appear from any point of the northern semicircle.

* It really of course would, from the cause of which we are speaking, have *no* motion at all.

The supply currents from the tropics toward the equator flow in the northern hemisphere over the tropical region as a constant north-east wind, and in the southern hemisphere as a constant south-east wind, because they come from parallels with less velocity to those with greater. Advantage has been taken by commercial navigators of these constant winds, and they have thus received the name of "trade-winds."

Where these two trade-winds meet and the equatorial current ascends there is produced a belt of calm, because two opposing currents of equal force will neutralize each other at the place of their meeting, and also because the continual upward motion of the air, being stronger than the lateral motion, will tend to produce the same effect. Another result of this constant upward current along the equator must be a belt of clouds above it extending all around the globe.

Where the equatorial current descends to the surface at the tropics two other belts of calm must be produced, for a current coming vertically downward must have the same effect as a current going vertically upward; it is only lateral currents that produce the effect of winds. As an ascending current decreases the pressure on the barometer, so a descending current must increase the pressure, and these belts of calm are therefore belts of high pressure. They have been called by sailors "the horse latitudes," the name being due to the alleged fact that the delay in these regions of sailing-vessels used as horse transports caused such a scarcity of water that the horses had to be thrown overboard.

As the sun at the approach of summer moves toward the northern tropic, and at the approach of winter toward the southern tropic, the belt of greatest heat—the belt of calm—at the equator, the region of the north-east and south-east trade-winds, and the two belts of calm north and south of these trade-winds, move with it—in the summer away from the equator, in the winter toward it. Indeed, all meteorological conditions of the whole atmosphere shift with the sun—in the summer toward the north, in the winter toward the south.

These different belts and regions would have exactly the same relation to the equator if there were all over the globe an equal distribution of land and water. But we find three times as much land on the northern hemisphere as on the southern. And the effect of the sun's rays on the land, and in consequence the air above it, is different from their effect on the water. The land is heated by the sun far more than is the ocean, owing to the fact that the heat of the solar rays is concentrated on the surface of the earth, scarcely penetrating an inch in the course of a day, while during the same length of time it is diffused through the water to a depth of several fathoms. This circumstance modifies considerably the regularity of the belts.

If we consider the region of greatest heat, or of calm, as the line of division between equal amounts of heat in the northern and the southern hemispheres, it must be found for the most part lying north of the equator, since the preponderance of land, and, therefore, of most heated surface, is in this direction. Experience proves this to be true.

In the Pacific Ocean the equatorial region of calm oscillates between 3° in January, and 10° 45′ in August, north latitude. Its central line moves in the course of a year about 5°. Its southern limit is therefore always north of the equator, and hence, the south-east trade-wind extends at all seasons over into the northern hemisphere. This trade-wind is, however, to be found in the Pacific Ocean only in that part which lies between the Gallapagos and the Marquesas Islands.

The north-east trade-wind, which begins about one hundred geographical miles from the American coast, extends to the neighborhood of the Marian Islands. The numerous islands in the western part of the Pacific Ocean cause different disturbances in the regularity of the trade-wind similar to those in the Indian Ocean.

As has before been said, the more heated air over an island or a continent in or near the region of the trade-wind may neutralize it or deflect it from its course, and high mountain ranges act in a similar way. The trade-wind is, therefore, mostly observable in open sea.

The little map (*Fig.* 4*) represents the average position of the limits of calm and of the trade-winds on the Atlantic Ocean. The dark lines refer to the months of July, August and September. The region of calm between the lines *c c* and *d d* stretches from the mouth of the Orinoco, on the South American coast, to the Islands of Cape Verde, on the African coast. The line *b b*, beginning at about 10° east of the coast of Florida, marks the northern limit of the north-east trade-winds, *c c* its southern limit; *a a* indicates the southern limit of the south-east trade-wind, and *e f* its northern limit.

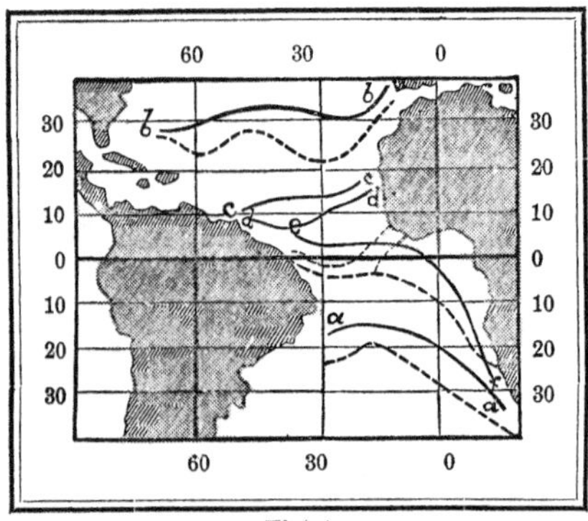


Fig. 4.

From this it will be seen that the south-east trade-wind extends during the summer months far north of the equator; according to Lieut. Maury, to 17° north latitude, and single oscillations doubtless extend still farther.

* From *Katechismus der Meteorologie von Heinrich Gretschel.*

Over the region between the African coast and the lines *d e f*, the regular course of the south-east trade-wind is changed into a south-west wind, by the influence of the upward current over the African continent.

The limits of the calm, of the trade-winds and of the region of the south-west wind on the coast of Africa for the months of March and April are marked by the dotted lines.

From the map it will be seen that the north-east trade-wind does not at any season extend south of the equator, except over a very small region. We observe also that in the Gulf of Guinea, on the coast of Congo and Angola to the cape, a south-west wind always prevails, while in a region farther west from the coast, which lies about equally on both sides of the tenth parallel of latitude, a south-west trade-wind prevails in the summer and a north-east during the winter.

In the Indian Ocean and the China Sea a similar influence on the trade-wind is produced by the continent of Asia. During the winter, when the air above the continent of Asia cools considerably, the regular north-east trade-wind prevails, and reaches far over into the southern hemisphere, toward the region of calm. But during the summer so much heat is developed on this continent, and the upward current is so strong, that the south-east trade-wind is drawn far over into the northern hemisphere, and north of the equator it is changed, on account of the rotation of the earth, into a south-west trade-wind.

These regular trade-winds, which change every six months—toward the winter into a north-east, and toward the summer into a south-west, trade-wind—are called *monsoons*. This word is derived from the Arabian word *mausim*, or from the Malayan *musim*, and signifies *season*. The change of the monsoons is characterized by variable winds and hurricanes, which are less violent south of the equator than north of it. The end of one monsoon is indicated by clouds moving in opposite directions. To the position and extent of the continent of Asia we must ascribe the fact that the south-west monsoon in the China Sea changes toward the south and south-east—that is, to a more direct course toward the continent. For the same reason the north-east monsoon changes toward north and north-west, because its cooler air is apt to flow toward the more heated region of Australia.

In the Red Sea there prevails, during the greater part of the year, especially during the summer in the northern part, a north and north-west wind; in the southern part, during the summer, a south-west by west; during the remainder of the year a south-east wind.

In the Persian Bay prevail, during the summer, south-east, and during the winter north-west, winds.

In the same manner the Gulf of Mexico and the Pacific Ocean near Central America have their monsoons. Here the north-east trade-wind changes its direction in order to establish the equilibrium disturbed over the heated plains of Utah, Texas and New Mexico.

The coast of Brazil has also a north-east monsoon in the spring and a south-west monsoon in the fall. The *etesien* (literally meaning *season*) of the Mediterranean Sea presents a similar phenomenon. During the summer the north-east trade-wind prevails here; during the winter, when the African desert cools below the temperature of the air above the seas, the wind flows from the south. On the Black and Caspian Seas similar phenomena take place.

If the sun produces such great differences on land and water by sending his rays obliquely over the regions of the trade-winds, so as to neutralize or change their course, his rays produce still greater differences over the region of calm, where they strike vertically. We find here, above islands, rocks, etc., such rapid upward currents that their supply currents, in combination with the regular trade-wind, cause the most sudden and violent local storms at regular times every day. Thus the most death-like calms alternate here with the most violent gusts and showers, with sudden and complete changes of the wind, so that this region has become the dread of mariners. The name of calm is therefore not very appropriate. Where no such varieties of the surface exist, however, vessels are sometimes detained for weeks.

In the regions of the tropical calms, where the equatorial currents $a$ and $a'$ (*Plate V.*) come down to the surface and flow as the currents $b$ and $b'$ toward the equator, the weather is fine and the sky clear, because the currents $a$ and $a'$ come to the ground almost deprived of moisture, and in flowing toward the equator their capacity to hold aqueous vapor increases. During this time these regions have their dry season. But with the motion of the sun north and south, the equatorial calm moves over this region, bringing to it the rainy season.

The *local* storms are therefore principally at home in the torrid zone, and there take place with the most gigantic violence. They are represented in the temperate zone by those sudden summer showers which originate over portions of the country more heated than the surrounding locality, and never travel far from their place of origin. The upward currents may be bent obliquely by a gentle lateral current, so that they discharge their condensation, or rain, somewhat distant from their place of origin, but never very far, the real storm remaining where it originates. They develop a great deal of electricity, and are therefore accompanied by thunder and lightning. Their thunder consists in short claps or explosions; their lightning is mostly directed vertically. They are generally harmless and of short duration, and have no marked influence on the temperature. They cannot well occur in the Arctic regions.

Their characteristic cloud is the *cumulus*, which may be seen forming some hours before the storm bursts. The formation of cumuli at a high dew-point, and with a falling barometer, is a sure sign of a storm of this kind during the day. These regular summer storms occur also late in the spring and early in the autumn, and frequently underneath the advance cloud of a north-east storm. The appearance of the clouds of two such storms one above the other is a sublime spectacle. Aristotle knew of this *courant ascendant*, and De Saussure showed its significance. Espy made it the basis for his theory of *all* storms, but it produces directly only the purely local storms, which are rich in rain, but generally not dangerous nor destructive. Espy proposed to originate storms artificially by burning forests to produce a *courant ascendant*, which would certainly have been more destructive than his storm even if the experiment could have produced one. Wherever the nature of the surface is uniform, so that the sun's rays cannot produce any difference of temperature, no upward current can originate, and, therefore, no storm of this kind. This condition is partly accomplished in the winter and in the polar regions by the earth's being covered with snow, and this is one of the reasons why these storms do not occur at this season or in these regions. Dr. Kane did not observe any cumulus clouds in his arctic explorations.

Plate V.

Summer
Winter
a
a'
b
b'
c
c'
N
S
A
B
B'
C
C'
Winter
Summer
Tropic
can
Equa
capric

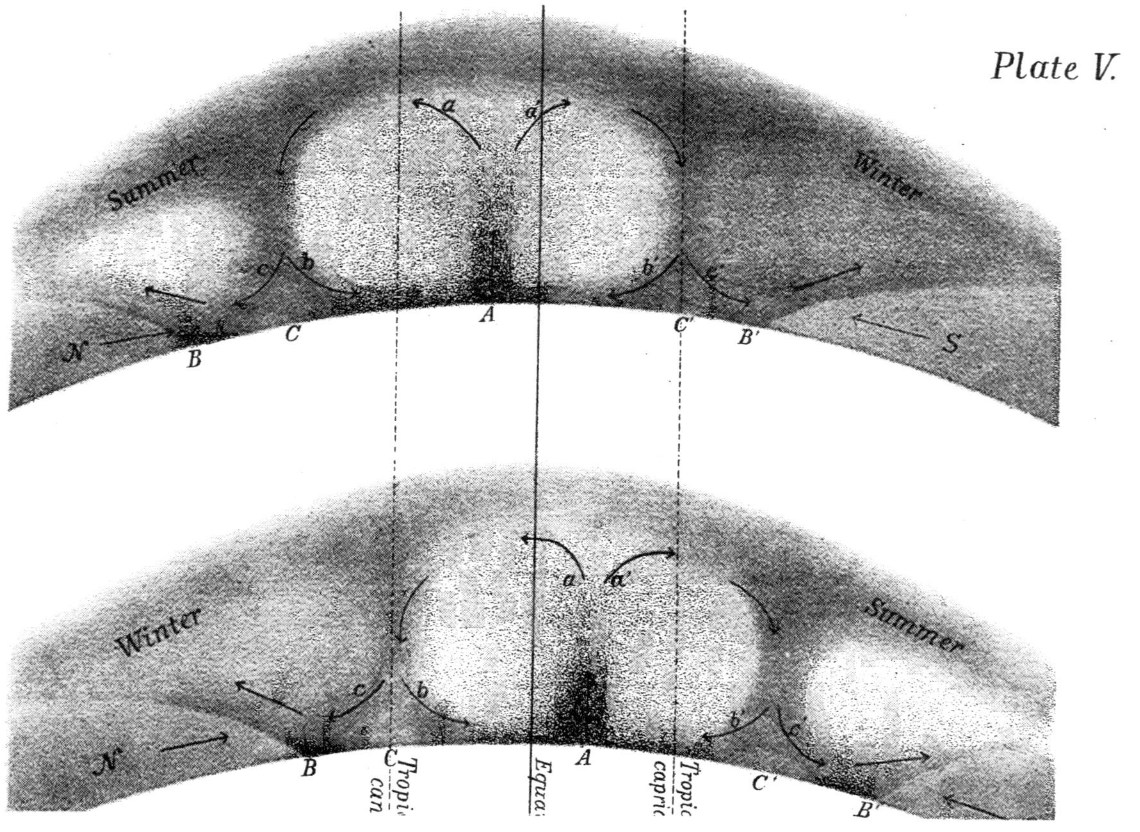

# CHAPTER V.

## *PROGRESSIVE STORMS.—EQUATORIAL OR NORTH-EAST STORMS—WINTER STORMS.*

IN describing the laws of the local storms, or those which originate by a disturbance in our atmosphere in a vertical direction, we found that the largest of this kind is going on continually along the line of the equator. There the heated upper current *A* (*Plate V.*) rises and divides in the upper regions into the two currents *a* and *a'*, which descend to the surface at the tropics and again divide each into two currents, *b* and *b'*, and *c* and *c'*; *b* and *b'* flowing toward the equator, and *c* and *c'* over the surface toward the poles in the direction of colder regions. The current *c*, coming from the equator and the tropics, is called the equatorial or the tropical current. As it comes from parallels of greater velocity to those of less velocity, it moves faster than the earth's surface at these places, and, therefore, appears to come from the south-west or west.

Having arrived at the surface, it soon becomes heated, and flows over the temperate zone as a warm south-west or west wind. The continual disturbances at the equator by the upward current causes necessarily also a pressure of the colder arctic air toward the equator, and this produces the real polar currents *N* and *S*, which will flow in the direction of the arrows toward the equator. For in the arctic regions the air becomes cooled principally from the surface below and contracts. It becomes thus heavier than air in the tropical regions of the same altitude, and will flow thither over the surface, the same as water or any other heavier fluid will flow under oil with which it is in communication. The polar currents, for the same reason as the trade-winds, will assume on the northern hemisphere a north-easterly, and on the southern hemisphere a south-easterly, direction.

It is evident that the currents *c* and *N* and also *c'* and *S* must meet respectively somewhere on the surface in the temperate zone at *B* and *B'*. (*Plate V.*) The warm equatorial currents *c* and *c'* will then rise a second time upward before the cool polar currents *N* and *S*, overlapping them obliquely, and will flow over them toward the poles, where, from contraction and the outflow from below, a deficiency in bulk has been created; while the polar currents press on the surface toward the tropics, where, from expansion and the outflow from above, a deficiency in density or weight has been created. Thus, from the tendency of the atmosphere to preserve equilibrium, the equatorial warm regions receive an afflux of air from below on the surface from the arctic regions, while the arctic cold regions receive an afflux of air from above from the equatorial. At these regions of meeting, *B* and *B'*, we must have belts of diminished pressure, or low barometer on account of the rising of the equatorial currents.

North of the region of diminished pressure, on the northern hemisphere *B*, and south of the region of diminished pressure on the southern hemisphere *B'*, regions of high pressure must be found on account of the banking-up of the polar currents *N* and *S*, having received an afflux of air from above. This gradual increase and decrease in pressure from the equator toward the poles can be seen from *Fig.* 5*.

We find thus around our globe several belts of low and of high pressure (*Plate V.*):

One belt *A* of low pressure at the equator.

Two belts *B* and *B'* of low pressure in the temperate zones.

Two belts *C* and *C'* of high pressure at the tropics.

* Taken from Flammarion's work on *The Atmosphere*, edited by Glaisher.

Two belts *N* and *S* of high pressure near the arctic and antarctic circles.

These meteorological belts, and in consequence the weather,

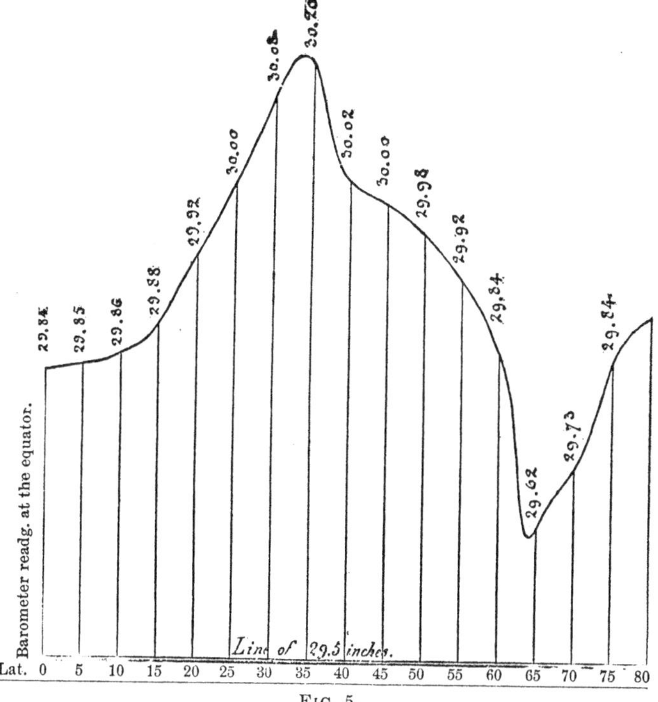


FIG. 5.

would have an equal distribution and remain unchanged in position if the earth's surface were wholly of the same nature, either all land or all water, and if the earth kept rotating always in the same position toward the sun.

From the motion of the earth round the sun these belts, and with them the whole atmosphere, make annually one general oscillation—that is, they follow the course of the sun, shifting in the spring toward the north and in the autumn toward the south. (*Plate V.*)

From the more or the less oblique direction of the rays of the sun upon these belts, those near the equator do not shift over so large a space as those near the poles. The region or belt of low barometer $A$ shifts annually over about 5°, the two belts of high barometer $C$ and $C'$ over about 10°, and the two belts of low barometer $B$ and $B'$ over much larger spaces in the course of a year. At and near the equator, and in fact all over the tropical regions, vertical movements predominate over the oscillation, while over the temperate and frigid zones the lateral oscillations predominate.

The shifting of the atmosphere with the motion of the sun toward the north during spring and summer, and toward the south during autumn and winter, does not, however, take place in one uninterrupted movement. As we see the waves of the tide rise by repeated oscillations, each wave advancing a little farther than the one before it, so does the atmosphere, with its belts of high and of low barometer, shift in minor oscillations, till it reaches the most northern or most southern limit, when oscillations in the opposite direction are begun.

As often as the region of low barometer $B$ and its adjoining regions of high barometer oscillate over us we must necessarily experience a change in temperature—a change in the direction of the wind and a change in barometric pressure—in short a storm. The ever-moving region of depression $B$ is therefore the region of storms in the temperate zone in the northern hemisphere, as is also $B'$ in the southern. Similar phenomena, more violent but less extended, we must expect from the shifting of the belts $C$, $A$ and $C'$, and the consequent meeting of currents of different temperature in the tropical regions.

If the surface of the globe were of a uniform nature, these belts would, as was before said, coincide with the parallels. If, on the other hand, the earth consisted alternately of strips of land and water extending from pole to pole, the tropical belt of high pressure would over the land during summer move much farther north, and the arctic belt of high pressure in winter much farther south, than the respective portions of these belts over the water, on account of the land's being much more readily heated or cooled. Now, this is to a certain extent actually the case, and therefore the belts must have a sinuous form around the globe, which is reversed respectively over land and water at different seasons. If such a strip of land increases in breadth toward the poles, the arctic belt of high pressure will move during winter still farther south, and may, if the tropical belt of high pressure is principally influenced by water, meet it toward the tropics, while in summer the tropical belt may approach the arctic belt toward the poles. Such circumstances seem to take place over Asia and America; and in the latter the arctic belts are in winter drawn far to the south, so that the real polar current may assume at times the place of the tropical current *b.* (*Plate V.*) The relative positions of the arctic and tropical belts of high pressure over adjoining sections of land and water must be taken into consideration in explaining the deflections of a current from the direction which the rotation of the earth alone would give it; the polar current does not always come directly from the poles, nor the equatorial current from the equator. Meteorology is fully as much a science of the earth's surface as of the air.

From the before-mentioned causes, we cannot expect to have the oscillations take place at the same time all around the globe. They will take place over different longitudes in separate waves or currents, at different times, as uneven distributions of the land and water influence them.

The aërial sea as a whole tends always to preserve its equilibrium; and whenever, by the modifying influences of land and water on these oscillations, a powerful disturbance in the regular circulation is caused in the torrid zone, we must experience a corresponding disturbance over the temperate zone to the arctic, and *vice versâ.*

When, therefore, by a more powerful local expansion, a depression or a deficiency of air occurs at the tropics, there will be over that longitude a corresponding motion of air, or a wave or current moving toward it from the arctic region; conversely, if, by a powerful contraction, a deficiency occurs at the arctic region, a corresponding wave or current will move toward it from the tropics. When, during the winter, when the region *B* (*Plate V.*), or that of low pressure, remains near its most southern limit, the prevailing wind of the northern United States comes from some point of the northern semicircle.

During the summer, when this region remains near its most northern limit, we have in the United States a prevailing southwest, south or west wind.

If the most northern limit of *B* during the whole summer, and its most southern limit during the whole winter, were fixed without movement in the same latitude—which is effected in the Indian Ocean by the influence of Asia, producing the monsoons—we should have in our temperate zone, in the summer, a constant south-west monsoon, and in the winter a constant north-east monsoon. If, by the continued flowing of the prevailing currents, a deficiency of air—diminished pressure—occurs in the region from whence the current comes, the opposing current will move toward that place and supply the deficiency—the want of pressure—and over the region where it replaces the prevailing current will produce a progressive storm.

The storms over the temperate zone consist of this conflict, caused by the prevailing current's being replaced by the opposing one. As often as the region of low pressure *B*, or the line where these currents meet on the surface, passes over any point, a storm is produced at that point; and a change of wind, a change of temperature, a change in the pressure of the air, in short, a change in the weather, takes place—*i. e.*, a change or disturbance in the regular circulation of the atmosphere.

The distribution of land and water, and the characteristics of the various bodies of each, have almost a greater influence on the direction of these oscillations than on the direction of the trade-winds.

The American continent is particularly favorable as a path for rapid oscillations of this kind, as is also the Atlantic Ocean. The elongated form of this continent from north to south, its mountains running in the same direction, and offering no impediment, favors them more than any other continent.

In Europe and in Asia the principal mountain chains run from west to east, and are thus a constant impediment to these oscillations, particularly to the progress of the cold polar current, which, being heavy, keeps to the surface. The weather is, therefore, not so changeable in that continent because these oscillations do not take place so rapidly and the storms are not so well defined and characteristic as in America. Many storms exhaust themselves before they have passed over the high mountain ridges.

But the region of low pressure, or the line of conflict, between two opposing currents shifts so rapidly over the American continent that we sometimes experience the greatest contrasts of heat, moisture and wind in less than fifteen minutes. These sudden atmospheric changes have undoubtedly a marked influence on the nervous temperament of the American people. The geographical position and configuration of America are, then, particularly favorable for the investigation of a storm from beginning to end, throughout its whole extent, in all its motions and appearances, in every phase of its development. Here we can obtain the full history and perfect picture of a storm which Herschel looked for in vain.

### (a.) *The North-east or Winter Storms.*

"About twenty years ago," writes the great Franklin, in a letter to Mr. A. Small, dated the 12th of May, 1760, "we were to have an eclipse of the moon at Philadelphia, about nine o'clock. I intended to have observed it, but was prevented by a north-east storm, which came on about seven, with thick clouds, as usual, that quite obscured the whole hemisphere; yet when the post brought us the Boston newspaper, giving us an account of the same storm in those parts, I found the beginning of the eclipse had been well observed there, though Boston is north-east of Philadelphia about four hundred miles. This puzzled me, because the storm began so soon with us as to prevent any observation; and being a north-east storm, I imagined it must have begun rather sooner in places farther to the north-eastward than it did at Philadelphia, but I found that it did not begin with them until near eleven o'clock, so that they had a good observation of the eclipse. And upon comparing all other accounts I received from the other colonies of the time of the beginning of the same storm, and since that of other storms of the same kind, I found the beginning to be always later the farther eastward."

We see in this simple account how a great natural philosopher arrives by apparently insignificant conclusions at one of the most important characteristics of north-east storms, which is at the same time a characteristic of all progressive storms, namely, that in approaching us they travel *against the prevailing wind.* It is true the fact puzzled him, and has puzzled all ever since, but Franklin was by his truly great simplicity of mind in such intimate relation with Nature, and therefore understood her so intuitively, that he would have found the explanation of this apparent anomaly long ago, had he lived. The motion of storms against the prevailing wind has not hitherto been explained by any theory. The cyclonists can-

Plate VI.—The Stratus in the North-east Storm.

not account for it, and do not seriously make the attempt. The centripetalists have very recently ascribed the principal motive power of storms to the rain, which they found spreads farther to the east than to the west of the depression of barometer. This is about as rational as if we were to say the wheelbarrow draws the man after it.

The approach of the north-east storm may be observed some time in advance. On a clear, cold day in the middle of the winter, in December or January, the prevailing wind being from a northerly direction, we sometimes see a long, thin, hazy stripe of cloud, the *stratus*, quietly appearing above the southern horizon. Its direction is generally from west-north-west to east-south-east and parallel with the horizon. This stripe rises very slowly, and after a little while a second, parallel with it, makes its appearance; then a third, a fourth and so on. (*Plate VI.*) Each stripe is a little denser, more visible and closer to its neighbor than the preceding one, but they always alternate with stripes of clear sky. They continue to move slowly and majestically toward the north-east, side forward, and seem to form arches supporting the dome of the heavens. This lasts sometimes half a day, sometimes a whole day, before the first stripes pass the zenith. Until they reach this point the meteorological instruments do not show any change; but when the first stripes pass the zenith, the barometer begins to fall slightly, the thermometer as yet indicating no change. As the first stripes move over us and downward toward the eastern horizon, the last stripes above the southern horizon have become so thick and broad that they unite and cover the southern sky, forming a complete screen. At this time the prevailing wind from the north-east generally begins to rise and blow more violently in the opposing direction to the march of the clouds. The denser clouds, which now begin to move over us, discharge rain or snow or sleet, according to circumstances. The single stripes sink one by one below the eastern horizon, apparently in the same order as they rose above the southern horizon. The barometer continues to fall, and the snow or rain is brought obliquely down from the northern quarter by the prevailing wind.

By and by the direction of the wind changes slightly; then comes a calm. At this time the thermometer rises suddenly and the barometer has reached its lowest point. The rain or snow falls vertically. After the calm has lasted for a length of time, varying according to circumstances, the wind has changed its direction, so that it comes from a quarter more or less opposite to that from which it came at the beginning of the storm; and it now begins to blow with greater fury than ever. The barometer rises again, but does not stand so high as before the storm. The wind keeps its direction for perhaps some hours, and may continue without change until the sky clears from the south, or it may change again to the direction it had before the storm, and the sky clears from the north.

In the latter case the barometer rises, the thermometer sinks and the state of the atmosphere existing before the storm is gradually re-established. This generally takes place in the middle of winter.

In the former case the barometer rises, and the thermometer also. The wind falls and the heavens clear from the south or south-west. This occurs generally in the late spring or early autumn. In this case the next change will come from a northerly direction in a manner hereafter described.

In the other case the next change will come from a southerly direction in the same manner as the approach of the north-east storm.

In some cases the stripes return below the southern horizon, going back in the reverse order to their approach, or else they vanish more or less suddenly before they have passed over us. This is an indication that the storm-wave has oscillated back again. It will then reappear a half day or a day later, and will pass over us.

Sometimes such a backward oscillation takes place when the region of calm has just passed over us, or is just about to do so, and is then indicated by the changing of the wind and by thermometric and barometric changes. In this case the storm will naturally last longer than ordinarily. A north-east storm can thus always be seen from one to three days beforehand by the appearance of its characteristic stripes of cloud. But when, in its progress, the region of calm has passed over us, and the sky is completely shut out by the clouds, the further movements of the storm must be judged by the changes of the wind and by the changes in the thermometer and barometer.

The explanation of the north-east storm, which may be observed once or twice every week during the winter, is as follows:

*Plate VII., Fig.* 1, represents a vertical section from north to south of the atmosphere of the temperate zone. $N\ S$ represents the surface of the earth along a meridian, $S'\ C'$ the height at which the first stripes of stratus are formed. The line $a\ b$ represents the section of the plane of meeting of the equatorial and polar currents. This plane of meeting, it must be remembered, is, from the overlapping of the two currents, always inclined to the surface of the earth, and the line where it strikes the surface is represented by $c\ d$, which, of course, must be imagined as at right angles to the line $a\ b$, and as running east and west. The arrow $q$ indicates the general direction of the equatorial current over the surface, and the arrow $e$ its direction obliquely upward. The arrow $p$ indicates the general direction of the polar current over the surface. The dotted line $m\ n$ represents the horizon from the point $a''$. At this point the sky is clear, the wind low and blowing in the direction $p$ prevailing at the season. The wind's being low indicates that there is no longer a want of air toward the equator, but in fact a deficiency toward the poles.

The equatorial current begins, therefore, its motion toward

the poles to supply this deficiency. It begins at its highest and most northern edge at *b*. Here it moves over the polar current in undulations, somewhat as the tide-wave moves up a river, until it reaches the point where the density of the polar current is less than its own. Here, the temperature being lower, the crests of its undulations cool, and the moisture they hold condenses into visible clouds. As the air in this region contains a comparatively small amount of vapor, the first cloud formed presents only a narrow, thin, elongated band.

In the process of condensation of the vapor in the first wave, latent heat is set free. This expands the surrounding air and facilitates the rise of a second wave from below. This second wave, coming from lower regions, contains a greater amount of moisture and therefore produces a thicker, broader and more visible stripe, stretched out in a line more or less parallel to the first. This process goes on until all the air along the inclined plane from *b* to *a* is set in motion, and proceeds in successive waves toward the arctic regions to supply the deficiency there.

When the air on the surface along the line *c d* begins to move obliquely upward the surrounding air will rush in from all sides to replace it. This process takes place both from the polar current at the north, and from its own current, the equatorial, at the south. The directions taken by the air of the two currents around this line *cd* are indicated by the arrows I., II., III., and 1, 2, 3, and *p* and *q*. The mingling of the cold and warm air of these southerly and northerly currents increases the amount of condensation, and in addition causes a region of calm along the plane *c d a b*, because, coming from opposite directions, the force of each is neutralized.

The area of the storm or the region of conflict between the equatorial and the polar currents must assume the form of an ellipse, and not that of a circle, which would be the case if the Rotary theory were true. The air in a storm, therefore, does

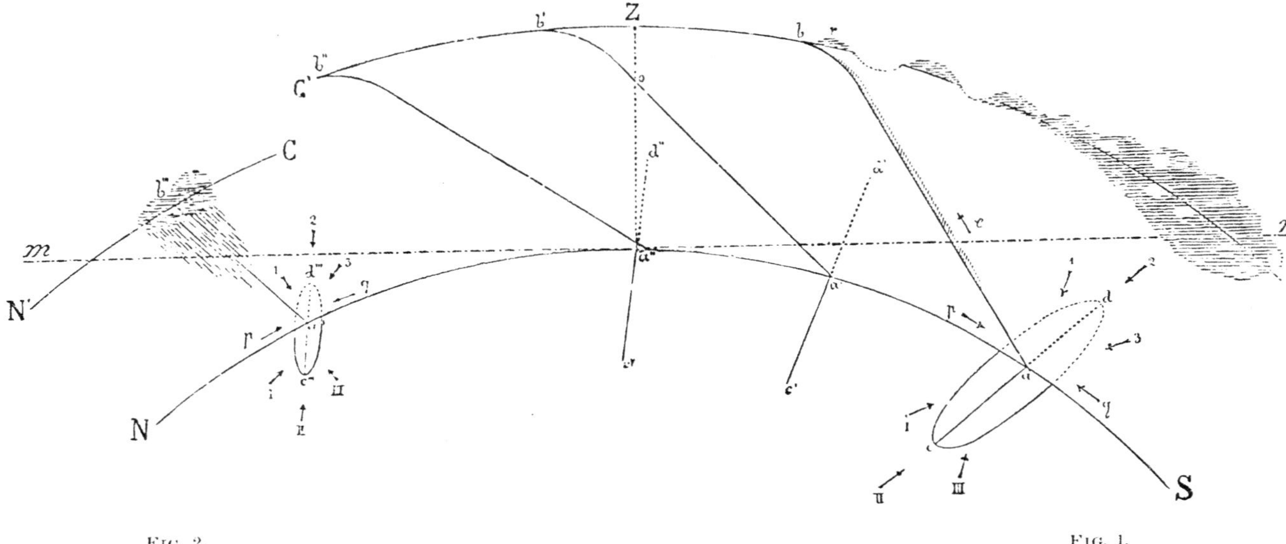


Fig. 2.

Fig. 1.

Plate VII.—Diagram of the Progressive Storms.

not move in a circle around one centre, as the Rotary theory maintains—much less around the line *c d*—but in straight lines from the circumference of the ellipse toward the region of the uprising equatorial current, the line *c d*. The storm will not consist in a single rotating current, but in different currents of different temperatures, blowing from all sides from the two main currents.

By the flow of the air of the polar current inward and upward immediately north of the line *c d*, room is made for the equatorial current to begin its advance toward the north over the surface. Thus the equatorial current, its motion beginning at the top, progresses northward toward the region of deficiency, replacing in its advance the polar current, of which the portion contiguous to the plane of meeting rises on account of coming under less pressure, and probably somewhat on account of its temperature's being increased by contact with the equatorial current and by the heat set free by the condensation which has taken place.

Now, it is evident that, as the line *c d* moves side foremost toward the north over any fixed point, all meteorological phenomena observed before the line *c d* has passed will be those of the polar current, and will be succeeded by the phenomena of the equatorial current, when the region south of the line *c d* begins to pass over this point after the region of calm existing between the two currents has gone by.

The wind changes, not in the manner generally supposed by the cyclonists, by the veering around of one and the same current, but by a succession of different currents, blowing inward toward the line of calm.

Thus a locality north of the line *c d*, near the left margin of the polar current, where the wind blows in the direction of arrow I., will, as the line *c d* passes over this locality, receive the wind successively from all points between I. and III., blowing in from the side, as before explained.

A locality north of the line, near the right margin of the polar current, where the wind blows in the direction of arrow 1, will receive, as the line *c d* passes over this locality northward, the wind successively from all points between 1 and 3.

A locality north of the line *c d* and in the middle of the main polar current, where the wind blows at a right angle to this line, will experience, as this line passes over it, at first a calm, and after this has passed the wind will blow from the opposite direction, as the arrow *q* indicates.

Localities north of *a d*, which are situated in the right half of the storm, will receive the wind in straight lines successively from all points of the arc *p*, 1, 2, 3, *q*.

Localities north of *a c*, which are situated in the left half of the storm, will receive the wind in straight lines successively from all points of the arc *p*, I., II., III., *q*.

In the middle of the storm opposite *a* the angle through which the changes in the direction of the wind over a locality north of the line *c d* take place is 180°. The angle will grow smaller as the locality lies nearer toward the margins *c* and *d*, where the wind always blows in the direction of the line *cd*.

We see, thus, that the directions from which a locality north of the line *c d*, situated in the right half of the storm, receives the wind, will change gradually while the line *c d* passes over, as the positions of the hands of a watch are changed in their movement, every different position representing a different current, and *not* a change in the direction of one and the same current.

A point situated north of the line *c d* in the left half of a storm will experience the same changes in the direction of the different currents, but in a manner as if the hands of a watch were moving backward. An idea may be formed of the changes in the direction of the wind in both halves of the storm by observing the motion of the two oars of a moving boat and the different directions they assume. This produces the appearance of one and the same current moving around a central point or line, and has doubtless given rise to the Rotary theory, while in reality there are *different* currents of *different temperatures* coming in straight lines from different points, and succeeding each other without intermission as the line *c d* passes over. If one and the same current were moving in a circle, it would be impossible to explain the meteorological changes which take place when a storm passes over us.

The error of this idea of a general rotation will also be proved by direct facts deduced by closer consideration of the West Cambridge tornado.

There must, necessarily, be a calm along the line *c d*, on account of the uprising of the equatorial current and its meeting with the polar current from the opposite side. This calm is of greatest extent and, therefore, of longest duration in any locality along the middle of the line *c d* or in the middle of the storm; for here the greatest quantity of air is rising, as all the different currents around this line are blowing toward it. This calm will grow smaller in extent toward the ends *c* and *d*, or along the margin of the storm, on account of the inblowing of air from the sides; and if the equatorial and polar currents come from exactly opposite directions, there will be no calm on the right or left margins of the storm.

With these changes of the wind from the polar into the equatorial current as the line *c d* passes over a certain locality, there must necessarily be experienced a rise in temperature. There is sometimes found in less than fifteen minutes a difference of from 15°–30° F.* Similar changes are found by the hygrometer in the amount of moisture north and south of this line *c d*.

From the difference in the tendency and nature of the two

* I have frequently found a difference of this amount in my own observations, and in severe storms other observers have found a still greater difference in as short a time.

opposing currents, it necessarily follows that the velocity of the wind around the line of calm *c d** is greater in the equatorial current south of this line than in the polar current, or north of it. For the equatorial current moves forward over the polar current to supply a deficiency in the arctic regions, while the polar current becomes passive because of this deficiency in its rear. The air of the equatorial current south of the line *c d* follows the uprising air above this line with a velocity increasing with the progress and development of the storm, while the air of the polar current north of the line *c d* flows toward this line only with sufficient rapidity to make room for the advance of the equatorial current. The greatest velocity of the wind in a storm will, therefore, be found in the equatorial current south of the region of calm *c d.* And as the tendency of this current is upward on account of greater heat and less weight, it must be more destructive than the polar current, the tendency of which is downward. Further on, in the consideration of the West Cambridge tornado, this important fact will be very clearly developed.

As has been said, the hazy stripes grow thicker proportionately as the air in which they originate comes from lower regions of the equatorial current, it containing most moisture nearest the surface. The clouds will therefore acquire the greatest thickness above the region *c d:* for the air here rises vertically from the surface of the ground, and taking the shortest way to the colder regions is subjected to the most rapid condensation. The formation of clouds then commences at *b* in separate, parallel stripes, as mentioned above, growing thicker and broader, and gradually uniting to form a screen completely covering the sky. When this screen of clouds has grown thick enough, it is precipitated as rain or snow, which of course increases as we approach the line *c d*, where it falls most copiously.

* This is really a *region* of calm; I speak of it as a line to simplify th explanation.

From this it is evident that the area of cloud and rain extends much farther—perhaps hundreds of miles—north of *c d* in the direction in which the storm moves than south of this line in the rear of the storm. For it begins with the first stripe to the north, and extends over the large area above the inclined plane of meeting, and over the area where the equatorial current ascends vertically.

If an observer at $a''$ sees the first stripe $r$ rise at $n$ above the horizon, he may know that the equatorial current—*i. e.*, a north-east storm—is approaching, although the barometer gives no sign of its approach, because no change has yet taken place in the pressure of the air at $a''$. When, however, the line *c d* advances into the position of the line $c'd'$, and the point $b'$, with the first stripe $r$, passes the zenith of the observer, the barometer will begin to fall, because the advancing end of the equatorial current has come above the barometer, and, being lighter and directed obliquely upward, causes the pressure to be diminished. The amount the barometer will fall is equal to the difference between the weight of the polar current of the depth of the line $o\,Z$ and the weight of the same depth of equatorial air, which has displaced it above the observer at $a''$. Manifestly, as the storm moves farther northward, the thickness of the equatorial current above the point $a''$ increases, while that of the polar current diminishes; the pressure upon the barometer at $a''$ must therefore decrease in the same ratio as the storm advances toward the north.

It is evident that the rapidity with which the barometer falls as the storm passes over $a''$ depends on the angle the plane of meeting makes with the surface—*i. e.*, the angle at which the equatorial current rises in overlapping the polar current. This angle seems to be dependent—first, on the relative velocity of the overlapping currents, and this on difference in temperature—second, on whether the equatorial or the polar current begins the oscillation, and whether the oscillation is in its beginning, middle or end. All these important questions must be answered by investigating corps, for I have not been able to arrive at any definite conclusion by individual observation. One result seems to be, however, tolerably certain: whenever, from the appearance of the clouds, the angle of the plane of meeting seems to approach a vertical, the velocity of the inblowing equatorial current and its destructiveness seem to increase, but the progressive velocity of the storm to diminish, and *vice versâ*. This result is also in accord with the dynamics of opposing air currents. The progressive velocity of the storm depends on the greater or less resistance with which the displacing equatorial current is opposed—*i. e.*, on the pressure or banking up of the polar current. The greater this becomes during the development of the storm, the more the plane of meeting must rise or approach a vertical position, the more the equatorial current is forced to rise vertically, and the greater must become the velocity of that laterally moving portion of the equatorial current which supplies the rising portion, but the greater, again, will be the resistance, and therefore the progressive velocity of the storm still less.

The velocity of the equatorial current will be greater the more vertically it rises, because it will then sooner reach a point at which its moisture condenses, and therefore the condensation will be greater, which, liberating a greater amount of latent heat, will cause the air to expand, grow lighter, and rise more rapidly.

In connection with this subject we may, perhaps, make a still further digression to note how the progressive velocity of a storm, and the position of its plane of meeting, change during its oscillation. The dotted line in *Fig.* 6 represents the variation of barometric pressure from the equator to the pole, *C* being the tropical belt of high pressure, and *N* the arctic belt of high pressure. If, now, in the winter the polar current, in a movement after displacement to reassume its prevailing position, has reached its most southern limit, the plane of meeting will occupy the position *a b*. The next movement will be that of the equatorial current toward the north, and this movement, beginning at *b*, will bend the plane of meeting over into the position *a′ b′*. Gradually, as the deficiency in the north becomes supplied, the pressure of the polar air toward the south increases, and the polar current banks up, bringing the plane of meeting into a more and more vertical position, until it finally, at the end of the forward movement, when the deficiency in the north is entirely supplied, takes the position *a″ b″*. The polar current, now pressing

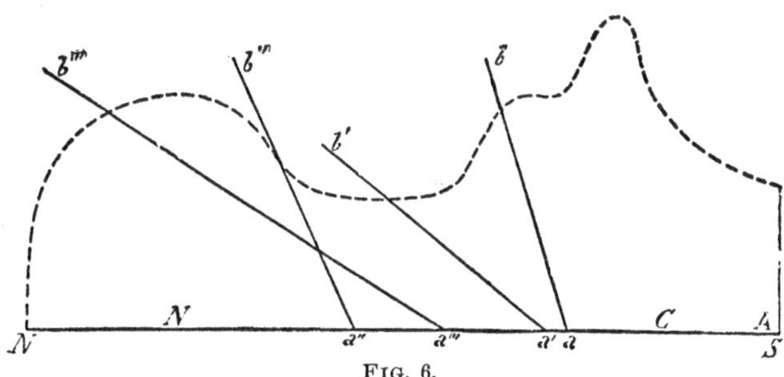


FIG. 6.

south, will begin its return movement at the surface, and will thus bring the plane of meeting into the position *a‴ b‴*, but in its progress will bank up again until the plane of meeting reassumes its original position *a b*.

From a consideration of these movements it is evident that the progressive velocity of the storm will increase from *a* to that point between *a* and *a″* where the inclination of the plane of meeting is greatest, from which point the velocity decreases, until the movement stops at *a″*; and the reverse order must be found in the return movement. The oscillation of a storm is thus like the oscillation of a pendulum, attaining its greatest velocity in the middle of a movement; but the velocity of the equatorial current follows a reverse rule.

But to return to the consideration of the falling of the barometer as the storm passes over us. When the line *c d* (*Plate VII., Fig.* 1) has assumed the position *c″d″*, the entire thickness of the light equatorial current has come over the barometer instead of the heavy polar current; and since the air here rushes upward, the pressure along this line must be lower than elsewhere, and the barometer fall to the lowest point. This line, therefore, where the plane of meeting of the two currents strikes the earth's surface, is *the line of lowest pressure.* It is represented on the plate successively as the storm progresses to the north by the lines *c d*, *c′d′*, *c″d″*.

When the line *c d* moves still farther north, and the region of calm or the region of uprising air has passed the observer at *a″*, that part of the equatorial current which blows horizontally toward this region will pass over him. As the air no longer rises, but moves horizontally, the whole pressure of the equatorial current comes upon the barometer, and causes it to rise again. It is easily seen that this rise will be more rapid than was the fall at the approach of the storm.

Before and during the time that the single stripes are moving over us toward the north-east the prevailing polar current is generally at rest, so to speak; but as the line *c d* approaches and the sky becomes covered with thicker clouds, the prevailing polar current increases in strength and blows toward the line *c d.* As its direction in our latitude is generally from the north-east, it has been thought that these storms *come* from the north-east, no one paying attention to the fact that the clouds, which generally cover the whole heaven when it begins to blow from this quarter, have really come from the opposite direction until Franklin observed this fact on the occasion before mentioned.

We find even now among many navigators, particularly the adherents of the Rotary theory, the mistaken idea that a storm comes from that quarter from which the wind is blowing at its beginning. They have not yet been taught that the clouds are the embodiment of the storm, and show by their motion that the storm arises in the direction opposite to that in which "the gale" begins to blow and travels against it. They do not seem to think that the storm stands in any causal relation to the clouds, and for that reason probably so little importance is attached to these.

It has been explained why the condensation and the precipitation increase as the point *b* passes over us toward the north and the line *c d* approaches. The vesicles of water formed by the condensation in the region *b S'* of the equatorial current will freeze by being precipitated into the denser, colder polar current below, if its temperature is below the freezing-point. As they fall slowly and quietly through this denser medium they will crystallize into the beautiful forms of snow. We can also easily understand why these snowflakes at first fly obliquely with this lower polar current toward the line *cd*, and why their direction becomes more vertical as this line approaches us.

Lastly, we can also understand why sometimes during the passage of this line rain falls instead of snow, because the precipitations do not pass through the polar current at all.

In this connection it is evident that the cause of an increase of temperature which is observed during and after the period of calm when the snow descends vertically is due almost entirely to being then in the equatorial current, which is always several degrees warmer than the polar. This phenomenon has been hitherto ascribed to the setting free of latent heat by the condensation; but as this takes place in the upper region, it is difficult to see how it could affect the temperature at the surface.

When the precipitation is profuse enough to form rain-drops above the plane of meeting, these rain-drops, in falling through the polar current, are frequently frozen into sleet; and the phenomenon is frequently observed that in the beginning of a storm snow falls, but as the region of conflict approaches, and the thicker strata of cloud come above us, the precipitation becomes profuse enough to take the form of sleet. As, however, the storm advances and the precipitation is still more profuse, the depth of polar air through which it falls, on the other hand, becoming constantly less, we find rain-drops reaching the ground unfrozen, mingled with the globules of sleet; and finally, when the region of meeting reaches us, the frozen rain-drops cease altogether. This change from snow into sleet, then into sleet and rain, and finally into rain alone, is familiar to every one, and is very difficult to explain on any other theory than the one presented here. Of course snow may change into rain without there being any sleet, all these formations being determined by the degree of condensation and the difference of temperature, but it will be generally noticed that in this case the snowflakes grow larger and wetter before they change into rain.

We have thus accompanied the movement of the equatorial current from a locality of the tropical belt of high pressure to a locality of a deficiency of air in the arctic region, and have seen how, in its conflict with the polar current, it produces all the phenomena observed in the passage of a north-east storm. As the first and highest edge of the equatorial current rises and flows over the polar current to the region of deficiency, replacing in its movement the polar air by tropical air in the cloud region, the line of high pressure in front of the equatorial current apparently shifts to the north, and there is a gradual decrease of barometric pressure until the lowest degree of pressure, indicated by the line *c d*, with its surrounding region of calm, has passed, and then the pressure of the equatorial current begins to be seen, and increases at a more rapid rate than was seen in the decrease of pressure in front of the storm.

In a north-east storm there is, therefore, a region of lowest barometer surrounding the line *c d*, with two regions of high barometer, one in front and the other in the rear of it. These three regions move onward in this order, the first region of high barometer far distant and in front of *c d*, the other region of high barometer in the rear keeping closer to it. The region of high barometer, which apparently moves far in front of the storm, is the receding polar current; the region of low barometer is the uprising, and the region of high barometer in the rear of the storm is the inblowing, equatorial current.

In the preceding explanation of the north-east storms we have assumed for the sake of simplicity that the equatorial current, which gives the storm its direction, moves in a due line from south to north; but it is well known that this current, from the rotation of the earth, changes its course gradually toward the east, and the longer distance it comes, the more easterly will be its course. The direction a north-east storm must have is, therefore, dependent on the geographical position —*i. e.*, on the longitude and latitude—of the locality from which it is observed, and on the geographical position of the point where the movement of the storm begins. And as the tropical belt of high pressure in which these storms originate shifts with the sun north or south and assumes different positions with the changing seasons, it follows, necessarily, that these storms approach any fixed locality from different directions according to the season, but generally from the quadrant south to west. Their general direction is, therefore, toward the north-east; hence the name north-east storms. A line at right angles to the first appearing stripe of clouds will indicate the general direction of the equatorial current, and therefore that of the storm. It has seemed to me, from observation, that such a line wheels around, generally speaking, from a southerly to a westerly direction from one autumn to the summer of the next year, at least in the United States.

The latent heat which evolves during the progress of the storm northward may draw the equatorial current farther north than it would have gone solely by the tendency to supply the deficiency in the arctic region; and thus this deficiency is over-supplied by the tropical air, and in turn there is created a preponderance of pressure here and a deficiency at the tropics. Thus the return oscillation of the storm or its retirement is initiated. The polar current returns and assumes the position it occupied before the storm, displacing the equatorial current, which had temporarily assumed the supremacy over the localities over which the storm had passed, by shifting over the surface like a wedge, with its thin end foremost.

In general terms, the meteorological phenomena brought by the storm in the forward movement of the equatorial current change in reverse order in the return oscillation into those of the polar current as the line *c d* passes southward. The wind which blows after the passage of the storm northward in the direction of the arrows III. and 3 will change first into the directions II. and 2 respectively, and then into those of I. and 1, and *q* will change into *p*. The thermometer falls and the barometer rises.

When a north-east storm is raging, and one of these two changes takes place, the return oscillation has commenced and the storm is retiring toward the south. Some hours—frequently half a day—after one of these changes has indicated the return of the polar current and the retirement of the storm, the sky clears in the northern semicircle—that is, in the north-east or north, or most frequently in the north-west. This clearing up of the sky is produced by the rising above the horizon of the upper line of the plane of meeting—*b*. The polar current in its progress to the south shifts the unprecipitated clouds lying suspended above the inclined plane of meeting to warmer regions; the capacity to contain aqueous vapor increases in both currents as they become more heated and the clouds dissolve in advance of the polar current.

If the polar current in the return oscillation flows back over the exact track of the storm, the meteorological phenomena will *all* change in reverse order, as before mentioned. This takes place frequently in the middle of the winter, when the line *cd* does not pass far to the north, and the polar current in the return oscillation has still the direction given by the rotation of the earth. The sky clears, therefore, to the north or north-east. But when the storm has moved far to the north with its line *cd*, the polar current comes from greater distances, and may be deflected from its original course by local circumstances, such as the presence of mountain ranges or localities where the air is more heated than in the surrounding regions. For the polar current, being cold and heavy, will not rise over mountain ranges, as the equatorial current does, but will be deflected at the same angle at which it strikes them. Thus for instance the polar current coming as a north-east or east current against the Rocky Mountains will be deflected, and will flow as a north-west or west current. A polar current passing west of a region over which the air is more heated than over surrounding regions will be deflected from its course and assume a direction from the north-west or west.

It appears that this effect is produced in this country by both of these causes, the Rocky Mountains and the Appalachian mountain system on the one hand, and the regions above the Great Lakes on the other. Therefore it occurs, particularly during the transition periods in the spring and autumn, that the polar current comes from the north-west or from the west, and the sky generally clears after storms from one or other of these quarters.

The forward and backward movement of the storm, or the forward and backward oscillation of the two currents, is in these cases comparable to the movement of an eccentric wheel, the right half of the polar current moving over an area in the backward movement, which in the forward movement of the storm its left half traversed. At any locality which lies in both the forward and the return movement of such a storm the wind will change around the whole compass.

In the winter the line *cd*, lying far to the south, does not move in the progress of a storm very far north, and therefore the observer at $a''$, a point some distance north of its winter position, will not generally remain long in the equatorial current before the return oscillation brings back the polar current and the sky clears from the north. In the late spring and early autumn, however, the line *cd* lies farther north, and therefore travels during a storm a much greater distance beyond the observer at $a''$, and the sky clears from the south before the return oscillation has brought the line *cd* past him again.

In describing the wind's direction over the area of the storm, we have for the sake of simplicity assumed that during the oscillations the main directions of the two opposing currents form a straight line 180°, or nearly that; when the two currents, however, meet at a smaller angle, the wind on one margin of the storm will be rather in the direction of the diagonal—*i. e.*, it will appear to flow along the line of low barometer, the direction of which is indicated, as we know, by the direction of the stratus.

Plate VIII.—The Cumulo-Stratus in the South-east Storm.

# CHAPTER VI.

## *PROGRESSIVE STORMS.—POLAR, OR SOUTH-EAST AND SOUTH-WEST STORMS—SUMMER STORMS.*

PRECEDING a storm of this kind the air is warm and sultry, the sky somewhat dim, but cloudless. A light southerly breeze rises which is just strong enough to decapitate any local storms that may possibly be forming. Suddenly the stillness of the day is interrupted by a long-continued, distant rumbling of thunder. About the same time the tops of black, round clouds (cumulus) are seen to rise above the northern or north-western horizon, and to arrange themselves in a long bank. It is the *cumulo-stratus*, the herald of the south-east storm. (*Plate VIII.*)

At sea high billows rise in front of and parallel to this long, black bank of clouds, and in some cases may possibly be seen before the clouds appear.

The mariner who is guided by the rules deduced from the Cyclone theory stands at his post, attentively watching the veering of the wind in order to find whether he is in the "dangerous" or the "manageable semi-circle" of the supposed cyclone.

All at once all hands on deck become active. The old sailor who was lazily lying about runs like a cat to the top of the mast and whistles his favorite tune. Some sails are furled, others are unfurled. The ship changes her course in order to avoid the centre of the storm and to clear the dangerous semi-circle, the captain following strictly the rules of the Navy Department, based on the theory that the storm is a cyclone, and therefore round. The rising wind strikes the sails with increased violence and the ship labors and trembles. The high swell of water comes nearer; all at once she finds herself in a death-like calm, the very place which the captain tried to avoid. Strange that here the waves are highest and the sea most terrible! The ship is tossed up and down and dashed from one side to the other "as if by two irresistible forces. One seems to draw her toward the storm, the other to throw her out of it." Air and water seem to be allied for destruction. One mast goes overboard, then another; one man after another is swept off. The ship is soon crippled, and the captain certainly knows by this time that, after all, he has gotten into the dangerous semicircle and near the centre, for he is in the so-called calm. Next the wheelhouse is torn away; the ship has become unmanageable, and soon its destruction is complete.

A storm of this kind is not a cyclone, and the dreaded region of low barometer, or calm, is not a circular space, but simply the elongated region surrounding the line of meeting of the polar and equatorial currents. In the typical case we have imagined, the captain, following the rules of the Cyclone theory, under the supposition that the storm was round, and thinking he is running out of the "dangerous semicircle," in fact runs into it; for the region of calm is elliptical, and its dangerous half is 90° from the place where this theory locates it. This is based on facts brought out in analyzing the West Cambridge tornado.

On land we observe analogous scenes. Instead of billows of water, we see clouds of dust arise before the storm. When the bank of cloud has reached a certain height, it sometimes advances more slowly. At last it becomes stationary. The thunder and lightning continue, the south wind increases. The farmer, unacquainted with the meaning of the apparent stop in the advance of the clouds, hurries once more to the fields to bring in another load of his harvest. He little anticipates that he is bringing it to destruction. On a sudden he hears a rattling, roaring noise; and looking in the direction from which it comes, he observes a fearful-looking, funnel-shaped black cloud, appearing in the distance like a volume of smoke, approaching with great speed. He hurries to a place of safety, but before he has reached it his barn, with his rich harvest, is swept away as if by magic, his house unroofed, his orchards destroyed. He may consider himself fortunate to find his family still alive. Such are the general appearances and movements of a progressive summer storm in its most severe aspects and ending in a tornado. In the majority of cases, however, after the storm has been stationary for some time, which is seen in the stoppage of the advance of the bank of clouds, it oscillates back; the clouds, having discharged themselves, dissipate, and the storm is over.

All these phenomena are caused by the conflict arising from the displacement by a cool, dense, heavy polar current of the prevailing warmer, lighter equatorial current. The movement of the polar current is caused by its tendency to re-establish equilibrium in a southern direction, or, in other words, to supply a deficiency of air which has been created either by a slowly continuous movement of the equatorial current over the polar toward the poles, or by a sudden, violent movement toward the uprising air at the equator. When, during the summer, the atmosphere, with its different belts of low and high pressure, has been shifted northward by the motion of the sun toward the tropic of Cancer, we, in our own latitude, have come into the prevailing equatorial or southern current (*Plate V.*) coming from points of the quadrant south to west, according to the season.

In summer the heat of the sun thus causes the air to move from the tropics, or the belt of high pressure, toward the arctic belt of high pressure, increasing the amount of the last belt and diminishing that of the first. Deficiencies of air will thus be created at the tropics, particularly over land, which is more heated than water. Part of the air of the arctic belt of high pressure will flow as a polar current toward these deficiencies, displacing the prevailing equatorial current and causing a south-east storm, which, it must be remembered, in approaching, comes from a direction opposite to and travels against the prevailing wind. So long, therefore, as we are in this prevailing equatorial current from the southern semicircle, we cannot expect any change of weather or any progressive storm except from the northern semicircle.

The polar current shifts over the surface like a wedge, with its thin edge in advance; for it is colder and heavier than the prevailing equatorial current, and, therefore, flows below it. The equatorial current is lifted up, and the great quantity of vapor it has received during the time that it was lying undisturbed on the heated surface begins to condense. The latent heat evolved by this condensation expands the air still more and assists its rise, thus making room for the movement southward of the polar current. By the rising of the equatorial current along the front of the polar current a region of lowest barometer is created, which will become more defined as the place of conflict or the region of depression moves southward. This is a general view of the phenomenon; we now pass on to a particular explanation.

The region of lowest pressure, or the rising equatorial current, is represented by the line $c''' \ d'''$. (*Plate VII., Fig.* 2.) The wind surrounding the area of lowest pressure $c''' \ d'''$ will in both currents take the direction of the arrows I., II., III., $q'''$, 3, 2, 1, $p'''$, whatever the general direction of the two currents may be. In these storms the line $N' \ C$, or the region where the clouds are formed, is lower than in the north-east storms. The dotted line $m \ n$ represents the horizon, $a''' \ b'''$ the plane of meeting of the two currents. North of $a''' \ b'''$ toward

*N* lies the polar current, south of $a''' b'''$ toward *S* the equatorial current.

When a south-east storm moves over us from north to south, we experience the same changes of the wind, of the barometer and of the thermometer as in the *return* oscillation of a north-east storm—that is, we experience the changes in the reverse order to that of those changes which the equatorial current produces in its displacement of the polar current.

On the right side of the storm the direction of the wind will change from that of the arrow III. to that of the arrow II. and from II. to I., or in the direction the hands of a watch move. On the left side of the storm the direction of the wind will change from that of the arrow 3 to 2 and from 2 to 1, or contrary to the hands of a watch. Along the line $c'''d'''$ it will pass through a region of calm, and change suddenly from the direction of the arrow $q'''$ to that of $p'''$.

Although the changes in the wind, the barometer and the thermometer are the same as in the return oscillation of a north-east storm, the accompanying effects are totally different, because the state of the two currents as to the amount of moisture is different. In the return oscillation of the north-east storm the polar current finds the equatorial current deprived of aqueous vapor, which it had just before discharged during its forward movement; but in the summer storm the polar current finds the equatorial current saturated with moisture by the immense evaporation going on during the time this current lies undisturbed on the heated surface of the earth. In the return oscillation of the north-east storm the clouds which still float over the inclined plane of meeting dissolve as the polar current moves southward; in this storm the polar current produces clouds as it progresses toward the south.

The storm begins to form by the forward movement of the polar current toward the south. Irregular masses of the polar air in advance shift over the surface, bank up and lift the equatorial air in an irregular manner, producing, if the storm develops above us, irregular globular masses of clouds, or cumulus. The latent heat liberated in the formation of the cumulus assists in raising the equatorial air, which moves obliquely over the polar current. The whole body of each current being set in motion, the pressure against each other is more regular, and therefore a more regular plane of meeting is developed. The cumulus arranges in a line along the upper end of the polar current. The clouds then look from *above* like small elevations arranged side by side in a long line (*Plate IX.*), and being the combination of the two elementary forms of clouds, the stratus and the cumulus, are called the cumulo-stratus, and are characteristic of the south-east storms. When the polar current begins to move in the upper region, this line of cloud becomes on its northern side more and more distinct; and as it shifts over us, the sky begins to clear in the north and to be obscured in the south.

As the storm progresses toward the south the condensation of vapor increases and begins to be precipitated; the clouds appear to travel with the storm, but in reality continually dissipate—being mostly precipitated, but also partly dissolved by the polar air—and form anew in advance of and above the polar current. The falling rain and the condensation formed between the two currents in the plane of meeting look in the distance like a gray sheet of uniform color spread out between the surface of the earth and the bank of clouds above. While in the beginning of the storm the cumuli are arranging themselves in a line in the upper region, a line of low barometer $c'''d'''$ develops, on account of the uprising equatorial air, on the surface between the two currents and parallel to the line of cloud.

In the undeveloped state of the storm the line $c'''\,d'''$ will pass us without our experiencing marked meteorological contrasts north and south of it, since the division between the cur-

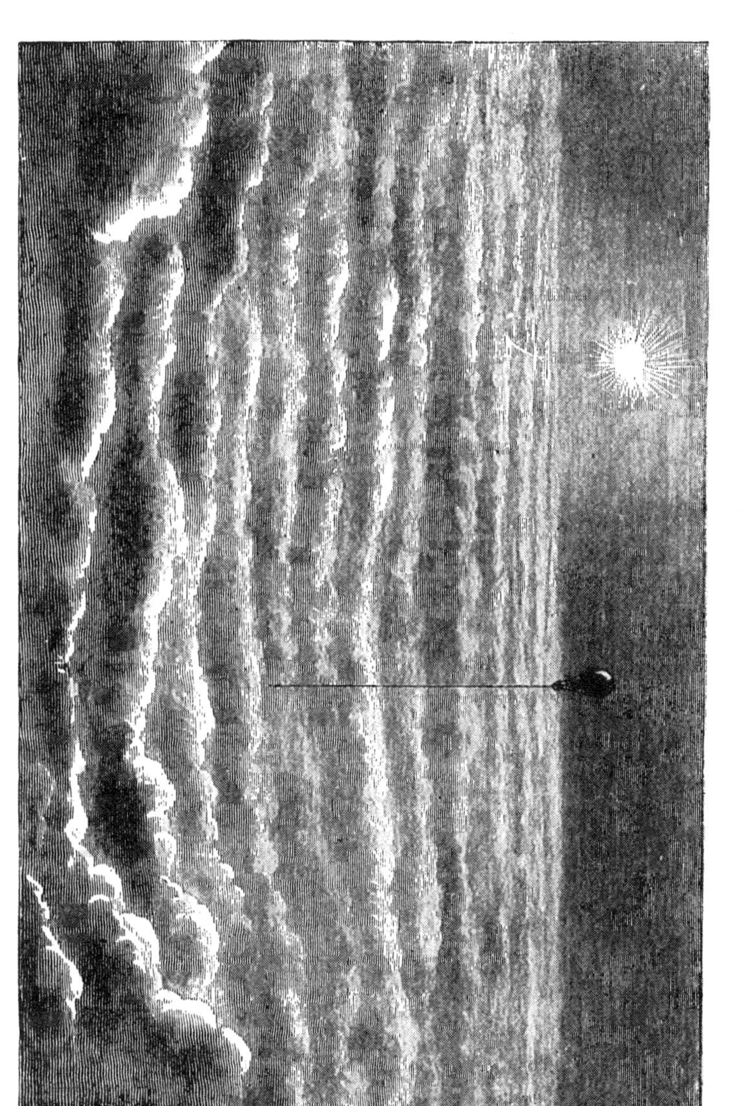

rents is not yet very distinct. But as the storm develops and moves southward these contrasts increase; thus the difference in temperature north and south of $c''' d'''$ increases; the equatorial current rushes up in greater volume and follows horizontally with greater velocity, particularly toward the end of the storm, while the polar current decreases in velocity; the barometer along the line $c''' d'''$ continues to fall, and the barometer in the regions north and south of this line continues to rise.

The process is the same as that considered in the north-east storm, but in reverse order. The plane of meeting, when the currents are *in equilibrio*, will have the position of the line $a'' b''$ (*Fig.* 6); but when the polar current begins a movement to supply a deficiency in density in the south, moving first at the surface it soon presses the plane of meeting into the position $a''' b'''$. But as the storm progresses the polar current, finding more and more resistance, banks up, and the plane of meeting rises into the position $a' b'$, and finally, when the movement stops, into $a b$. About this time tornadoes are likely to occur. The deficiency will now be somewhat over-supplied, the liberation of latent heat by the profuse condensation having caused great volumes of equatorial air to ascend, and thus drawn the polar current farther to the south than required to establish equilibrium, and the return movement begins, the plane of meeting assuming its successive positions, until, when equilibrium is finally established, it occupies the position $a'' b''$, as before the storm.

The rule of velocity, it is evident, is here the same as in the north-east storm, the velocity of the storm decreasing and the velocity of the equatorial current increasing as the angle of inclination of the plane of meeting grows larger, and conversely.

As the storm progresses the regions of high barometer north and south, particularly north, approach nearer to the line of lowest barometer $c''' d'''$, and the area of the storm narrows, the isobars, or lines of equal barometer, approaching each other. We find thus a gradual development in this kind of storm, as in all others. If it originates above us or not too far away to the north, it will pass quickly and harmlessly, without much or any rain; but it may become violent and very dangerous to those south of us. If it approaches us in a more developed state, it may become dangerous to us. It may originate so far north of us that its oscillation brings it near, and it appears very threatening, but does not reach us.

A little acquaintance with the appearance of the cumulo-stratus, and a knowledge of its progressive velocity in particular cases, will enable one to judge as to these points.

In these storms the condensation sometimes takes place so rapidly and on so large a scale that the whole process becomes plainly visible. In this case, as the equatorial current rushes upward along the plane of meeting, it deposits its cumulus along the upper edge of the polar current, and the newly-formed clouds appear like the spray produced by the sea dashing against rocks.

The great violence with which the equatorial current rushes upward over the polar current, so different in temperature and density, produces, doubtless by the friction and the profuse condensation, the great amount of electricity so characteristic of these storms. The long continuous thunder in the south-east storm is probably caused by the extensive development of electricity along the whole plane of meeting, while the short explosive thunder in the summer showers—the local storms—is produced by the development of electricity in a limited space.

There occur no discharges of electricity in a north-east or winter storm, and the cause of this probably consists in the fact that in these storms the two currents overlap each other more obliquely, and consequently their friction is less.

Whenever, in a north-east storm in the early spring or late autumn, thunder and lightning occur, we may be sure that a local storm takes place underneath the main storm or that a south-east storm collides with it, as will be explained further on.

From the fact that the plane of meeting must assume a more nearly vertical position, on account of the banking up of the polar current in its progress, the line of lowest barometer $c''' d'''$ is not so distant from the line of clouds which marks the meeting of the two currents in the upper regions as it is in the north-east storms. Hence there will not be so long an interval between the appearance of the cumulo-stratus and the passing by of the line $c''' d'''$ as there is in the north-east storm, especially as the line $c''' d'''$ precedes the bank of clouds and the main rain-area, while in the north-east storm it follows the clouds and the main rain-area. Toward the end of the south-east storm, when the plane of meeting becomes more nearly vertical, the rain-area lies on both sides of the line, but always is more extensive to the north of it. In general, it does not extend so far from the line on either side as in the north-east storm, since the plane of meeting is at all times more nearly vertical, and these storms are therefore of less duration, but more sudden, and accompanied by more rapid condensation, producing a more violent rain-fall. So sudden and violent is this rain-fall frequently that it is pictured by the popular expression of a *bursting* of the cloud.

For the preceding reasons the characteristic cloud, cumulo-stratus, can generally be seen only from one to eight hours, or in the most violent storms perhaps twelve, before the middle of the storm or the line $c'''d'''$ reaches us. They cannot therefore be predicted by the appearance of the cloud so long in advance as the north-east storms, but their approach seems to be slow in the ratio of their violence; and thus Nature gives us warning proportionately in advance to the danger we are to incur.

In these storms, which are the most violent and destructive, the barometer is utterly useless as a predictor, because the line of lowest barometer $c'''d'''$, the region of greatest danger, travels in *front* of the inclined plane of meeting. Part of the most dangerous region of the storm, the in-rushing equatorial current, has therefore already passed over us before the barometer indicates by its sudden fall the uprising current or the line $c'''d'''$, the place of greatest danger.* The clouds, however, if rightly understood, will not only indicate these storms early enough for safety, but also tell how to avoid them.

The breadth of the south-east storms is not so extensive as that of the north-east storms, probably because the polar regions from which they come are less extensive in breadth than the equatorial regions from which the north-east storms come.† Therefore a vessel may more easily sail around them and avoid the region of greatest danger *in front* than in the north-east storms.

These two kinds of storms differ also in the distance which they travel, this being much less in the south-east storms. Another marked difference consists in the fact that the course of the south-east storms depends much more on the configuration and other physical circumstances of the earth's surface, and on the extent and shape of the arctic and tropical belts of high pressure, than that of the north-east storms.

* From an account of the terrible and destructive typhoon which occurred in the summer of this year (1874), at Nagasaki, Japan, and which I take to have been a storm of the kind under discussion in connection with a tornado on a large scale, it appears that a change in the barometer was first observed when the rain had begun to fall. Thus, by waiting for a fall in the barometer, which could not take place until the line $c'''d'''$, the middle of the storm, had already arrived, the warning came too late to take measures preventive of the terrible destruction that took place. The clouds, doubtless, if understood, would have given warning probably as much as eight hours in advance, and thus have saved many lives and much property. Compare also Prof. Mohn's and Mr. Gaster's remarks, chapter XI.

† This may perhaps be more readily understood if we think of the currents of air as occupying a certain proportion of the parallel of latitude from which they start. Thus a current of air starting from 60° N. lat., and measuring in width say half a degree of longitude, will measure much less in *miles*—that is, in actual measurement—than a current which starts from 30° N. lat., measuring half a degree in width.

The course of the south-east storm is determined by the direction that the polar current takes. If this current were influenced only by the rotation of the earth, these storms would come from the quadrant north to east and travel toward the quadrant south to west, and should then be called south-*west* storms; but I have called them south-*east* storms* since in this country and in Western Europe they mostly come from the north-west and go to the south-east, because the polar currents which produce them evidently become deflected by local circumstances. In considering the return oscillation of the north-east storm, some of the causes that may produce a deflection of the polar current from a north-easterly to a north-westerly direction have been already indicated.

The high mountain chains in North America running mainly from north to south, the lake regions and the Gulf Stream, with the more rarefied air above it, must exercise a positive influence on the direction of the polar currents starting from the different longitudes of the arctic region north and north-east of us. They also exert an influence on the form of the arctic and the tropical belts of high pressure at the different seasons, drawing them more to the north at some points and more to the south at others, thus giving them a sinuous form.

The equatorial current is little, or not at all, influenced in its course by these local circumstances, since, as its tendency is to rise from the surface, it is enabled to surmount those obstacles that deflect the polar current, which, of course, lies upon the surface. The course of the north-east or winter storms is, therefore, almost wholly dependent on the rotation of the earth, and is defined by it and by the season. The course of the south-east storms being determined by these local circumstances,

* If by future investigations it should be found that in some longitudes along the belt of high pressure, for instance on high sea, the polar currents, and in consequence the south-east storms, retain the direction given to them by the rotation of the earth, *south-west* storms would be a more scientific appellation, and should therefore be adopted.

however, they may be expected to come from all points of the northern semicircle. Their accommodation to the configuration of the ground naturally leads them to make pathways of valleys; and as each valley has its stream of water, there has arisen a popular belief, based merely on observation, that "storms follow rivers."

The greater the extent over which the polar current passes, and the greater the number of irregularities in its path, manifestly the more will it be deflected from the course originally given to it by the rotation of the earth. In the summer, when the belt of arctic high pressure has its most northern position, the polar current comes from its greatest distance, and is, therefore, more deflected from its original direction than during the winter in the return oscillation of the north-east storms.

A deflected polar current may, of course, be deflected again should there be the causes spoken of, and this may also occur should the deflected current strike obliquely against the tropical belt of high pressure; and the more or less sinuous form of this belt adds to its complications. The movements of the current resulting from these various modifying causes are apt, therefore, to obscure the main principles which pervade the whole.

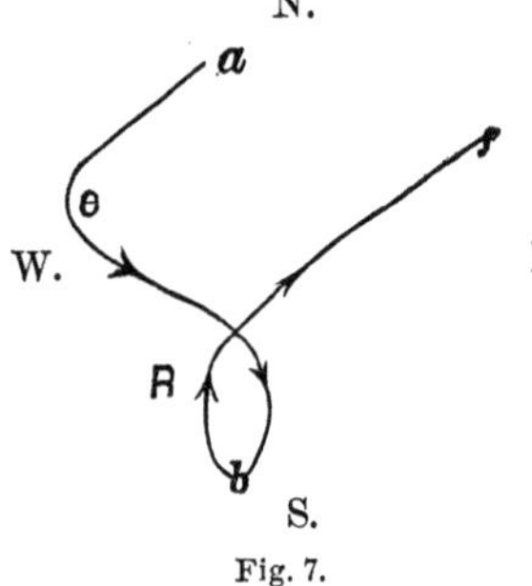

Fig. 7.

For the sake of illustration the following hypothetical case is assumed, in which some of these complications take place. (*Fig.* 7.) Let it be supposed that somewhere in the arctic regions a polar current begins a movement to supply a deficiency in the tropical region near *b*. At first, being only influenced from its direct course southward by the rotation of the earth, it flows to the south-west; but striking at *e* a range of mountains running north and south, it is deflected to the south-east. At the bend in the tropical belt of high pressure at *R* it is again turned from its course by the greater pressure of the equatorial air, and takes a more easterly direction, but is soon, by the rotation of the earth, brought again to a southerly, and perhaps even south-westerly, direction. When it reaches *b*, the deficiency is supplied, and here a tornado may originate in the manner hereafter explained, and will travel from west to east through the region of calm between the opposing equatorial and polar currents. When the deficiency at *b* is fully supplied, the return oscillation begins—that is, the equatorial current flows back to take the position it had before the storm. It may do this at first toward the north-west in the direction in which it was displaced by the polar current, but soon it will be influenced by the rotation of the earth and bend to the north, and then to the north-east toward *f*, producing on its way a north-east storm by displacing the polar current.

This north-east storm, or return oscillation, of course begins immediately on the cessation of the south-east storm, and at the point where it ends. The region of low barometer, the line $c'''$ $d'''$ of *Plate VII.*, *Fig.* 2, in this case would, therefore, travel from *a* to *e* and from *e* to *b;* from which point it would travel as a *new* storm, in the return oscillation, first to the north-west, but soon turning to the north-east and travelling as a north-east storm, ending probably at *f*.

Those who consider that storms exhibit themselves principally in "depressions," and are guided in their observations almost entirely by the barometer, will naturally conclude that these two storms are but one, which travels from north-west (*e*) to south-east (*b*), describes a circle and travels, at a right angle from its first direction, to the north-east (*f*). This is the error into which the Signal Service and Professor Loomis have fallen, and which was inevitable from the method of observation pursued. The truth, however, I am convinced is, as before stated, that we have here two different storms—a south-east storm originating at *a*, travelling to *e* and then to *b*, where it ends, immediately followed by a north-east storm, beginning on the backward track of the other, and then turned by the influence of the earth's rotation in the direction of *f*. *Continuous* observations throughout the duration of both of these storms would show that they differ essentially in the mode in which the wind changes, the order in which the temperature and pressure change, and in the forms of the clouds, and are in all respects characteristic of the two different kinds of storms. The Signal Service observations fail to manifest this, because they are made only three or four times in the course of twenty-four hours. The region of low barometer between the opposing currents frequently does not remain in the same position for five minutes at a time, and it is impossible to observe its changes of position and the great contrasts north and south of it—the things most essential to a knowledge of the individual nature of the storm—by only three or four daily observations, or even eight, as was agreed on by the late Meteorological Congress at Vienna. Such a method of observing will, in at least the majority of cases, only serve to indicate the whereabouts of the storm. I am thoroughly convinced of this, and that *continuous* observations are essential to scientific investigations.

We have described the south-east storms on land, and at sea their main characteristics—the clouds, changes in wind, temperature and pressure—are the same. There are, however, some differences due to the different nature of the surface over which they move. The principal of these is that there is in the storm at sea a high hill of water rolling before it.

In reference to this phenomenon the *Nautical Directions for Manœuvring in the Case of Hurricanes*, a pamphlet issued by the United States Hydrographic Office, says:

"The undulations and currents of hurricanes appear to be the constant results of these violent atmospheric shocks. These two phenomena deserve to be the subject of serious study and research.

"The undulation of the hurricane is a mass of water of greater or less diameter, according to the force of the tempest, raised above the ordinary level of the ocean by the atmospheric pressure or other cause. This mass is driven before the storm in its course until it encounters some obstacle, as the mouths of rivers, bays or coasts, when it often produces serious inundations or heavy bores."

Redfield and the other cyclonists hold that this undulation is the water in the centre of the vortex rising on account of the rarefication of the air above it. If this were so, it would appear as a *round* hill, and not as an elongated one, as it certainly is; above all, it should be, according to this theory, underneath the storm-cloud, whereas, in reality, it is in advance of it. The centripetalists, on the other hand, hold that it is produced by the air rushing in on all sides and rising vertically above a superheated surface; but this theory would also locate the undulation underneath the storm-cloud instead of in advance of it. The true explanation of the phenomenon is simply this: North of the region surrounding the line $c'''d'''$ (*Plate VII., Fig.* 2), the polar current, being denser and heavier, exerts more pressure upon the surface than the upward-rising equatorial current south of it. The water will then stand higher immediately south of the line $c'''d'''$, being relieved from pressure, and the polar current in its rapid advance ploughs it up, so to speak, into a still higher undulation. This line $c'''d'''$ is invariably in advance of the storm-cloud and the greater extent of the storm, although the wind south of $c'''d'''$ is even more violent than north of it.

A consideration of these matters will also clearly explain the phenomena detailed in the following extracts from the pamphlet that we have before cited:

"A remarkable trait of the rotary gale is the increase of the wind in the vicinity of its centre, although at the centre itself it blows so irregularly and by squalls as to render it impossible for a ship to complete a manœuvre. The nearer the centre is approached, the more sudden are the changes of the wind, which, instead of shifting point by point, as is the case at the entrance of the circle of the tempest, shifts all at once sixteen points. The ship is enveloped in a terrible squall, and gathers stern-board against a frightful sea, the disastrous consequences of which it would be unnecessary to detail. . . . There are also in every hurricane two forces, independent of that of the wind, which act upon a vessel, the one drawing her directly in the line of the path of the storm, the other drawing her toward the circumference of that portion of the rotary circle where she is placed. . . . Electricity seems to take a great part in hurricanes, though very often it may escape observation.

"Among the thirty-two hurricanes of the Indian Ocean of which the *data* is precise, eleven have been accompanied by thunder and lightning, while in twenty-one no electric phenomena were observed. Thom says that these phenomena are five times more frequent on the north side of the curve of translation of hurricanes than on the south side—that is, in the position where the monsoons of the W. prevail. He adds that it was so common for lightning in the N. and N. W. to precede a gale that the Dutch captains, when going from the Cape of Good Hope to India, had orders to reduce sail and take every precaution when they saw lightning.

"In addition to the menacing aspect of the sky which generally precedes all storms, that thick circle around the sun or moon, clouds heaped up and distended with their gloomy lines of light and their fantastical colors, often of copper color, forming a heavy curtain at the horizon, with menacing points and lines of pale lightning, is known to every sailor. These clouds rise little by little, covering soon the whole horizon. In approaching the zenith squalls form before the strength of the tempest, the rain falls in torrents, and at the same time the hurricane bursts.

"The barometer and sympiesometer are most valuable instruments in the region of hurricanes, and should be attentively consulted. In these regions a great fall of the mercury below its ordinary level never takes place without being followed by a tempest. . . . On each secant the barometer falls gradually to the instant of the passage of the point nearest the centre, then it rises progressively from this moment until the end of the tempest, which corresponds to the extremity of the secant. But, says M. Lefebvre, the violence of the wind is no more connected with the diameter of the vortex than the fall of the barometer is. The wind increases as the centre is approached, and the barometer constantly falls; this is all that can be said. To attempt to establish a general rule on this point would most likely lead to error."

In considering these extracts it is perhaps necessary to premise that, as the notions of the nature of storms are somewhat vague, the terms used in the different theories do not convey very exact impressions. I have therefore avoided the use of terms such as "centre," "secant," etc., as not being applicable to all kinds of storms. The word "centre" means for instance in the Rotary theory necessarily a circular space in the middle of the storm around which the air rotates; in the Inblowing theory it means either a circular or an elongated space in the middle of the storm toward which the surrounding air blows.

In fact, however, the portion of the storm which the cyclonists and centripetalists call "the centre" possesses a shape, position and meaning so different from that which these theorists assign to it that the term would, if used in our theory, produce only confusion and false impressions. It should, however, be borne in mind that "the centre" of the other investigators is in reality our *region of meeting of the opposing currents,* the region of calm around the lines *cd* and *c'''d'''*. (*Plate VII.*) This, we have seen, is not, except in the local and loco-progressive storms, either in the centre of the storm or circular in shape; it is toward the rear of the storm-clouds in the north-east storms, and in front of them in the south-east storms, and in both cases elongated.

Understanding, however, that the term "centre" is intended to mean that portion which we call the region of calm, we can easily see why the wind increases "in the vicinity of the centre," why "at the centre itself it blows so irregularly and by squalls as to render it impossible for a ship to complete a manœuvre," why the changes of the wind "are more sudden the nearer the centre is approached," why it here shifts, not point by point, as on the margin, but "all at once sixteen points," or 180°, for it changes from the direction of the wind of the equatorial current into that of the wind of the polar current as the region of calm between them, where the wind is fitful and of no definite direction, passes by.

That the wind increases in violence as we approach "the centre," and decreases as we recede from it, may be easily illustrated by the picture of a crowd of men pressing against a door; those standing nearest the door will have the greatest velocity when it suddenly opens, being subjected to the greatest pressure; those standing in the rear, the least. The uprising equatorial current over the region of calm is to the surrounding air what the door suddenly opening is to the crowd; those portions lying nearest to it will flow with the greatest velocity irregularly, from opposite directions, into and over this region.

The surface of the water underneath the uprising portion of the equatorial current, being relieved from pressure, is higher than the surface subjected to the full pressure of either current;

and this, in connection with the *ploughing* action of the polar current before described, is indeed calculated to produce "a frightful sea," disastrous in its consequences, over the region of calm, the waves rising and falling in the most tumultuous manner. Neither the Cyclone nor the Centripetal theory can explain these phenomena, which seem to us so plain.

The two mysterious forces, "independent of that of the wind, which act upon a vessel, the one drawing her toward the storm, the other drawing her away from it," find here also their only natural explanation in the unequal and opposite actions of the equatorial and polar currents on the water. The oblique pressure of the polar current on the water will evidently act mostly on that part of the ship lying below the surface, and will push it toward the south, away from the storm, while the action of the equatorial current is on the surface-water, and rolls it up against the upper part of the ship's hull, and presses it to the north against the storm. Both forces thus tend to lay the ship on its side, with the masts bent toward the storm-cloud. The ship has thus to battle in the region of calm with the two opposing currents of air above the water, and with the two opposing effects these currents have on the water.

In the consideration of the constant aërial currents (in treating of local storms) it was stated that the monsoons are nothing but the polar and equatorial currents fixed by local circumstances for six months in one position. If they change that position, one displacing the other, it is done over an extensive region in a shorter period, and therefore much more violently, than is the case in similar displacements upon our continent, which are generally in successive oscillations.

The displacement of one current by the other begins to take place in any part of the globe at the time or soon after the sun begins his movement in the opposite direction from one tropic to the other—that is, at the equinoxes. There is therefore to be expected at these times the most severe and the most frequent storms in those latitudes over which the line of meeting of the opposing currents passes. This explains the equinoctial storms and the frequent typhoons at the time when the equatorial current assumes its summer position, and at the time the polar current assumes its winter position. It becomes equally evident that in the displacement of the north-east monsoon by the south-west monsoon there will occur storms analogous to our north-east storms, and in the displacement of the south-west or west monsoon by the north-east monsoon, storms analogous to our south-east storms, only in both cases more violent. We therefore understand the remark in the above extract that some of these storms are connected with thunder and lightning and others not. We understand the observation of Thom that these electrical phenomena "are five times more frequent on the north side of the curve of translation of hurricanes than on the south side—that is, in the position where the monsoons of the west prevail"—and that the thunder and lightning comes from the north or north-west, and precedes a storm brought by a deflected polar current. The Dutch captains, in following their instructions, had therefore better warning of approaching danger than the present theories furnish in the use of the barometer. The twenty-one hurricanes mentioned as not being accompanied by thunder and lightning were doubtless the storms resembling our north-east storms. For as has before been stated, these electrical phenomena are in every probability produced by friction and condensation, and therefore are mostly manifested in the displacement of a warm current by a cooler one, rather than in the displacement of a cool current by a warmer one.

From the preceding explanations of different kinds of storms, it is apparent that the barometer has not the value to navigators as a storm prophet hitherto ascribed to it, and it is a matter of easy proof from actual occurrences that just in the most violent storms the fall of the barometer comes too late to allow of any arrangements for the safety of vessels.

As has already been shown, in the same degree that the storm becomes violent and destructive its area grows smaller, and its conflicting forces come closer together; or, in other words, the regions of high pressure approach nearer to those of low pressure. When the barometer begins to show a depression in these violent storms, the most dangerous part is already passing over the vessel, and a consultation of the barometer of no avail. This is particularly the case in the south-east storms of the temperate zone and in the so-called hurricanes and typhoons of the torrid zone. In the loco-progressive or rotary storms, such as tornadoes, water-spouts, hail-storms, real hurricanes or typhoons, which, as I shall show, originate at the crisis of a south-east storm, the barometer is utterly useless. It is of more avail in the north-east storms, for obvious reasons, and of most use in the local storms to vessels over which a storm is developing, giving them a warning in time to escape danger.

The cumulus cloud above the uprising current will, however, indicate this kind of storm, almost at the same time, and with more certainty, and in the north-east storms the first hazy stripe of stratus indicates the approaching storm sometimes a whole day before the barometer gives any sign of it.

The idea that a diminished pressure of the atmosphere must be in some connection with a disturbance in it is quite natural. Otto von Guerike, who invented the barometer and first measured such changes, narrates in the twenty-first chapter of the *Mirabilia Magdeburgica* in Schott's *Technica Curiosa*, a remarkable observation:* "In the year 1660 the air had become so uncommonly light that the finger of the little man pointed to the lowest mark on the glass tube. When I saw this, I told to those present that doubtless somewhere a large storm must have originated. Scarcely two hours had elapsed when the hurricane, although with less violence than it had on the ocean, arrived in our locality."

* *Klimatologische Beiträge von Prof. Dove.*

The barometer became at once a valuable instrument in the estimation of those interested in foreknowing the weather, and instrument-makers marked on the tube the kind of weather that would take place at different heights of the mercury; but its frequent fallacies have since injured its reputation as a weather guide. Prof. Dove says in the work which we have already cited: "Although the barometric minima occur almost always at a time when the atmosphere is violently disturbed, we see the barometer frequently very low when gentle, warm spring breezes seem to bring us out of the winter into a more genial season." Although the barometer has lost, in a measure, its reputation, it is nevertheless considered in navigation the only guide for safety. We have seen, however, its limited range of usefulness in some cases, and the cause of its frequent fallacies and utter uselessness in others. The navigator will find a far better guide and counsellor for safety in the forms of the clouds; for they not only foretell the approaching storm much earlier, but instruct him, also, in what position his vessel is to it, and how he best can escape its danger.

The observation that a strong north-west wind produces on rivers and on coasts phenomena similar to those of the undulations on high sea has been made by others. Klœden observes* that a strong north-west wind (the deflected polar current in our preceding consideration) presses the water in the North Sea so much toward the coast of Germany that the tide rises always higher, whilst in the Thames (over which the wind flows toward Germany) it does not rise so high as usual.

"The tide may even be hindered in its progress by large storms. During the strong hurricane on January 8, 1839, the tide in the Trent did not come for twenty-five miles up the river—a thing that never happened before. At Saltmarsh, five English miles from the Humber up the Ouse, a low tide

* *Handbuch der Physischen Geographie.*

instead of a high tide occurred until the river became dry. At Ostend (toward which the north-west polar current in this tempest blew) the reverse took place."

Col. Reid (*Law of Storms*, page 521) says: "In most detailed accounts of great hurricanes near the sea statements are found of extraordinary high tides occurring at the time. We read instances of great disasters from inundation, which lead to the belief such occurrences could not take place without the agency of some powerful cause yet unexplained. Thus, on the 21st of October, 1831, three hundred villages, with ten thousand inhabitants, were swept away by inundation at the mouth of the Hooghly. And on the 21st of May, 1833, near the same place, when the sea rose several feet higher than is reported in the gale of 1831, it is stated in the *Asiatic Journal* of November, 1833, that fifty thousand people were drowned.

"We have the authority of the learned secretary of the Bengal Asiatic Society, Mr. James Prinsep, for observations that at this time the barometer fell nearly two inches, and that the oil from the sympiesometer retired entirely from the tube.

"The intendant of Martinique, in making his report upon that island to the French government in 1780, says: 'The sea was more destructive than the wind; in the suburbs of St. Pierre the surf rose twenty-five feet.' And in the same report, speaking of St. Vincent, which then belonged to the French, he says: 'In Kingston, out of six hundred houses, only fourteen were left.' The Jamaica reports state that in that year Savanna-la-Mar was entirely submerged. At St. Vincent, in 1833, various marks on the shore, showing that the sea had risen twelve feet during the hurricane of 1831, and overflowed the roads below that level, remained distinctly visible. He states that after having moved his vessel forty to fifty yards from the sea to what he thought a place of security, the sea, notwithstanding, reached it, and lifted the vessel several feet.

"During the Bermuda hurricane in 1839 the sea was observed to rise more than two feet higher than usual at a spot which was not only on the leeward side of the island, but within the camber of the dock-yard; neither did the tide at this place ebb as usual.

"I was told by Sir Thomas Hastings that he had observed the ebbing tide in Portsmouth harbor suspended during a rapid fall of the barometer, and begin again to flow, which he ascribed to the influence of diminished atmospheric pressure. A fall of two inches in the barometer indicates a diminution of a fifteenth part of the atmospheric pressure, which would cause water to rise a little more than two feet."

The great floods on the northern coast of Germany are doubtless caused by the pressure of the north-west deflected polar current in the south-east storms.

The undulation or the swell receives thus not only an explanation, but a meaning. It is the line or region where the two currents meet on the surface of the water—the dreaded region of calm, the so-called centre. It runs parallel to the cumulo-stratus, and furnishes another means to the navigator of determining the position of his ship toward the storm.

In deserts little or no clouds may be formed in these storms on account of a want of moisture; here the sand, analogous to the clouds, will show which way the wind blows. Thus Nature has provided the means to protect ourselves under all circumstances.

# CHAPTER VII.*

## *LOCO-PROGRESSIVE STORMS.—TORNADOES, HAIL-STORMS, DUST-STORMS, WATER-SPOUTS.*

THE loco-progressive is an offspring of the south-east storm, and is totally different from other kinds in origin, motion and appearance. The result of the coincidence of a peculiar configuration of the earth's surface and a certain condition of the atmosphere during a south-east storm, it unites somewhat the characteristics of both a local and a progressive storm. It is, therefore, the most complicated and most difficult to understand. With a smaller area than any other of the storms of the temperate zone, it is, nevertheless, by far the most violent and destructive. The north-east storm, which sometimes extends over our whole continent east of the Rocky Mountains, is harmless compared with a tornado, which seldom moves over a larger track than twenty miles in length and six hundred yards in width; and the south-east storm, although more characterized by great meteorological contrasts than the north-east storm, does not approach the destructiveness of the tornado.

We followed the south-east storm in its gradual development to its crisis—that is, to the point where the polar current balances the equatorial current and the region of conflict has become stationary or nearly so.

The two currents thus balanced are now of course in a state of extreme tension, and the compression of the air at their region of meeting is the cause of the sultriness so universally observed just before a tornado.

* Before reading this chapter it will be well to read the analysis of the West Cambridge tornado, Appendix B. It is here frequently referred to.

If in this critical condition of the storm no disturbance takes place in the plane of meeting of the two balancing currents, the return oscillation toward the north sets in. If, however, a disturbance from any cause takes place, a tornado or rotary storm is generated, which travels in the diagonal of the forces of the two currents through the region of calm between them. Its course is delineated in the sky by a long black bank of cloud accompanying the south-east storm, for it will travel in the direction of and underneath this cloud. The polar current coming from north-west, its pressure is supposed to be from this direction, while that of the equatorial current is from the south-west.

The polar current, in its course toward the south, held in suspense by the equatorial current, may be compared to a body of water confined by a dam, except that the dam has here also a positive force, and, if released, a motion of its own. If, now, this aërial dam is broken at some point on the surface of the earth, the air of the polar current above the break will sink into it, coming in the main direction of the current, and there will be formed in its upper regions a depression or trough corresponding to the break. That portion of the equatorial air which has opposed the sunken polar air will rush with great force into the depression. It cannot, however, do this in the main direction of the equatorial current toward the north-east, but must take the direction of the trough in the polar air—that is, it must go to the north-west—and this change of direction will produce an eddy or whirl.

This process becomes apparent by the sudden appearance of a cloud darker than ordinary, which whirls around, and at first, from below, is seen as a round disk. This cloud is formed by the sudden and profuse condensation of the moisture contained in the air of the equatorial current, which was thrown suddenly into higher and colder regions.

If the polar current continues to flow out below, it will also continue to sink down from above. Thus the opposing air from lower regions of the equatorial current will rush up and join this eddy, and new condensations will be added from below to the rotating disk of cloud. The rotating cloud grows darker and appears to lengthen downward.

The centrifugal force and the rapid evolution of latent heat from condensation will soon create a space of rarefied air inside of this rotating cloud, and this increases again the rushing up of air from lower regions of the equatorial current, thus adding new condensations from below and still further lengthening the rotating cloud downward. After a vortex is thus formed, while the latent heat evolved by the condensation would increase the temperature of the cloud on the outside, the rarefication in the inside produced by the centrifugal force would cause this part of the vortex to be much colder. That the cloud assumes the shape of an inverted cone follows from the action of the centrifugal force on the spirally ascending cloud. For the longer the parts of the cloud rotate on their way upward, the farther they will be thrown from the axis. Thus the conical shape of the tornado-cloud is formed, and it lengthens gradually down to the surface of the earth.

In this kind of storm, as in the others, the invisible motions of the aërial currents become visible, written in the clouds.

When the tornado-cloud has approached the ground, the surrounding air on the surface will rush into the space of rarefied air of the vortex with a velocity proportionate to the difference of pressure outside and inside of the vortex. This current will be made visible by a mass of detached objects, such as sand, dust or water, which it whirls up off of the ground. Thus a second cone, looking like a cloud, with its base on the earth, will be attached to the inverted cone of the tornado-cloud, which has its base in the cumulo-stratus of the south-east storm.

When the cloud of loose objects has all been whirled up, the lower part of the rotating current becomes again invisible, and the cloud seems to rise.

Applying these principles to the facts in the case of the West Cambridge tornado, which may be taken as a type of all rotary storms, the situation at Waltham, where it first made its appearance, is easily understood. It is important that the configuration of the ground over which the tornado travelled should be borne in mind, particularly the elevation above the level of the sea of Prospect Hill and surrounding points; the heights of these points are indicated on the map. (*Plate I.*) In this analytical map of the West Cambridge tornado, *Fig.* 1 depicts the track of the destruction, *Fig.* 2 the manner in which the equatorial and polar currents acted on each other to produce the tornado and its effects, and *Fig.* 3 the forms of the tornado-cloud at different points along the track.* These three figures have been lettered to correspond with each other.

Just before the commencement of the West Cambridge tornado the south-east storm had nearly reached its crisis, and the plane of meeting of its two currents stood about in the position of the lines *A B* in *Figs.* 1 and 2, the polar current, being a deflected one, coming from the north-west, and the equatorial current coming from the south-west, so that the two stood nearly at right angles to each other.

Prior to this no essential disturbance could well have taken place in the plane of meeting, because the storm was advancing over a plateau only slightly undulated, and the equatorial current was not prevented by any obstructions from forming an

* The map of the cloud in its progress was not made from my own observations, as I did not witness the tornado, but was deduced from facts discovered in the destruction and in the state of the atmosphere. My drawing I was afterward able to verify by the observations of the assistant at the Cambridge Observatory, who had sketched the clouds from the window, and by the observations of Dr. Gould of Boston, who had particularly noticed the changes of the cloud in its progress.

unbroken dam against the slowly advancing polar current. But when the storm reached the valley *M*, which was at its deepest point some four hundred feet lower than the highest point of Prospect Hill, the dam was undermined by the polar current's sinking into the valley at its upper end; and not finding the same resisting force on the surface from the equatorial current as hitherto, on account of the obstruction of Prospect Hill, it rushed down the valley *M*. The sinking down and the rushing forward over this part of the valley caused a corresponding depression in the upper portion of the polar current, forming a trough corresponding in direction and form to the valley on the surface. That part of the equatorial current balancing the sunken part of the polar current rushed up through this trough, changing its direction from S. W. to S. E., and this caused the first eddy and the embryo tornado-cloud *B'* (*Fig.* 3), appearing from below as a disk.

The south-east storm advanced slowly. As the line *A B* moved southward it came over wider and deeper parts of the valley *M*. The breakage grew larger, and the air of the polar current rushed in greater quantities forward and sank proportionately above. This caused the air of lower regions of the equatorial current which had opposed the sunken portion of the polar current to rush up and join the rotating cloud, which progressed in advance of the main body of the polar current toward the south-east, and seemed at the same time gradually to lower itself in proportion as the equatorial current rushed in from lower regions, as shown at *B'B''B'''B''''*. (*Fig.* 3.) (See *Analysis*, 80*.) When the tornado-cloud had reached a position south-east of Prospect Hill, with its lower end still above the inclined plane of meeting of the two currents, the storm must

* All through this article references are made to the analysis of the tornado, Appendix B, the paragraphs of which are numbered; and for the sake of conciseness, these paragraphs are here referred to by number only.

have reached the position represented in *Fig.* 2, the black portion *A B F E* representing the polar current, with a projection of the more advanced part in the valley *M*, and the shaded portion representing the region of meeting. The white and black arrows indicate the direction of the polar and equatorial currents respectively.

To judge from the sudden gust at and near the house No. 1 (*Analysis*, 68), the polar current must have travelled with great velocity down the valley *M*. This we can easily understand, from the fact that the rush upward of the equatorial current in the rarefied space of the vortex must have rapidly increased, thus removing the slight resisting power this current still possessed east of Prospect Hill.

But when the projection of the polar current had arrived south-east of Prospect Hill, its farther progress was suddenly checked by the full force of the equatorial current over the ground from the south-west, rolling the vortex around and over the face of the inclined plane of meeting toward *b*, where it was compelled to stop on account of the resistance opposed by the compressed polar current. This motion must have taken place when a cloud was seen moving toward the main cloud. (*Analysis*, 78.) While the vortex was thus rolled by the equatorial current toward *b*, it sucked into its lower opening the air over the surface south of Prospect Hill, and above the lower part of the inclined plane of meeting, with such velocity that trees and other objects over this area not protected by the much compressed polar current were broken and carried toward *b*, thus producing the first area of destruction *a b c*. (See description—*Analysis*, 12 to 23.)

We can thus understand why the carriage of the physician was pushed by this in-rushing air in the direction of Waltham (*Analysis*, 12); why ex-President Hill was obliged to close the shutters of his house (*Analysis*, 69); how the supper was thrown from the table in house No. 2. (*Analysis*, 13.)

We also understand why the air became compressed into smaller space at and toward *b* in order to rush into the small opening of the vortex, and also that the destruction increased toward *b*. (*Analysis*, 10.) In short, the direction of the destroyed objects toward *b* over the whole area *a b c*, and particularly the distinctly marked limits (*Analysis*, 18) of this area near *b*, explain themselves. There may be, and doubtless is, a great deal of electricity developed by friction and condensation, but the withering of the leaves (*Analysis*, 18) is not necessarily the effect of electricity, as is generally assumed. It is more likely produced by the mechanical effect of the sand's being blown violently against the leaves and destroying the cellular tissues or by heat from compression of the air. The fact that the leaves were all injured from the side from which the wind blew seems to indicate this.

In the analysis the important conclusion was reached that of the two contending forces the polar current's action is more downward, rather sustaining and protecting, while the equatorial current's action is upward, lifting and destroying, which might have been expected from the different natures of the two currents in respect to gravity and elasticity. The position of the two currents at the commencement of the tornado explains, therefore, why all the left side (*A B F E, Fig.* 1) of the first portion of the track north of *E F*, and all the objects in the valley *M*, even over the north-western part of the area of destruction *a b c*, remained uninjured. They had been submerged by the polar current, over which the equatorial current rushed without touching a leaf of the trees.

The areas of destruction and the areas left uninjured furnish the data to mark the position and extent of the polar current each moment of its progress, and the depth of the polar current and the angle of inclination of the plane of meeting at every step might have been determined with almost mathematical precision. (*Analysis*, 15, 16, 19.) Generally, the trees will break at the height where they emerge from the polar current into the equatorial current rushing over it in the opposite direction. The height of the breakage from the ground will give thus the depth of the polar current at that spot.

The facts in reference to the covering of objects with mud (*Analysis*, 19 to 22) have been observed in this and all tornadoes by others, and have always remained unexplained. It has been said that the mud was carried by the vortex from a distant pond; but why, then, in this instance do we not find it promiscuously at all heights and all around the trees? why only seven feet high, and with such sharply-defined limits? why, also, should it be found in places where there is no water, and where no rain falls? The rational explanation seems to be that the row of trees east of Lyman's road were submerged in the polar current only to the height of seven feet, this submerged portion thus being cooled, while the rest remained warm; and when the warm equatorial current saturated with moisture rushed over the ploughed field (*Analysis*, 20) toward *b*, and into the vortex coming from the south and south-east, it forced the polar current from around the trees. The moisture of the equatorial current would certainly condense in large quantities on the cooled portion of the trees, and at the same moment the dust from the ploughed field, mingling with the condensation, would produce the mud on that side of the trees against which the equatorial current blew, and just as high as those trees had been standing before in the polar current. The portions above seven feet from the ground had not been in the polar current, and were not cooled; no condensation could, therefore, take place upon them, and they remained free of mud.

The row of trees on the other side of the road had been to their tops submerged by the polar current on account of its greater depth at this point, and were, except a few branches at their crown, not touched by the equatorial current.

Farther on in the track the same phenomena were observed,

but more on the south and south-west sides of the trees. The reason for this is to be found in the fact that in the former case the polar current had reached so far to the south-east in the valley *M* that the air from the equatorial current, rushing into the vortex at *b*, over the first area of destruction, came from the south-east, while in the latter case it came from the south-west, its normal direction.

The case of the mud-covered house, however (*Analysis*, 14), seemed at first not to be accounted for by the same process of reasoning, since the mud was observed to be on the north-east side of the house; but in considering the action of the two currents at that locality, Nature is found to be at work in the same way as at the elm trees on Lyman's road.

The polar current had evidently submerged only the north-eastern side of the house when the equatorial current came from the south-west, blowing the supper from the table (*Analysis*, 13), and pressed the polar current toward the north-east in the first gust far enough to leave the house entirely in the warmer air.

This warm current, heavily laden with moisture and dust, either struck the cool side of the house in an eddy, perhaps produced by the position of Prospect Hill, or else was driven back against it by a reaction of the polar current. Either action would explain this deposit of mud, which is unaccountable on any other hypothesis.

The forces of Nature are few and simple; it is the endless combination of circumstances that produces the variety and difference of the phenomena she exhibits. She requires no "convective discharge of electricity," as Peltier, Dr. Hare and others thought, no complication of unknown forces, to produce the phenomena of a tornado; but only the two opposing currents of air, in a peculiar but not uncommon condition, combining with a particular configuration of the earth not at all infrequent.

Although the tornado received its first impulse from the earth, it is nevertheless a product of the air. It manifests itself first in high regions by a little disk of a cloud. This enlarges, descends rapidly over and in advance of the inclined plane of the polar current, betraying the action of the currents at every step until it is almost on the ground.

Every sudden forward movement of a portion of either current is followed, on account of its elasticity, by a reacting movement from the opposite direction; when, therefore, that portion of the polar current which flowed in a rush down the valley *M*, pushing the descending vortex in front of it, assumed the position indicated in *Fig.* 2, it was checked and partially repulsed by the full power of the whole equatorial current, acting not only in the upper regions, but on the surface as well. The vortex, having come by this time nearer the ground, was brought into the full influence of the equatorial current south of Prospect Hill, and received by it another direction in being rolled along the inclined and compressed plane of meeting in the direction of the arrows 2, 3, 4, 5, 6, *Fig.* 2. (*Analysis*, 77, 78 and 80.) As the vortex is still in contact with the compressed polar current it is not pushed but *rolled* along the face of this current, its rotary motion being increased thereby. In this progress it descended still lower, being joined by equatorial air from still lower strata; and reaching the ground at last at *b*, it caused the first destruction on the surface over the area *a b c* by sucking the equatorial air into its hollow, rarefied body. This explains why all destroyed trees over this area were pointing to *b*. By the reacting movement of the equatorial current to stop the forward-rushing portion of the polar current above the valley *M*, the vortex was rolled to *b*, where it was stopped in its progress in this direction by the compressed polar current.

After the up-rushing of the surface air of the equatorial

current at *b*, in front of the polar current, the latter in its turn makes naturally a movement forward over the surface, in which it is assisted by the following process: By the stop in the progress of the vortex new masses of equatorial air above the inclined plane south-east of *b* follow through the vortex from lower and lower regions, making more room for the polar current to shift at that point into the position of *a' b'* (*Figs.* 1 and 2), repeating, but nearer the ground, the action which took place in the air above the valley *M.* The plane of meeting of the two currents is now *a' b' F.* A second breakage in the dam was thus produced, so to speak, by the removal of the equatorial current in front of the polar current through the vortex, which is gradually becoming more developed and growing wider. The shifting of the polar current over the area *b d b'* (*Fig.* 1) brought the vortex in advance and above the inclined plane over the path *b e*, in the main direction of this current, the vortex gradually descending a second time as it was added to by the equatorial current. The vortex had not yet approached sufficiently near the ground to do much injury; it showed its effects over this path only in the tops of the trees, a few of which were broken. (*Analysis*, 40 and 41.) The area *b d b'*, being submerged and protected by the polar current, is left, with the above exceptions, uninjured. (*Analysis*, 11.) When the second forward-rushing portion of the polar current, with the vortex in front of it, has reached the position *a' b'*, coming again into the full power of the equatorial current, its further progress is checked a second time by reaction, and the vortex, having been thrust again into the full force of the equatorial current, is rolled in the direction of the pressure of this current to *b'*, its rotary motion being increased thereby as when it was rolled in the direction of the arrows 2, 3, 4, 5 and 6 to *b*.

The rushing into the vortex of the surface air of the equatorial current at *b'* produces the second area of destruction *a' b' c'* (*Fig.* 1), throwing all objects in the direction of *b'*.

(*Analysis*, 9.) Here the cloud appears to touch the ground a second time, and assumes the shape as at $b'$. (*Fig.* 3.)

When the equatorial surface air in front of the polar current has been whirled up through the vortex to regions above, a portion of the polar current flows for the third time forward and assumes the position $a''\ b''$, the line of division being now $a''\ b''\ F$ (*Figs.* 1 and 2), at the same time pushing the vortex before it over the track $b'\ e'$. By this movement it submerged the area $b'\ d'\ b''$ (*Fig.* 1), and protected it from being injured by that portion of the equatorial current which lay opposite to it, and which reacts against the polar current, checking its advance.

The vortex, being thrust into the power of the equatorial current at $e'$, is again seized and rolled to $b''$, and a third area of destruction is produced by the in-rushing portion of the equatorial current throwing all objects toward the point $b''$ (*Analysis*, 9); and the cloud appears to touch the ground a third time, and assumes the shape as at $b''$. (*Fig.* 3.) This play goes on in this manner between the currents and the vortex, producing similar phenomena at intervals in regular order. The result is that we find areas of destruction of a similar and almost mathematically defined shape alternating with areas left uninjured over the right side of the first portion of the tornado's track. *The destruction is here entirely produced by the more elastic, warm equatorial current,* whose tendency is obliquely upward and in straight lines. *The polar current acts at this stage of the storm only as a resisting, protecting power.* We find, therefore, the whole left side north of the line $E\ F$ (*Figs.* 1 and 2), which was submerged by this current at the beginning of the tornado, entirely uninjured; and those areas on the right side of the track, which at each step of the tornado forward were submerged by the polar current, before the destructive equatorial current rushed successively into the vortex at $b$, $b'$, $b''$, etc., were also protected; while those areas on the right side of the track over which the destructive equatorial current rushed into the vortex at the points *b*, *b'*, *b''*, etc., were all destroyed.

By the first breakage or disturbance in the plane of meeting the vortex was pushed with the forward-rushing portion of the polar current down the valley *M* toward the *south-east*, where above the area 50 (*Fig.* 1) the equatorial current took hold of it and rolled it toward the *north-east*, in the direction of the arrows 2, 3, 4, 5, to *b*, where it touched the ground and was lifted up by the in-rushing equatorial air and thrown again back over the inclined plane toward north-west, in the direction from whence it came. It is lifted up because, the mouth of the vortex being as yet small, only a part of the up-rushing air enters, and the rest in its upward course strikes against the inclined sides of the vortex, lifting it bodily. It also follows, because the vortex cannot carry off all the in-rushing air, that the pressure at the mouth will be very great; and, therefore, would produce great heat, which would seem to account for the apparent scorching of the grass observed on portions of the track of a tornado. While the polar current at that point occupies the place on the ground left by the up-rushing equatorial air, the vortex is again pushed by the polar current toward the south-east, and is drawn downward at the same time by the addition of equatorial air from lower regions. The process above the valley *M* is repeated, but the track from *b* to *e* cannot be so long as that down the valley. For the vortex is more developed, receives greater quantities of air from the surface, and, therefore, remains nearer the ground.

Arriving at *e*, the vortex is again rolled by the equatorial current to *b'* and lifted up by the equatorial surface air which rushes over the area *a' b' c'*, but here it cannot be lifted so high as at *b*, because the mouth of the vortex is larger, and, therefore, more of the equatorial air enters. Besides this, the forward-rushing mass of the polar current could not have been so great as in the valley *M*, and, therefore, the reacting, checking and uplifting power of the equatorial current would be less. Therefore the vortex approached the ground successively at shorter intervals of its track, and was kept for a longer distance near the surface—*i. e.*, the successive distances over which it was brought by the polar current became shorter, and the successive distances over which it was carried by the equatorial current became longer. The distance from the house 1 to the south end of the valley *M* is longer than *b e*; *b e* is longer than *b′ e′*, etc. The distance from the area 50 to *b* is shorter than *e b′*; that of *e b′* is shorter than *e′ b″*, etc. (*Fig.* 1.)

As the vortex over the first distances is entirely in higher regions and over the latter approaches nearer the ground, which it reaches every time a little sooner, it follows that the vortex with each vertical oscillation remains a shorter time in the air and longer on the surface, until at last it fastens itself permanently to it, and that in conformity with this movement the destruction caused by it is visible first in the tops of the trees only, and then gradually appears on the ground, increasing in violence with each successive area of destruction. (*Analysis*, 38.) Intimately in connection with these vertical oscillations of the vortex are its lateral oscillations north and south; for both are the consequence of the opposite action of the overlapping currents.

The natural tendency of the pressure of the equatorial current in repulsing the successive rushes of portions of the polar current is evidently to re-establish the original line of the plane of meeting, which was in the West Cambridge tornado straight; and in this tornado the action was assisted by the fact that the main storm, to which the tornado was an adjunct, was just beginning its return oscillation northward, and the equatorial current had taken the aggressive.

The lateral oscillations must, therefore, grow shorter, until at last they cease entirely, when the vortex, driven forward by the combined action of the two currents, will travel in their diagonal, which is the plane of meeting. From this tendency of the two currents gradually to force the vortex in the diagonal $E\ F$, it follows that the angles that the equatorial current in its successive rushes into the vortex forms with the diagonal grow less, which is evidenced by the facts in the survey of the tornado. Since the angle $c\ b\ E$ is greater than $c'\ b'\ E$, and this greater than $c''\ b''\ E$, and so with the angle $a'b'E$, which is greater than $a''b''\ E$, and $a''\ b''\ E$ greater than $a'''\ b'''\ E$, etc. Thus the lines in which the vortex is successively rolled to $b'$, $b''$, $b'''$, etc., approach gradually nearer to the diagonal, until at last they coincide with it.

From the continuous action of the two currents on the vortex, it follows equally by a mechanical law that there is an increase in its progressive velocity. This is most beautifully verified by the facts in the survey. (*Analysis*, 7.) For we find that the distances $b\ b'$, $b'\ b''$, $b''\ b'''$, etc., which measure the progress of the vortex during the successive oscillations, increase each time two hundred and fifty yards with mathematical precision.

An increase of the width of the path over which the rotary motion takes place is also found. (*Analysis*, 38.) This follows of necessity from the combined mechanical and chemical actions of the two currents. The latent heat liberated by the condensation of the moisture of the upward-rushing air expands the wall of the vortex, thus producing a larger space of rarefied air within, and thus also increasing the amount of air which rushes through it.

By the mechanical action of the centrifugal force, and that of the equatorial current in rolling the vortex along the paths $e\ b'$, $e'\ b''$, etc., the air around the vortex will join it as long as the velocity of the equatorial current is greater than that of the vortex. From these causes the diameter of the vortex grows larger, and the destruction of it spreads over a larger area, as it travels forward.

That the vortex first had an oscillation up and down, and then fastened itself to the ground until at last it dissolved suddenly, is shown in the survey of the destruction caused by it, and is also a necessary deduction from our theory. As often as the vortex was rolled by the equatorial current along the lines $e\,b'$, $e'\,b''$, etc., until stopped by the general plane of the polar current $E\,F$, it was pressed upward by the sudden in-rushing of equatorial air, being then drawn down by additions from below, as explained in the first part of this consideration. But we observed that these horizontal oscillations grew less violent as the direction of the branch axes approached that of the main axis. Therefore this oscillation upward at $b$, $b'$, $b''$, etc., must have been less and have stopped almost altogether when these horizontal oscillations stopped—that is, when the vortex ran in the diagonal of the two forces.

We have thus found that the theory we have set forth is deduced from existing facts, and that these facts in their turn are only those which would be expected from our theory.

We saw the embodiment of the tornado, its cloud, form in higher regions, appearing as a small disk, descend and assume a conical shape, with its base in the clouds, its apex lengthening downward. Another cone attaches itself to it from below and vanishes from time to time, giving the appearance of up-and-down motions to a greater extent than it really possesses them. We see it move at the same time in a zigzag, which appears, however, differently to distant observers according to their positions toward the track—to one as having a sinuous motion, to another as in a straight line.

We found also that it increases its rotary motion and the diameter of its vortex, and also its progressive motion.

"Where will this increase stop?" the reader may ask. For if it goes on the whole atmosphere will soon form one enormous cyclone terrible to think of. Uneasy thoughts of this kind would be very natural when we read of cyclones with diameters of a hundred miles, increasing to even a thousand miles, travelling with a velocity of thirty miles an hour, and rotating with a velocity of ninety miles an hour.* For knowing the fearful destruction in our miniature cyclone, the tornado, which has a diameter of only about four hundred yards, and assuming the destruction of a cyclone of 9° of the terrestrial arc† to be in proportion, we might almost expect the end of the world. There would seem to be no good reason why the increase in diameter of a cyclone of this sort should not continue indefinitely until the whole atmosphere of the globe is involved; at least, the cyclonists do not tell us how it is to stop. They do not consider the cyclones caused by and dependent on the aërial currents, as we do the tornado, but rather that the currents are caused by the cyclones; for they tell us that cyclonic storms bring the warm air of the tropics up into the temperate zone.

But the facts of the case are that the only rotary storms in the temperate zone are tornadoes, water-spouts, hail-storms and dust-storms—all alike produced by a peculiarity of the surface in connection with a south-east storm; and the rotary storms of the torrid zone are in every probability not different.

The cyclonists tell us of cyclonic hurricanes of the West Indies which they say travel up into the temperate zone, but even if these hurricanes are cyclones, it is a matter of proof that they do not carry the same characteristics into the temperate zone. From that point of the parabolic curve at the tropics from which the hurricanes, as hitherto represented, take a north-easterly direction‡ through the temperate zone, the hurricane is not a cyclone, but a north-east storm. This I know from personal observation of these storms over the United States, where they develop themselves so characteristically,

* As, according to Redfield, they sometimes do.

† See extract from U. S. Hydrographic Office's nautical directions, quoted in the chapter on cyclones.

‡ See chapter on the Cyclone theory.

through a series of twenty years. The north-east branch of the hurricanes is a different kind of storm from that branch which is represented as travelling from the West Indies through the torrid zone to the west or north-west, and has nothing in common with it except that it commences at the time when the other stops. That this is true may be concluded from the fact that the north-east storm, or the second branch, occurs in many cases without the occurrence of the first branch. That the second branch of the hurricanes represented by the cyclonists as travelling from the tropics to the north-east is not a cyclone, but simply our north-east storm, is, however, principally proved by the fact that none of these storms pass without showing the marked contrasts in temperature, pressure, humidity and change in the wind north and south of the line *c d* (*Plate VII.*) described in the consideration of north-east storms.

If they were cyclones, or were centripetal storms, as described by Espy, no such meteorological contrasts would be observed in front and in the rear of the region of calm, because in either case the air, being of one and the same current, would not show these contrasts in passing over any locality.

These changes can readily be observed, and the failure of other investigators to remark them can only be accounted for by the present method of making observations only at certain fixed periods of the day.

We have followed the tornado to that state of development when it is travelling in the diagonal of the two currents, and increasing in its progressive velocity as well as in its rotary motion; but there need be no fear that it will grow to the size of a cyclone of 9° of the terrestrial arc. It is, unlike those gigantic imaginary storms, under the control and guidance of the two opposing currents, and carries, as all bad things do, the germ of destruction and dissolution within itself.

As both forces act continually on it, the vortex will assume first the progressive velocity of the slowest of the two currents, then that of the other. This seems to be the point when the rotary motion, which was also continually increasing, comes to its full development and spreads over the greater width of the track, obliterating the destructive action of the equatorial current. The section at West Cambridge, first surveyed, must have been produced during that time. (*Plate II.*) The effects of the rotary motion extend here almost over two-thirds of the whole track. This portion is to be found in all tornadoes in about the middle of the whole length, and well illustrates the *rotary* motion.*

When the vortex by the continued and combined action of the two currents has acquired a progressive velocity greater than the single velocity of either of them, it becomes independent of their guiding influence. Its progressive velocity rises now rapidly to that of the combined forces of the two currents, and by the momentum so obtained it runs with lightning speed in its wild career to its own destruction.

As it now travels faster than either of the two currents, its progressive motion must soon slacken, because it is running against the wind, and this the sooner occurs if the plane of meeting is not straight, when the vortex, travelling independently in a straight line, will plunge into that current which happens to oppose its course.

The rotary motion, it is clear, would begin to decrease from the moment the progressive velocity became greater than the velocity of the equatorial current, since the rotary motion is

* It was therefore quite natural that Mr. Redfield, whom I had the pleasure of taking over the track, grew here quite enthusiastic, and condemned that part at Waltham as unfit for a survey, because incompletely developed. When I afterward studied the sections which Mr. Redfield had selected in other tornadoes, particularly that of the New Brunswick tornado in 1835, I found that they were similarly situated and quite analogous to this in West Cambridge. There is no doubt that in the middle of tornadoes the rotary destruction is fully developed and is the only one visible.

largely due to the equatorial current's having a greater velocity than the vortex; and when this condition of affairs is reversed, the action of the current on the vortex must be reversed also. From this cause the outside layers of the vortex are rapidly peeled off until it has entirely dissolved.

In this way the tornado-cloud is seen to dissolve, ascending rapidly upward in the air as it came down. The tornado during the last part of its existence is graphically described by the Rev. Charles Brooks as "seeming as if a vacuum had travelled (if we can say so), . . . and the wind had rushed in with violence, not only behind it, but on each side toward its central line of motion," drawing all objects toward it. Here the air from both currents would rush into the vortex, and also into the vacuum left behind it by its rapid motion forward.

The track of destruction becomes narrower during this time, as will be seen by Mr. Brooks's report, given in the Appendix.

That the rotary action during the last half was exhibited only exceptionally, may follow from the fact that the progressive velocity was so great in proportion to the rotary velocity that the latter had little action on objects in the path of the vortex.

If the vortex toward the end runs out of the region of calm, plunging into one of the two currents, and its progressive velocity has become less than the velocity of that current, it must of course move with it, and may change a little from its first direction. Mr. Brooks seems to have observed a small deviation from the general course toward the end. It seems even possible that having arrived on the left side of the storm in the region, where the wind stands in the direction of the arrows 1, 2, 3 (*Plate VII., Fig.* 2), the dying vortex may be revived again, and a new tornado may be created, which will travel in the opposite direction and with a reversed rotation; and this is more probable if the two currents are opposing each other in exactly opposite directions.

The last part of the tornado's track at Medford, if taken alone, would thus go to prove that Espy's or the Inblowing theory is the true one; the middle portion over West Cambridge, that Redfield's or the Rotary theory is the true one; and the greater portion of the first half near Waltham, that *neither* of these two theories is the true one. The whole proves that tornadoes cannot be made the base upon which to build up theories of storms, as has been done. Theories of storms must have a different and broader foundation if they are to prove worth anything.

It will not be difficult to understand now almost all the facts presented in the analysis of this tornado and in others, by considering place, time and circumstances; only a few are therefore reviewed here, the explanations of which are likely not to be so evident.

(*Analysis*, 25.) That the flower-pots were not crushed by the falling branch, I ascribe to the fact that the branch must have found great resistance in falling from the compressed, dense air of the polar current.

(*Analysis*, 26.) The house must have been submerged to the roof in the cooler current, and this was repulsed by the equatorial air which advanced far enough to come in contact with the cooled southern side; the consequent condensation wetting the side of the house. As the southern air rushed over a meadow where no dust was found, no mud could be deposited.

(*Analysis*, 28.) The facts here set forth may have been caused by the air nearest to the vortex in its progress from $e'$ to $b''$; the air entering the vortex at $b''$.

(*Analysis*, 33, 34, 35, 36, 37.) As often as a rush of air from the southern current entered the vortex, a rush or gust from the northern side in the opposite direction was the consequence. The sand flying with such a gust may have injured the leaves, which the sun the next day withered. This may have been produced also by the heat from the compressed in-rushing air. The carrying up into the air of men, animals and other objects, the unroofing and destruction of houses, twisting of trees, shifting around of houses, the throwing of one half of the roof of a house in one direction and the other half in the opposite direction, can be explained by the action of the vortex and the rushing of air from opposite sides into it.

The oscillations over the fourth and fifth areas of destruction are doubtless caused by the rushing of air into the vortex at different times and from different directions over the same area.

(*Analysis*, 49, 50.) The action here was produced by air rushing into the vortex from opposite sides, throwing the one side by a southern gust to 49 (*Plate I., Fig.* 1), and the other side by a northern gust (which, however, became deflected by a new one from the south) to 50. By the last gust from the south the side building of the house 10 may have been shifted with one corner away from the house.

(*Analysis*, 53.) The cause of the convolutions at $\beta$, $\beta'$, $\beta''$ are somewhat obscure; they are perhaps produced by a violent rebound of the vortex in striking the polar current at the end of the paths $e''$ $b'''$ and $e'''$ $b''''$.

(*Analysis*, 54.) The destruction here was produced by the passing of the vortex over the south side of the building, while an in-rushing gust from the north immediately afterward throws the half left by the vortex inside of the house.

(*Analysis*, 55.) To produce the action here, the vortex must have passed between the two houses left uninjured, as was the case with 6 and 8 on each side of the destroyed house 7 of *Analysis*, 46.

(*Analysis*, 56, 57, 58.) The board was doubtless brought by the vortex, and had thus required an enormous velocity. A pebble must have produced the phenomenon in *Analysis*, 57, brought in the same way. The granite block in *Analysis*, 58, had doubtless been struck by the vortex.

A great many facts, usually related as wonders and puzzling

mysteries, become intelligible by determining the localities in reference to the track and the time of their occurrence.

In the case of the car mentioned by the Rev. Mr. Brooks (*Analysis*, 59) the relation of the car to the railroad is well determined, but the position of the railroad and dépôt to the track is not mentioned. Therefore the fact remains to those unacquainted with the locality a puzzle. It will be understood at once if it is added that the railroad crossed the track at an angle, as North street does, and that the dépôt lies north of the track. Judging from the destruction, the vortex must have passed south of the dépôt, where about one hundred yards off it carried away a two-story brick house. Now we understand how one of these gusts from the north rushing into the vortex rolled the car in this direction over the railroad into the opening of the vortex, which took it up and carried it sixty feet to the east.

Tornadoes occur only in connection with south-east storms when at or near their crisis. A tornado is not known to occur in a north-east storm, although there is perhaps a possibility of its doing so. The cause for this may be found in the different nature of the two storms. In the north-east storm the equatorial current is drawn toward the north and overrides the other more readily, and produces a more inclined plane of meeting; there cannot, therefore, be so great a compression of the polar current as in the south-east storms.

Tornadoes develop only when the polar current in its displacement of the equatorial current has reached its most southern limit, and occur, therefore, in the temperate zone only in the warm half of the year. As the region of this southern limit of displacement travels, with the belts of high and low pressure, north and south, following the sun in the ecliptic, it would seem that even in the temperate zone the liability to tornadoes shifts north and south in the same way.

In North America at least, since the equatorial and polar

currents in south-east storms meet at such an angle that the diagonal of forces takes an easterly direction, tornadoes will, as a rule, travel from west to east. In the southern hemisphere the law will be reversed.

### *Apparently Intermitting and Parallel Tornadoes.*

For the sake of simplicity it has been assumed that the plane of meeting of the two currents is a straight one, but this is not always exactly the case, especially in the beginning of the conflict; for the motion of air currents, like the motion of water, is in waves more or less curved. But when the curve is very large the section where the tornado occurs may be practically a straight line; this must more be the case in the equatorial wave than in the polar, because it is much wider. Irregularities in the plane of meeting may occur on account of local circumstances; and it sometimes happens that the polar current is divided by a chain of mountains such as the Alleghanies, one branch flowing down the valleys east of the mountains and the other west of it. In this case tornadoes may occur at the ends of both branches in the same latitude, and so nearly at the same time as to apparently warrant the conclusion that they are only parts of the same tornado which has in some way been broken in two, but they are in reality entirely separate phenomena, except as connected with the same south-east storm. If by parallel mountain-ranges the polar current should be divided into several branches, it would be even possible that tornadoes should so occur as to appear to be one and the same tornado broken into several sections. It is evident from our view of the subject, however, that a tornado is without possible exception a purely local phenomenon whose whole existence is embraced between its first appearance and its disappearance. In further confirmation of the fact that it is originated by the configuration of the ground, is the significant statement that tornadoes have been known to occur several times in different years at the same locality and travelling over almost the same track. Such an instance is mentioned by Prof. Loomis as having occurred near Natchez.

Parallel tornadoes frequently occur at different points of the same storm, though either not in the same longitude or else not at the same time. In the former case the plane of meeting would be bent to the north or south at one or more of the points where tornadoes occur; and in the latter case one or more of the tornadoes may take place before the crisis of the south-east storm, and would, therefore, not be of so great violence.* There are of course other possible combinations and complications.

## *HAIL-STORMS.*

Hail-storms are in their origin and nature very different from the fall of sleet which frequently accompanies the north-east or winter storm, and must not be confounded with it. They are in connection with south-east storms, and, like tornadoes and in fact *all* rotary storms, originated by purely local circumstances; and are therefore liable to occur at the same places at a certain season of each year. This fact is so well known in Europe that companies for the insurance of crops hesitate to take risks on

*Some months after I had made the survey of the West Cambridge tornado I delivered a public lecture on the subject in Woburn, a small place two or three miles north of Medford, and suggested the possibility of such a thing without knowing that it ever had happened. After the lecture Dr. Drew of Woburn informed me that a tornado had actually occurred at that place in the same afternoon that the West Cambridge tornado occurred. Dr. Drew had the kindness to take me over the track the next morning, and I became convinced that it was a similar phenomenon in respect to origin and development, only smaller. It had, however, destroyed several orchards and forest trees of one foot in diameter. Its length was about two miles and its width proportionate. It had not attracted attention until the possibility of the occurrence was mentioned in my lecture, and I was at the time delighted to find my theories thus confirmed.

certain farms because they are almost regularly visited by hail-storms.

Hail is almost invariably an accompaniment of tornadoes, and is found in one or sometimes two belts outside of the track and parallel to it. If hail does not occur there is to take its place an excessively violent rain-fall; this is dependent on temperature, and was the case in the West Cambridge tornado. (*Analysis*, 72.)

Hail forms only in the summer season.

Its crystallization is not of the same appearance throughout, giving evidence that it is formed under circumstances which change during its formation. If a large hailstone is cut in two, the section shows alternate concentric rings of compact snow and of transparent ice. The nucleus resembles a miniature snowball, then comes a ring of clear ice, then a ring of the snowball-like conglomerate, and so on. This would indicate the repetition alternately of two different influences.

Volta's theory that the different appearance is due to the formation of the hailstones between two clouds, one above the other, charged with opposite electricity, which alternately attract and repel the hailstones, is generally felt to be defective, and the action and condition of a tornado's vortex offers a much more ready explanation.

In the case of a tornado we have an immense quantity of warm air in the highest state of saturation and compression, coming suddenly on entering the vortex under conditions of much diminished pressure, in consequence of which the temperature is much reduced and the moisture condenses and freezes. The sudden and profuse congelations in the form of large snow-flakes are kneaded together and balled by the commotion of the air on its spiral road upward, being tossed in all directions inside of the vortex. Each of the little snowballs thus manufactured forms the nucleus of a hailstone, and having finally reached the top of the vortex will be thrown by the centrifugal force upward and outward. Those balls which are thrown into the equatorial current in *front* of the vortex will of course first fly up into its clouds, and after their momentum is exhausted fall toward the ground, covering themselves during their passage with a coating of transparent ice, the congealed moisture of the clouds and of the equatorial current. In falling they will drop again into the vortex, the upper opening of which will by this time have come underneath them, and falling through the cold rarefied space in the middle to the mouth, they are caught up by fresh in-rushing warm air in the region where the snow-flakes are formed. Here a covering of snow is packed on the hailstone, which is followed by another coating of ice when it is thrown out into the moist current again. This process may be repeated until the hailstone grows weighty enough to be thrown out of the top of the vortex sufficiently far to reach the ground before the vortex comes underneath it, or is thrown to the side or rear, which latter case may occur, of course, at any stage of its formation. The number of rings will thus tell how many times the stone has gone up and down.

The formation of a coating of clear ice around a very cold body may be observed quite frequently in the spring upon the branches of trees and upon other objects when a moist equatorial current replaces a cold polar current.

As the vortex of a tornado is inclined to the north, lying against the face of the polar current, the hail will mostly drop to the north of the track of the vortex, and parallel belts of hail will be accounted for by parallelly-travelling vortices.

Such seems the probable explanation of hail formation, and the following interesting account by Prof. John Wise of one of his balloon experiences is valuable as strong confirmatory evidence:

"According to announcement I started on Saturday last on my forty-first aërial excursion from the Centre Square of Carlisle, at precisely fifteen minutes past two o'clock in the afternoon, it being on the 17th of June, 1843. A slight breeze from the west wafted me a short distance in its direction horizontally, after which the ascent became nearly perpendicular until the height attained was about twenty-five hundred feet, when the balloon moved off toward the east with a velocity much greater than that of its ascent. . . . When I had reached a point about two miles east of the town, there appeared a little distance beyond and above me a huge black cloud. Seeing that the horizontal velocity of the balloon would carry it underneath and beyond the cloud, preparations were at once made to effect it by throwing out some ballast as soon as its border should be reached. Harrisburg was now distinctly in view, and the balloon moving directly for it; I was hesitating, with the bag of ballast in my hand, whether I should throw it out for the purpose designated, or continue straight on as I was then going to the place just mentioned. By this time I had reached a point underneath the cloud, which was expanding, and immediately felt an agitation in the machinery, and presently an upward tendency of the balloon, which also commenced to rotate rapidly on its vertical axis. I might have discharged gas and probably have passed underneath it; but thinking that it would soon be penetrated, and then might be passed above, as it appeared not to be moving along itself, I made no hesitation in letting the balloon go on its own way. This part of the feat, however, I had reason to regret soon afterward, although at the present time it gives more real pleasure in contemplating its terrific grandeur and reality than anything that has ever transpired in my aërial adventures. The details that shall here be given of this terrible scene may be relied upon, as I was sufficiently composed to appreciate its grandeur and observe its physical operations. The cloud, to the best of my judgment, covered an area of from four to six miles in diameter; it appeared of a circular form as I entered it, considerably depressed in its lower surface, presenting a great concavity toward the earth, with its lower edges very ragged and falling downward with an agitated motion, and it was of a dark smoke color. Just before entering this cloud, I noticed, at some distance off, a storm-cloud from which there was apparently a heavy rain descending. The first sensations I experienced when entering this cloud were extremely unpleasant. A suffocating sensation immediately ensued its entrance, which was shortly followed by a sickness at the stomach, arising from the gyrating, swinging motion of my car, causing me to vomit several times in quick succession most violently; this vomiting, however, soon abated, and gave way to sensations that were truly calculated to neutralize more violent symptoms than a momentary squeamishness. The cold had now become intense, and everything around me of a fibrous nature became thickly covered with hoarfrost, my whiskers jutting out with it far beyond my face, and the cords running up from my car looking like glass rods, these being glazed with ice, and snow and hail was indiscriminately pelting all around me. The cloud at this point, which I presumed to be about the midst of it from the terrible ebullition going on, had not that black appearance I observed on entering it, but was of a light, milky color, and so dense just at this time that I could hardly see the balloon, which was sixteen feet above the car. From the intensity of the cold in this cloud I supposed that the gas would rapidly condense, and the balloon consequently descend and take me out of it. In this, however, I was doomed to disappointment, for I soon found myself whirling upward with a fearful rapidity, the balloon gyrating and the car describing a large circle in the cloud. A noise resembling the rushing of a thousand milldams, intermingled with a dismal moaning sound of wind, surrounded me in this terrible flight. Whether this noise was occasioned by the hail and snow which were so fearfully pelting the balloon I am unable to tell, as the moaning sound must evidently have had another source. I was in hope, when being hurled rapidly upward, that I should escape from the top of the cloud; but as in former expectations of an opposite release from this terrible place, disappointment was again my lot, and the congenial sunshine, invariably above, which had already been anticipated by its faint glimmer through the top of the cloud, soon vanished, with a violent downward surge of the balloon, as it appeared to me, of some hundred feet. The balloon subsided, only to be hurled upward again, when, having attained its maximum, it would again sink down with a swinging and fearful velocity, to be carried up again and let fall. This happened eight or ten times, all the time the storm raging with unabated fury, while the discharge of ballast would not let me out at the top of the cloud, nor the discharge of gas out of the bottom of it, though I had expended at least thirty pounds of the former in the first attempt, and not less than a thousand cubic feet of the latter, for the balloon had also become perforated with holes by the icicles that were formed where the melted snow ran on the cords at the point where they diverged from the balloon, and would by the surging and swinging motion pierce it through.

"I experienced all this time an almost irresistible inclination to sleep, notwithstanding a nauseating feeling of the stomach, causing me to vomit several times, and the terrible predicament I was placed in, until, after eating some snow and hail mixed, of which a considerable quantity had lodged on some canvas and paper lying in the bottom of the car, I felt somewhat easier in mind and in body (for it is no use to say that I cannot be agitated and alarmed), and I grasped a firm hold of the sides of the car, determined to abide the result with as much composure as the nature of the case would admit; for I felt satisfied it could not last much longer, seeing that the balloon had become very much weakened by a great loss of gas. Once I saw the earth through a chasm in the cloud, but was hurled up once more after that, when, to my great joy, I fell clear out of it, after having been belched up and swallowed down repeatedly by this huge and terrific monster of the air for a space of twenty minutes, which seemed like an age, for I thought my watch had been stopped, till a comparison of it with another afterward proved the contrary. I landed, in the midst of a pouring rain, on the farm of Mr. Goodyear, five miles from Carlisle, in a fallow field, where the dashing rain bespattered me with mud from head to foot as I stood in my car looking up at the fearful element which had just disgorged me.

"The density of this cloud did not appear alike all through it, as I could at times see the balloon very distinctly above me, also, occasionally, pieces of paper and whole newspapers, of which a considerable quantity were blown out of my car. I also noticed a violent convolutionary motion or action of the vapor of the cloud going on, and a promiscuous scattering of the hail and snow, as though it were projected from every point of the compass.

"Such is the history of this short but magnificent trip, and I can assure my readers that when I again meet clouds of this character (which I shall name the cloud of terror) I will endeavor with all my skill to avoid them."

The origin of tornadoes and simple hail-storms is, I am satisfied, the same, the difference being only one of degree; as for instance if the disturbing cause in the West Cambridge tornado had not been so great, the vortex would not have been drawn down to the earth, but would have remained in the air. In other words, hail-storms are only tornadoes on a smaller scale travelling through higher regions of air and not touching the surface.

Those tornadoes which have two belts of hail are probably preceded or followed by a lesser whirl which does not reach the ground.

The loud rattling noise described by many as heard in the approach of a tornado may be accounted for by the clashing of the hail-stones in the vortex; and it is a significant fact that in the West Cambridge tornado, where no hail fell, the noise was of a different character.

### *Dust-Storms of India.*

The dust-storms are doubtless of the same origin as tornadoes, which seems to appear from the following extract from a report made by Dr. P. F. Baddeley, surgeon in the Bengal army. He says: "They come on a sudden, without barometric warning. All that we notice is a low bank of dark cloud in the horizon. After the first sudden burst, violent gusts or squalls succeed one another at intervals, becoming weaker toward its close, when the wind gradually veers and subsides. The electric fluid continues to be discharged without intermission during the storm, and with increased intensity at the recurrence of the gusts or squalls which mark the passage of a fresh batch of spirals.

"It seems probable that in an extensive dust-storm there are many of the columns moving on together in the same direction, and during the continuance of the storm. In all cases, from those of a few feet to fifty miles in diameter, toward the close of the storm of this kind a fall of rain does take place."

He evidently does not distinguish between the storm and "the whirl;" therefore the assumption of such large diameter.

In an extract from the *Meteorological Journal* at Lahore we read: "The air before a dust-storm is calm and sultry. On its approach, a vane, before unaffected by any wind, turns slowly and points toward the advancing cloud." This rise of the wind in advance of the cloud and the condition of the air beforehand indicate a storm of the nature of our south-east storms.

### *Water-Spouts.*

A water-spout is simply a tornado travelling over water; this is evident from the fact that tornadoes have frequently been known to pass over small sheets of water in their course, producing phenomena identical with the water-spouts observed at sea. The reverse may also happen, a water-spout striking the land and passing over it as a tornado.

The cause disturbing the equilibrium of the conflicting currents is, in the case of water-spouts originating at sea, an island above which the air is more heated and therefore more rarefied, or sometimes a warm ocean current, as the Gulf Stream, above which the air is in the same rarefied condition. In *Fig.* 8. the line *h a e* represents the plane of meeting of the two currents; and if a portion of this, *a h*, comes over the Gulf Stream, as the air here is more rarefied, the pressure which has opposed the advance of the polar current is more or less removed; the polar air rushes in advance over the rarefied space, and the break is produced, with its consequences, as in the origin of the tornado, the vortex which is formed travelling along the plane of meeting *a e*. As the plane of meeting makes an advance into the position *b f*, the same thing may be repeated, and another vortex travel off parallel to the first; and so on until there may be several, as is in fact generally the case. When the plane of meeting passes over an island, the same process would take place; and if there should be a group of islands, we may look for several parallel or intermittent water-spouts.

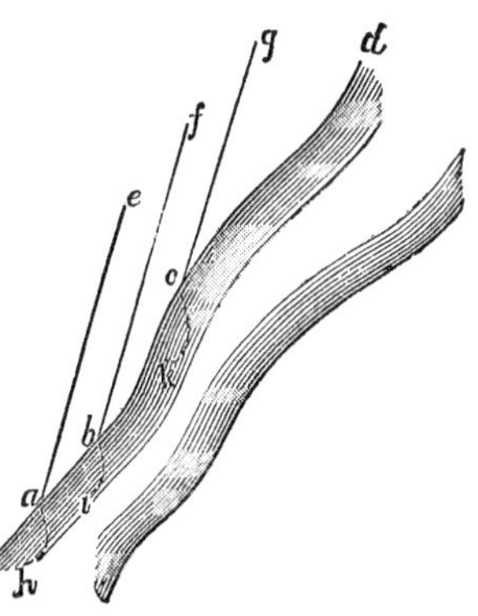

Fig. 8.

It is a matter of common knowledge that water-spouts as a rule occur in the neighborhood of islands or warm ocean currents, and without doubt the only exception to this rule would be in the case of land tornadoes passing from the land to the water.

The following account of a water-spout at Langley, South Carolina, August 12, 1874, illustrates the theory:

"A dense cloud was first seen approaching the pond, being apparently a considerable distance up. Nothing particular was thought of it, the citizens of Langley being at the time occupied in trying to keep cool—a hard thing to do with the thermometer at one hundred degrees in the shade. But presently a startling circumstance occurred. The cloud had halted over the pond and established connection with the latter. A genuine water-spout had in fact been evolved, and an immense quantity of water was rushing skyward through the liquid conductor. When first seen, the water-spout was near the dam, and travelled slowly across the pond until it reached the railroad trestle-work, a distance of a mile and a quarter from its starting-point, when it disappeared, and the cloud moved majestically off, carrying with it thousands of gallons of water which had been drawn from the pond. The latter, covering an area of six hundred acres, was, in fact, lowered fully two inches. The huge column which joined the upper region to the expanse of water below resembled a cone in form, and rotated horizontally with exceeding rapidity. The marvellous speed with which the column turned impressed the beholder immediately with the idea that it was associated with a whirlwind. This was most probably the case, as a tremendous wind passed over Augusta from the direction of Langley some hours afterward. The heavens were brilliant with incessant flashes of lightning after the spout described above had disappeared. There was no rushing noise connected with it, as is the case in some instances. The water underneath the clouds just before the spout formed was in a state of great agitation. Waves rolled angrily, and a perceptible bulge was seen. As the cloud halted a sort of funnel protruded from it and dropped slowly down, becoming larger as it lengthened, the broader portion or base being at the surface of the cloud. When it reached a point about one-fourth the distance between the cloud and the pond, the bulge on the surface of the latter rose to meet it, and the two at length joined, when the water from the pond commenced ascending into the cloud, which moved slowly toward the trestle-work, the waves in the water all leaping and tending toward the spout, and the spout itself continued the vertical motion referred to above. The outside of the watery funnel was dark and not well defined, while the centre was much lighter, being rather of a bluish cast. This would seem to indicate that the column was partly hollow, the dark portions representing the sides. There can be no doubt but that the immense quantity of water which was transferred from the pond to the cloud was literally sucked up. The spout finally disappeared, as if it had been drawn bodily up into the cloud, while the latter quietly moved off to parts unknown. Not a drop of rain fell during the occurrence or afterward. The formation and subsequent motions of the spout are described as having made up a spectacle grand in the extreme. Nothing of the kind was ever before seen in that section. The strangest part of the phenomenon was the fact that the cloud, so burdened with water, moved off without dispensing any of it in the form of rain in the neighborhood.

"The following interesting statement was furnished by a civil engineer: Area of mill-pond, 600 acres; depth of water diminished, two inches by a water-spout, which prevailed for about ten minutes. The superficial area of one acre is 43,560 square feet; the decimal for the depth of two inches is 0.166 of a foot; hence 43,560 × 0.16 = 6969.60 cubic feet is the quantity taken from one acre; and then 6969.60 × 600 gives us 4,181,760 cubic feet as the whole quantity taken from the mill-pond. The cube root of this last is about 161 feet, so a cube of that size would nearly measure the quantity of water taken off. This quantity would make a column ten feet diameter, 53,243 feet high—rather more than ten miles. At 62½ pounds to a cubic foot, the above 4,181,760 cubic feet would weigh 261,360,000 pounds."

# CHAPTER VIII.

*STORMS OF THE TORRID ZONE, AND THEIR PROBABLE INTIMATE CONNECTION WITH THOSE OF THE TEMPERATE ZONE.*

THE storms of the torrid zone are without much question not very dissimilar to those of the temperate zone; for the general conditions of the aërial currents in both are alike, the only difference being that in the torrid zone the predominant disturbances are in a vertical direction, while in the temperate zone they are in a lateral direction, and the effect of this is that in the first case the progressive storms are developed in a smaller area, but with greater violence.

Glaisher* found by many balloon ascensions that up to five hundred feet the temperature decreased in winter 0.46° C. and in summer 0.77° C. per one hundred metres, and others found similar results. If we apply this law to warm and cold latitudes, which on general considerations will be safe, the decrease in temperature vertically upward will be more rapid at the equator and less at latitudes nearer the poles, while the temperature in a lateral direction decreases more rapidly in going toward the poles. We will have, therefore, toward the equator a preponderance of vertical disturbances, and toward the poles a preponderance of lateral disturbances. In the re-establishment of a disturbed equilibrium between cold and warm regions the greatest contrasts in the torrid zone lie in a vertical direction, while toward the frigid zone they lie in a lateral direction. Small differences in a lateral direction will therefore, in the torrid zone, be accompanied by very violent disturbances, because the main contrasts lie vertically. This conclusion is verified by the well-known

* *Report of the British Assoc.*, 1863, p. 426.

fact that a lateral difference of only 5° C. in the temperature at the northern and at the southern limit of each trade-wind, which is equal to about $\frac{1}{5}$° C. in one degree of latitude, is capable of keeping these mighty currents unchangeably in the same direction. In the temperate zone there must be much greater contrasts before similar effects are produced. In connection with this, it is found that in higher latitudes the velocity of progressive storms is greater, but the destructiveness less, and also that the plane of meeting between the two currents is most inclined as we go toward the poles, and approaches the vertical position as we go toward the equator.

In treating *local storms*, which are caused by vertical disturbances, it was stated that they are unknown in the arctic regions, and are represented in the temperate zone only by sudden and insignificant summer showers, while in the torrid zone they are developed on the most gigantic scale. The ever-rising current along the equator and the belt of cloud above it, with the two supply-currents *b* and *b'* (*Plate V.*), the trade-winds, were spoken of as an everlasting storm of this type on the largest possible scale. This mighty storm, encircling the whole globe with its sinuous belt of calm, and oscillating north and south, is differently affected and modified in different longitudes as it passes in its oscillations from land to sea, or the reverse; and the vibrations of these special disturbances are felt vertically upward, producing violent local storms, and also horizontally toward the poles, originating progressive storms. Experience teaches that both these kinds of storms exist in the torrid zone.

The local storms of the torrid zone are manifestly of the same character as those of the temperate zone, and therefore have already been considered. We will now endeavor to show how the progressive storms are also similar. We shall assume that the track of the hurricanes of the West Indies is a curve, as the cyclonists describe it (see *Fig.* 1), although this does not seem to be established definitely as yet.

The transition from a warm to a cold region is much more rapid in a vertical direction than horizontally, and the contrasts are much sharper. This is clearly instanced by the comparison of the geographical distribution of plants in the ascent of high mountains in the torrid zone, with the corresponding distribution in travelling toward the poles, where there will be found within a vertical distance of less than three miles the same gradations that are spread over a lateral distance of more than three thousand miles, which of course is a matter of common knowledge.

The re-establishment of an equilibrium between cold and warm regions taking place mostly in a vertical direction in the torrid zone, greater contrasts of temperature will therefore be produced in storms here than in the temperate zone, although we shall not see them in a lateral direction.

The currents *b* and *b′* (*Plate V.*), coming down vertically from cold regions which are at a comparatively short distance from the warm regions of the surface, will be proportionately colder when they reach the ground at the tropics, particularly as the storm develops, than the polar current will be when meeting the equatorial current in the temperate zone—*i. e.*, in the torrid zone, a proportionately small difference in temperature laterally on the surface will have a greater disturbing effect than in the temperate zone. The two currents *b* and *b′*, after they reach the ground, flow horizontally as supply-currents toward the region of the rising equatorial current *A*, forming, as before remarked, the two trade-winds, from north-east and south-east respectively. It will be remembered also, from the consideration of the local storms, that these two currents alternately displace each other in their annual oscillation, due to the motion of the sun north and south, either gradually or, if they have been fixed by local circumstances for six months in the same position, periodically, as in the case of the monsoons.

The one of the two currents *b* and *b′* which has in the annual oscillation reached into the region of the other will be the most heated from traversing a longer distance on the surface, and will assume the office held in the temperate zone by the equatorial current. The other current, which, from traversing a shorter distance on the surface, is less heated when it begins the return oscillation to regain its former position, displaces the warmer current in a similar manner to the action of the polar current in the temperate zone. But as the return oscillation, which would otherwise have taken place gradually, extending over half the year, has been delayed by local circumstances, it must traverse its whole distance in a much shorter time, and the displacement of the other current is, therefore, attended with much greater violence.

The region of calm *A* is, in such a case, somewhat compressed by the pressure of the conflicting currents, but nevertheless, for manifest reasons, remains of greater dimensions than the region of calm in the storms of the temperate zones. It must be remembered, however, that this conflict of currents is produced by local circumstances, and, therefore, does not take place at once along the whole equatorial belt of calm; and for this reason this belt of calm may be bent to the north or south by the storm in its oscillations.

The continent of North America has an influence on the south-east trade-wind in the Atlantic Ocean similar to that of Asia on the south-east trade-wind in the Indian Ocean and China Sea, although not to as great an extent. It is drawn, according to Maury,* as far as 17° north latitude, and may reach in some cases farther north of the West Indies. It, therefore, may be treated as a monsoon, although it does not preserve its direction continuously for six months, except in one locality. The displacement of it by the north-east trade-wind, therefore, when the return oscillation is begun, must necessarily produce the most violent south-east storms.

As there is no obstacle north-east of South America to de-

* Wind and Current Charts.

flect the north-east trade-wind, the current *b*, nor the south-east trade-wind, the current *b'*, from their respective courses, they will meet at an angle; the plane of meeting or diagonal of forces *m n* (*Plate X.*) will lie from east to west or from east-south-east to west-north-west, and the storm will travel toward the south-west. The "northers" in the Gulf of Mexico (*m' n'*, *Plate X.*) are doubtless storms of this kind, but may sometimes be produced by the real polar current instead of the north-east trade-wind, because the arctic belt of high pressure approaches the tropical belt of high pressure during winter in this longitude.

The storms of the torrid zone will not move over so great a distance as those of the temperate zone, because the annual oscillations of the meteorological belts near the equator are not extensive as those of the belts nearer the poles; but they will be much more violent because of the much greater contrast in the temperatures of the conflicting currents in a vertical direction, in addition to the reasons before stated.

If one of these storms at its crisis arrives over the West Indies, its equilibrium may be disturbed in the same way as in the origin of water-spouts. A tornado on a large scale, or perhaps a series, apparently parts of one intermitting tornado, will then originate and travel in the direction of the diagonal of the two currents toward the north-west. This would account for the first branch of what the cyclonists suppose is a cyclonic hurricane travelling first to north-west or west-north-west and then curving to north-east, as was described when setting forth the Cyclone theory. When by such a storm the current *c* (*Plates V.* and *X.*) has been thrown with the current *b*, making the whole volume of the current *a*, toward the region of the uprising current *A*, it would seem to follow that in the return oscillation the current *b* will join the current *c* in its movement toward the arctic regions. For the movement of the current *c* to join *b* in its movement to *A* will, it is manifest, stop the supply of the equatorial current of the temperate zone, and thus af-

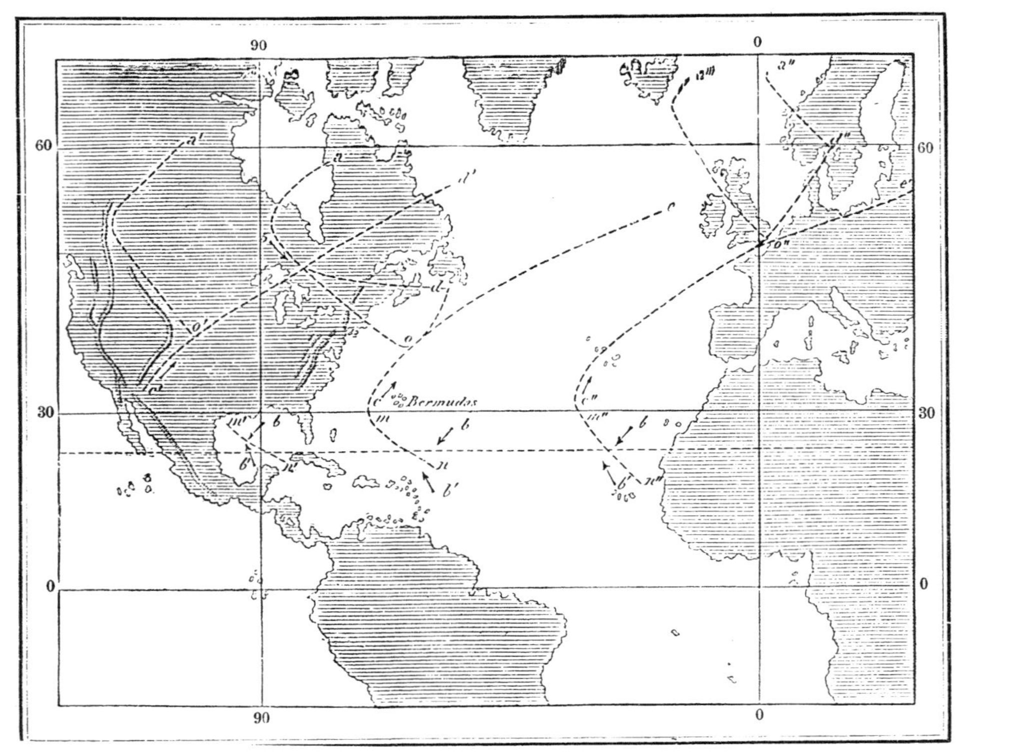
90
0
60
30
0
Bermudas
90
0

ford room for the advance south of the polar current *N*. (*Plate V*.) Thus the same cause which draws *c* toward *A* also draws *N* in the same direction. But this advance of the polar current will create a deficiency in the arctic belt of high pressure of such an extent as to draw toward it not only the current *c*, but also *b*, thus originating a north-east storm through the temperate zone travelling at right angles to the first storm, and closely following it from *c* to *d* or *e*. (*Plate X*.) If the south-east trade-wind *b′*, reaching some degrees north of the equator, should have been changed into a south-west wind in the Gulf of Mexico, the continuity of the two storms would be still closer.

The general resemblance of hurricanes, typhoons, tornadoes and water-spouts becomes more striking if we compare the places of their origin, the time of their occurrence and the appearance of the clouds as far as they have been described. The pamphlet issued by the U. S. Hydrographic Bureau, which has before been quoted, basing its statements on the treatises of Keller and others, says:

"Hurricanes take place in the three great seas of the globe: the Atlantic, the Indian and the Pacific Oceans.

"In the Atlantic Ocean the West Indies is the centre of the most terrible hurricanes known. In the Indian Ocean it is about the position of Rodriguez, Mauritius and Reunion Islands. In the Pacific, where very few observations have thus far been made, it is supposed to be in the vicinity of the Tonga Islands.

"In the West Indies and their vicinity the season during which hurricanes may be expected includes the months of August, September and October; at this period the navigation of the West Indies, of the Gulf of Mexico and south coast of the United States should be avoided as much as possible.

"If it is necessary to winter in these localities, a perfectly protected port should be chosen. Hurricanes seldom occur in June or July.

"In the Indian Ocean hurricanes take place from December to April—that is, during the warmest months of the southern hemisphere; they seldom occur in November and in May, and are unknown during the other months of the year.

"In the Pacific Ocean, to the south of the equator, the known hurricanes have taken place in November and in December, and they appear to have much similarity to those of the Indian Seas.

"In the Atlantic Ocean, to the north of the equator, the supposed extent of the zone where hurricanes are experienced is comprised between the latitude of 10° and 50° N. and the longitude of 50° and 100° W.

"In the Indian Ocean the extent of this zone in longitude is three thousand miles, from the west coast of Australia to that of Madagascar, and is comprised between the latitude of 6° or 8° S. and 22° S."

It will be noticed that in all cases the seat of the most violent hurricanes is, like water-spouts, in the vicinity of islands. It will be noticed, also, that the time of occurrence is on both the southern and northern hemispheres during the hot season, and principally at the time when the monsoons change, or the south-east trade-wind is displaced by the north-east trade-wind, and *vice versâ*.

The clouds characteristic in the temperate zone of the advancing equatorial current and those of the advancing polar current have also been observed in the torrid zone in the advance of the south-west (deflected south-*east*) trade-wind, and of the north-east trade-wind, and in each case moving against the prevailing current, thus indicating a similarity of cause and action to those of the north-east and south-east storms of our latitude.

The fact that the hurricanes of the torrid zone—that is, their rotary portion—originate always at definite localities, and travel in a definite direction corresponding to what must be the diagonal of the forces of the two currents at the seasons of the year when these storms take place, makes the resemblance of the whole phenomenon to our south-east storm ending in a tornado very striking.

The slow progressive motion observed in the most violent typhoons* bears also a strong likeness to the irregular and tricky progress of the south-east storm.† The similarity is still further carried out, as will appear from the following extract from Col. Reid's *Law of Storms*, page 46, which agrees exactly with the description of a south-east (here south-west) storm, accompanied by a tornado:

"At Antigua it happened on the 12th of August, 1835; the wind during the first part blowing from the north, and during the latter part from the south, with a calm of twenty minutes in the middle of it. The barometer was observed to fall 1.4 inch. . . . Trees were blown down as if forming lanes—an effect which has been remarked in many other descriptions of hurricanes—and at its commencement the wind was described as coming in gusts."

According to Reid, the most furious hurricanes of the West Indies seem to commence with a wind from the north, north-west or north-east; after this comes a calm, and this is followed

* Piddington tells us in the thirteenth memoir, with reference to the law of storms in India, an instance of a stationary storm, illustrated by the movement of a ship in the storm from 22d to 27th of Feb., 1815.

Capper (*Observations on the Winds and Monsoons, London,* 1801) found some of these storms stationary.

† I feel still more inclined to think the two branches of the hurricane presented as travelling in a parabolic curve (*Fig.* 1), in which the one branch stands at a right angle to the other, two different kinds of storms —1. Because I know the one branch in the temperate zone to be our north-east storm, and 2. it will appear from investigations made by Meldrum that the hurricanes at Mauritius are, as I expected, really produced by two opposing currents which form an elliptical region of low barometer between them. That Meldrum calls them elliptical cyclones, as will appear, proves only how difficult it is to get rid of the Cyclone idea.

by winds from either the south, the south-east or south-west. They are preceded by gentle breezes or sultry calms and black, threatening clouds, coming from the north or north-east, accompanied by thunder and lightning and a heavy swell of the sea.

The kind of destruction on land resembles that of our tornadoes. There appears to be sometimes an oscillation of the region of conflict north and south, and the south-east storm (in this case really a south-*west* storm) may assume for a period the character of a north-east storm, which, as has been observed, sometimes takes place in the temperate zone at the point in the storm's duration when the two currents are almost balancing each other.

Although the hurricanes of the West Indies seem mainly to be storms of the south-east kind, still there must be also storms of the north-east character. These may not be well developed, or rather may assume the character of south-east storms, on account of the plane of meeting's becoming more vertical. The north-east storm will here, then, differ from the south-east storm only in the formation of the clouds and the direction of progress. The clouds even are likely to lose somewhat their characteristic stratified form, and the hazy stripes assume that modified shape of the different kinds of cirrus, as "mares' tails," etc., produced by the action of the powerful upward warmer current.

Comparing the movements of the storm over the Atlantic Ocean and over the continent of North America, it appears as if there exist two systems of storm-tracks in these longitudes, indicated on *Plate X.* by the dotted lines. These two systems, one over the continent, the other over the ocean, although separate, are in some connection on account of their proximity and common origin; and sometimes they collide on the coast, the south-east storm of the continental system falling into the north-east storm of the oceanic system.

Let us take an illustration.

The arrows *b* and *c* (*Plate X.*) represent the down-coming currents at the tropics, *c* the equatorial current of the temperate zone, *b* the north-east trade-wind of the torrid zone, and *b′* the south-east trade-wind, reaching far over into the northern hemisphere. (Compare *Plate V.*) If, now, in any longitude, by a powerful vertical disturbance, for instance over the West Indies or South America, *b′* is displaced by *b*, *c* will join *b*, and a south-westerly oscillation or south-east (here south-west) storm originate with its region of meeting in the direction of *m n;* and a rotary storm or hurricane may travel toward north-west from *n* to *m*. The flow of both the currents *b* and *c* toward the south will stop the supply of the equatorial current *c* in the temperate zone, and originate the advance of the polar current from the north, or a south-east storm in the temperate zone, probably in the storm-system on the continent at *a*. This creates a deficiency in the arctic regions, causing a north-east storm from *c*. In this north-east storm, or return oscillation, *b* will join *c*, flowing toward the arctic deficiency and producing a north-east storm over the Atlantic, travelling from *c* to *d*, and possibly to *e* or farther. The south-east storm before mentioned, having in the mean time become deflected in the direction of the arrow 5, owing to the physical character of the earth's surface, and in addition being attracted by the region of low barometer of the north-east storm, will strike the north-east storm off the coast at *o*, at a right angle to its track. The north-east storm, in sliding along the coast, will finally double up the south-east storm at *d*, re-establishing the equilibrium at that point, and will either begin a return oscillation or will continue on toward Europe. This coalescing of the storms of the two systems would account for those violent storms which are frequent on the coasts of Nova Scotia and New Jersey. We have described such a meeting on the continent in the hypothetical case when we treated the storms represented by the Signal Service Bureau as changing their direction at a right angle in the west at *o′*. Currents never change their direction unless they are deflected by obstacles or deficiencies, and it does not seem possible that one and the same storm can travel in right angles, as is said to take place in hurricanes and in certain storms mentioned by the Signal Service Bureau.

It seems highly probable that there exist over the Eastern Atlantic Ocean and Western Europe systems of storm-tracks similar to those of the Western Atlantic and North America.

If future investigations should prove these theories of the connection between the storms in the torrid and temperate zones to be correct, the storms all over the globe would prove to be nothing but modifications by local circumstances, or particular developments, of the general circulation of the atmosphere, as we found to be the case in the storms in the temperate zone, and we should then be enabled to telegraph coming storms in the temperate zone weeks ahead from the knowledge of those occurring in the torrid zone.

The aërial sea around us could then indeed be likened to a living organism which keeps its material in perpetual health by circulation, in the same way as the body is kept healthy by a regular circulation of blood. The region of greatest heat, its heart, would send the air, its blood, through the currents, $A$, $a$, $a'$, etc., its arteries, to the colder regions, its lungs, from whence they return in a similar manner to the equator. Storms would appear as special impulses in this circulation, by which the blessings of heat and moisture become more equally distributed all over the globe, and by which poisonous matter becomes scattered and changed. An uncommon disturbance at the equator would be felt in its palpitations through the whole atmosphere, as a disturbance in the heart is felt in the pulsations of the farthest branches of the arteries.

At the equator we should then have the first cause of all storms.

# CHAPTER IX.

## *CORROBORATIVE EVIDENCE FROM OTHER SOURCES.*

THE operations of Nature, at least in their beginnings, are not complicated, and she attains her greatest ends by the simplest means. The deeper her secrets are penetrated, the more clearly it appears that the most complicated phenomena in this visible world are due to a few forces which seem to start from one common source, as the blood of the many veins in the body receives its impulse from the heart. The force that makes the apple fall to the ground causes also the worlds to move in their orbits. Obscure and complicated explanations are therefore always to be regarded with suspicion.

The theory that I have set forth in the preceding pages is not thus complicated, nor is it dependent on the action of unknown forces, but upon those that are familiar. Its basis is the phenomena of the motion of locally heated air, which are commonly known, and which may be seen around any fire and in the interchange of cold and warm air through the open window of a heated room. It was not first assumed and then the facts sought for its corroboration, but it grew out of facts which had been gathered together with the simple desire to discover their true significance. The phenomena upon which it is built, so far as they are to be seen in the temperate zone, I have observed to follow each other as cause and effect in regular order without fail through a period of nearly a quarter of a century. They can be verified by any intelligent and careful observer, and are unexplained by any theory which has heretofore been published to the world. But the proof of my theory does not depend on my own investigations, being supplied also by facts brought out in recent investigations in Europe and this country, the results of which are of the more value, as they are opposed to the inclinations of the investigators, who, being cyclonists, are at a loss to explain them.

The attempt to reconcile them with the Cyclone theory has led to numerous complications, and has necessitated the assumption of new hypotheses without foundation in fact; but to me they not only appear easily explainable, but are welcome as strengthening the conclusions to which my own investigations have led.

## I.

*Conclusions as to the storms of Northern Europe drawn by Hildebrandsson from the study of weather charts, based principally on hourly observations at Upsala, Sweden.**

1. Regions exist of high and low barometer, which are surrounded by isobarometric lines of a more or less regular form.

2. The isobars surrounding the areas of maximum barometer are further separated from each other, the winds are feebler and are variable, and the sky is generally serene; these are thus the centres of fine, calm weather.

3. On the contrary, around the lowest barometer the isobars are more crowded together (at least on one side), the wind stronger in proportion as the isobars are nearer, and the direction of the wind is determined at any point by the law of Buys-Ballot, so that the air seems to move about the centre of depression in a direction contrary to the movements of the hands of a watch. At the very centre itself is sometimes found a region where the isobars are farther separated from each other, and where, consequently, the winds are feebler.

4. All centres of depression come from the north.

5. The path of a storm is generally preceded by a cloudy sky and rain or snow; the rear is, on the contrary, less cloudy.

* Taken from Prof. Spencer F. Baird's "Scientific Record" of *Harper's Magazine* for December, 1873.

6. An intimate connection exists between changes of the various meteorological elements during a storm. In the more southern countries various perturbations obscure more or less the relation that in Sweden appears in a striking manner. By studying principally the barometric minima of winter nights we have almost entirely eliminated these perturbations, and find—

7. That the wind varies with a surprising regularity, so that from it we can fix at any time by Buys-Ballot's law the direction in which the centre of low barometer is to be found.

8. The nearer the centre passes the place of observation, the greater becomes the velocity of fall and rise of the barometer, and the quicker the wind veers if the centre is to the north, or backs if the centre passes to the south, of the station.

9. If a new storm centre approaches, the wind changes in the direction called "backing" toward the south when the maximum barometer has passed.

10. The pressure of the air and the temperature change in opposite directions, the daily curves of barometer and thermometer being, in fact, nearly contrary to each other.

11. The changes in the pressure of aqueous vapor nearly follow the changes of temperature.

From the above Mr. Hildebrandsson appears as a cyclonist, but his observations have been so accurate that for our purpose it is only necessary to explain and connect what seem to him to be independent phenomena. To any one who has comprehended the theory I have advanced, it will be clear that Hildebrandsson's regions of high barometer are identical with the regions of the polar and the equatorial currents, and the regions of low barometer, or "centres of depression," the region of calm between them. By this light the facts noted in *Results* 1, 2 and 3 are also explained.

The region of calm or of low barometer being produced by the upward flow of the equatorial current in front of the polar current, it is readily seen why its size, and the consequent distance between the isobars, varies in different storms; for the size and form of the region of calm are dependent on the nature of the conflict of the two currents, the velocity with which the displacing current moves, and the amount of resistance opposed by the other.

If the isobars of low pressure approach each other more nearly on one side of the storm than on the other, it shows that the currents meet at an angle, and therefore compression is greater on one side than on the other. The isobars toward the middle are farther from each other than toward the margin of the storm, but that the calm is greater in the middle than on the margin is not the effect of the greater distance of the isobars, but because the currents of the storm are directed centripetally toward the line of meeting, and the greater mass of air rises here. The isobars are on one side of the region of low barometer more crowded than on the other, for the reason that the equatorial current overlaps the polar current obliquely. If it were rising vertically, as in local storms, we should find the isobars on both sides equally distributed.

*Result* 4 I cannot understand in connection with the statements in *Result* 5, and should suppose that there is either a typographical error in substituting "north" for *south*, or that the observations on which it is founded were made at a different season of the year from the others; for it would clearly refer to our south-east summer storms, while *Result* 5 and others as clearly indicate north-east winter storms. The discrepancy would probably be accounted for if the result has been arrived at by the system of *averaging*, which almost invariably proves deceptive. If Mr. Hildebrandsson had indicated the forms of the clouds, the point could be cleared up.

*Results* 6, 7, 8, 9, 10 and 11, if viewed from our standpoint, appear simple and easily explained.

We thus see in these results, with the one exception noted,

conditions set down as existing that are at the least not *satisfactorily* explained by the Cyclone theory, if, indeed, it is attempted at all, but are, on the other hand, not only accounted for by our theory, but are those which it *necessitates.*

Mr. Hildebrandsson gives so many true and important data because the observations were made *hourly.* Mr. William Clement Ley has come to somewhat similar results in relation to the winds of Western Europe.

## II.

*Prof. John Wise's experience in his balloon ascension of July* 30, 1874. (See Appendix D.)

The first course of the balloon after having ascended was in a southerly direction, being, therefore, in the polar current; this course continued for several miles, until the balloon arrived at a point above League Island, which lies in the Delaware River at the mouth of the Schuylkill. Here it remained stationary, as related by Prof. Wise. I happened to be watching its course and observed the same thing, although my observation, if standing alone, would, in the nature of things, be somewhat indefinite. At this point Mr. Wise made his first observation, and found that the barometer indicated an altitude of 5400 feet, and that the thermometer registered 81° F. This was at nine minutes past four o'clock in the afternoon, eight minutes since the balloon left the surface, at which the thermometer had registered 72°; so that in these eight minutes the thermometer rose 9°. The balloon was here in a calm. In the next three minutes the barometer indicated an altitude of 5500 feet; thermometer 81°, atmosphere "hazy." Three minutes later a rise of 100 feet was indicated, and a temperature of 82°. Five minutes later still a fall of 200 feet; thermometer 79°, "balloon slightly agitated." Five minutes after this a rise of 200 feet; thermometer 86°. After this the fluctuations of the thermometer and barometer were considerable, the greatest temperature recorded being 90°, when the barometer indicated an elevation of 2250 feet, and three minutes afterward the same temperature at an indicated elevation of but 1450 feet. Mr. Wise, finding here a reversal of the ordinary rule of a diminished temperature proportionately to the elevation attained, thinks that it must be due to some unknown influence of Coggia's comet passing between the earth and the sun, but our theory supplies a simple explanation.

That the balloon started in the polar current is evidenced by its taking at first a southerly course, and by the temperature at the surface, which was low for the season. At the altitude of 5400 feet it evidently emerged into the inclined region of meeting of the two currents; and as this region is mostly occupied by the up-rising equatorial air, the thermometer stood nine degrees higher than at the surface. That the balloon had emerged from the polar current is not alone indicated by the heat, but also by its being in a region of calm, and by the fact that it suddenly almost ceased to ascend, taking three minutes to rise one hundred feet. The haze observed was, of course, the condensation of the moisture of the equatorial current, in contact with the polar current. In the next rise of one hundred feet the heat had slightly increased, and no haze is noted; the balloon, therefore, appears to have risen into the full equatorial current. Mr. Wise next descends two hundred feet; the thermometer falls 3°, and the balloon is "slightly agitated," being probably only partly in the polar current. The next change is a noteworthy one, the thermometer in five minutes rising 7°, while the balloon ascended but two hundred feet. The next change is seen to be a diminution of temperature of 4° in an ascent of three hundred feet, which may be accounted for by a shifting of the plane of meeting bringing the balloon out of the full equatorial current into the mixed air of the region of calm; this is indicated by the haze here observed. It is probable that the course of the balloon after this was mainly along the plane of meeting of the two currents, at times being entirely in the polar current, at others entirely in the equatorial current. This seems the more probable from the fact that at five o'clock the thermometer stood at 82°, the barometer indicating an altitude of 3450 feet, and two minutes later the thermometer registered 90° at an altitude of but 2250 feet, there being in the next three minutes a further fall to 1450 feet. The inference to be drawn from this sudden increase of temperature, 8° in two minutes, is that the balloon had come entirely into the equatorial air, the descent of 2000 feet in five minutes being due to the balloon's having come into air much lighter than the cooler air in which it had been floating.*

And again, at twenty-five minutes past five o'clock, the thermometer stood at 81°, and seven minutes later at but 70°, the balloon having risen in the mean time 1200 feet, and the next three minutes showing a further rise of 550 feet, the next five of 850 feet, the temperature remaining unchanged. The sudden diminution of temperature by 11° indicates that the balloon had gone into the polar air, which being heavier, a rise would at once take place, and we accordingly have the balloon rising 2600 feet in fifteen minutes.

These phenomena remain utterly unaccountable, unless our theory is true, Mr. Wise's supposed cometary influence being as much of a puzzle as the phenomena themselves.

The optical effects observed by Mr. Wise are capable of a like easy explanation from our standpoint, and go to confirm the fact of the overlapping of two currents of different temperatures coming from opposite directions. From a point in the equatorial

* Since the up-rising equatorial air would exert less pressure on the barometer than the dense polar air at the same elevation above the surface, the altitudes calculated from barometric observations in this case are not altogether to be relied on; and calculations of heights generally should be made with reference to the different characteristics of the two currents. The rules to do this may be readily deduced from the considerations I have offered.

current above the plane of meeting, objects on the surface of the earth, by the refraction of light in passing from the denser medium of the polar current, which is also in the shape of a prism, would not appear in their true position. Thus that which Mr. Wise mistook for the shadow of the comet was in all probability the shadow of the bank of clouds which he describes as skirting the horizon. Also, what he thought was the "river-bottom grasses" in the Delaware must have been simply the reeds and long grass growing in the marshes on its banks; it is simply impossible that the river bottom should have been visible from his elevation, since it cannot be seen even from the surface of the water. It will be noted here that Mr. Wise says: "There was also during the two hours of observation more than ordinary refraction of light through the surrounding portions of air." The electricity observed is, as has been explained in treating of summer storms, to be looked for as a production of the friction between the currents and the condensation in the plane of meeting.

It is easy to supply an explanation as to how Mr. Wise could have made so many previous ascents without finding anything to conflict with the established law of a regular diminution of temperature in ascending, even if he had always made as careful thermometrical observations as on the present occasion. If, instead of being in the polar current underneath the inclined plane of meeting, the starting-point had been in the equatorial current, the changes of temperature would have accorded with the well-known law, as also would have been the case if the starting point had been in the polar current far enough to the north to have cleared the plane of meeting in the ascent of the balloon.

Mr. Wise's experience seems to have been, in part at least, repeated by Brunelle in a balloon voyage of some length made in Russia, as reported in a paragraph in Prof. Spencer F.

Baird's "Scientific Record" of *Harper's Magazine* for September, 1874. Prof. Baird says:

"The most remarkable feature of the voyage consisted in the fact that the lower strata of air were colder than those above; and even at night-time the former were found to be rushing along the earth's surface with great rapidity, while the upper currents of the atmosphere were in comparative quiet." From this Brunelle would appear to have made his ascent in the polar current near the region of meeting, where the air would have a considerable velocity, and have travelled principally in the plane of meeting or region of calm.

## III.

### *Prof. Loomis's examination of the Signal Service maps of* 1872 *and* 1873.*

The daily weather maps of the Signal Service Bureau have afforded to Prof. Loomis little other opportunity of deducing results than by averaging, and the conclusions arrived at from them are, therefore, mostly indefinite. The two or three definite general facts at which he is able to arrive agree with my theory, although he himself comes to other conclusions.

Prof. Loomis says:

"These results (as to velocity and direction) are derived from observations made at intervals of twenty-four hours. They represent, therefore, not the actual progress of storms from hour to hour, but the average progress for a period of twenty-four hours."

Prof. Loomis found, however, that there was little information to be gotten from these averages except that a considerable variation was manifested in the velocity and direction of particular storms; and going on to the observations made at shorter intervals, he finds a still greater diversity: "The observations made under the direction of the chief signal officer

**American Journal of Science and Arts for July*, 1874.

are made three times a day, and enable us to determine the change of position of a storm's centre for every period of eight hours. A comparison of these observations shows much greater variations in respect both to the direction and velocity of storm-paths than what is stated above. . . . On the 6th of April, 1873, the path of a storm centre near the Mississippi River, in latitude 40°, was such as is shown by the upper curve in the annexed cut (*Fig.* 9), and on the 17th of April, 1873, the path of a storm centre near Chicago was such as is shown by the lower curve. In the latter case the direction of progress changed 360° in a little more than twenty-four hours, and in both cases the actual motion of the centre was for several hours westward at the rate of from ten to fifteen miles per hour. If, then, we take into account the actual motion of a storm's centre from hour to hour, we find that the storm-path"—*i. e.*, of an individual storm—"may have every possible direction, and the velocity of progress may vary from fifteen miles per hour toward the west to sixty miles per hour toward the east.

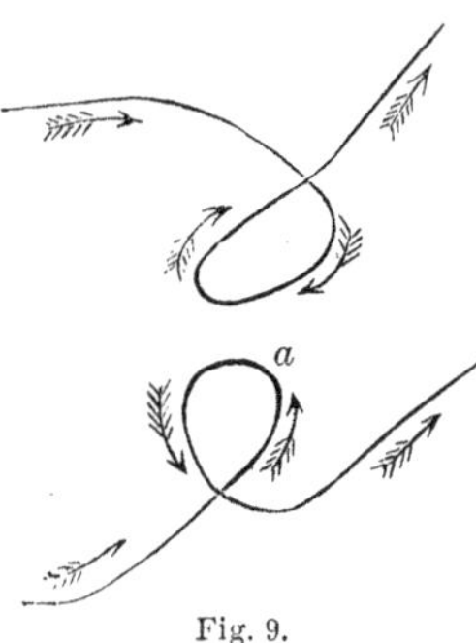

Fig. 9.

"It thus appears that the inequality in the direction and velocity of storm-paths is so great that a knowledge of their mean value affords but a very uncertain guide in predicting the progress of a storm from day to day."

It certainly would be a very discouraging prospect for a scientific knowledge of storms if it were true, as Prof. Loomis thinks it is, that a storm may go to all points of the compass, with a varying velocity guided only by what may be called accidental circumstances. Meteorology could then at best be but more or less empirical.

There are no recognized theories to explain the phenomena

that Prof. Loomis has investigated, and the explanation he himself offers we shall show to be untenable. Now, if, in the absence of explanation, we can show that the principles we have set down will, without any violent assumptions, here apply to a solution of the difficulty, it will be admitted that these principles are at the least a step forward. Let us, therefore take the case of the storms of April 6 and 17, 1873, represented in Prof. Loomis' figure, which I take to *substantially* indicate their paths. The first one of these storms is almost identical with the hypothetical case introduced on page 102, and is there fully explained on our basis. The other storm is a movement that has come under my personal observation many times in the last twenty years, and with some modifications is a similar phenomenon to the first case.

The equatorial current is drawn toward a deficiency at *a* in the cut. Having reached that point and somewhat oversupplied the deficiency, a return oscillation takes place for a short time, generally about half a day, and then the equatorial current again moves forward in a northerly direction to supply another deficiency. I am satisfied that the conjunction of circumstances necessary for such movements frequently occurs.

In the return oscillation the storm often changes its character from a north-east to a south-east storm, these being really two individual phenomena. The equatorial current and the region of calm in this oscillation make the movement of an eccentric wheel; one side passes over places in the return oscillation over which, in the forward oscillation, the other side of the equatorial current has passed, and the wind changes around the whole compass, either with or against the hands of a watch according to circumstances.

This, to any one who has comprehended the theory, will, I think, seem perfectly consistent with the principles laid down, and I am satisfied that it is the true explanation. If in a case of this kind the clouds are closely observed, they will be seen to retire below the horizon in the return oscillation in the same direction from whence they came, and a short time afterward, probably the following day, to reappear, generally with their direction slightly altered. This observation will enable one to make general predictions with considerable accuracy, falling weather being to be looked for only in the forward movements of the storm. Movements of the above description occur most frequently in the spring and autumn, the seasons of transition, when one current moves to displace the other and to take up for a few months a comparatively settled position.

Prof. Loomis, in his investigations of the direction and velocity of storms, finding here no clue to the motive and directing power, naturally seeks to find some other attendant phenomena that shall solve the problem. He investigates the extent of rain area of a portion of the storm of April 25, 1874, and finds that it lies much more in advance than to the rear of the region of low barometer, as indicated in *Fig.* 10,

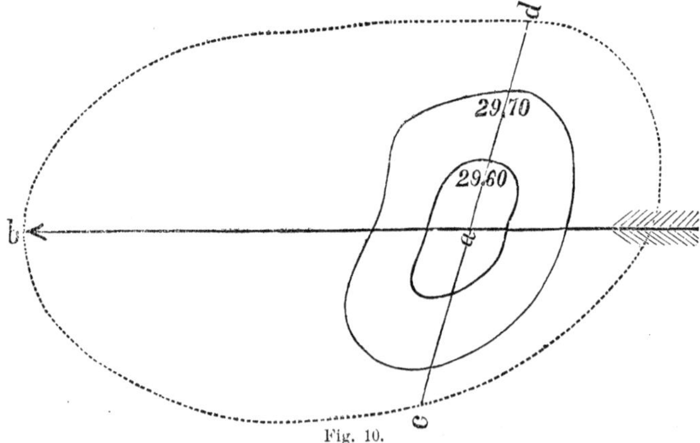


Fig. 10.

which (with the exception of the lettering and the line *c d*) is taken from his article. The dotted line marks the rain-area and the solid elliptical lines the regions of low barometer. Prof. Loomis accounts for this as follows:

"The connection here discovered between the progress of storms and the extent of the rain area cannot be regarded as accidental, and it is not difficult to discover, at least in part, the origin of this connection. The fall of rain—that is, the precipitation of the vapor of the atmosphere—is generally accompanied by a fall of the barometer. According to the theory advocated by the late Mr. Espy, when the vapor of the atmosphere is condensed, its latent heat is liberated, which raises the temperature of the surrounding air, causing it to expand and flow off laterally in all directions in the upper regions of the atmosphere, thus causing a diminished pressure over the region of precipitation, and an increased pressure on all sides beyond the area of the rain.

"The progress of the storm eastward * is not due wholly to a *drifting*, resulting from the influence of an upper current of the atmosphere from the west, but the storm works its own way eastward in consequence of the greater precipitation on the eastern side of the storm. Thus the barometer is continually falling on the east side of the storm and rising on the west side, in consequence of the flowing in of colder air upon that side."

Now, even if it were true that the rain-fall is the origin of motion in a storm, and its chief guiding power after its movement has begun, we should not have advanced, because the question as to the causes producing the rain area would be fully as imperative as the other.

But that it is impossible is established by known facts, as for instance that storms frequently travel over a considerable distance unaccompanied by any rain-fall at all, and that in most cases the motion of the storm has already begun before the rain begins to fall. And then, on this theory, how could the backward movement which Prof. Loomis has noticed in several instances, and which I have often seen, possibly be ac-

*The cut has here been reversed, so that it may better be compared with *Plate VII.*; the arrow should be understood to point to the east.

counted for? or how could the south-east storms travel, having the rain area in the rear? It is true that the motion of storms is due to traction, but the attracting force is not the rain area, but a deficiency of air in another locality.

A simple comparison of Prof. Loomis's figure with *Plate VII., Fig.* 1, will explain *why* in north-east storms the rain extends so far in advance of the region of low barometer. Recollecting that the region *c d* of the plate is identical with the region of low barometer of the figure, and that *b* of the plate is directly above *b* of the figure, it will be seen that the rain area of the figure is exactly underneath the clouds of the plate, which is certainly the proper place for it.

Prof. Loomis next investigates the influence which the velocity of the wind in front and in the rear of a storm has upon the storm's progress, and arrives at important results.

He says: "The averages were taken both of the velocity of the storm's progress and the velocity of the wind in the east and west quadrants of the storm, when the following results were obtained:

| Velocity of storm in miles per hour. | Velocity of wind in E. quadrant. | Velocity of wind in W. quadrant. |
|---|---|---|
| 32.1 | 8.8 | 9.0 |
| 18.1 | 7.8 | 11.3 |

"These numbers indicate that the stronger the wind on the west side of the storm, the less is the velocity of the storm's progress. The velocity of the wind in the west quadrant generally exceeds the velocity in the east quadrant by twenty-two per cent. When the velocity in the east quadrant is equal to that in the west quadrant, the velocity of the storm's progress is seven miles per hour *greater* than the mean; but when the velocity of the wind in the west quadrant exceeds that in the east quadrant by forty-four per cent., the velocity of the storm's progress is seven miles per hour *less* than the mean.

"Some persons might have anticipated that an increase in the velocity of the wind in the western quadrant of a storm would have the effect of driving the storm eastward more rapidly—that is, of increasing its velocity. But we shall see hereafter that upon each side of a storm's centre the wind blows obliquely inward, and hence we must infer that in the central region of the storm there is an upward motion of the air; and this is the cause of the precipitation of vapor—that is, the cause of the rain-fall. An increase in the velocity of the wind in the western quadrant is accompanied by an increase in the velocity of the upward motion in this quadrant —that is, an increase of precipitation. This increased precipitation of vapor tends to depress the barometer on the western side of the storm—that is, tends to retard the eastward motion of the storm's centre; and this cause may operate with sufficient force to carry the storm's centre westward, as actually happened in several instances in the years 1872 and 1873. On the other hand, an increase in the velocity of the wind in the eastern quadrant tends to produce a greater precipitation on the eastern side of the storm's centre—that is, tends to push the storm's centre eastward, or increase the velocity of its progress."

The explanation Prof. Loomis gives of the facts he has found shows the incapability of the present theories, and is manifestly unsatisfactory; while, on the other hand, the facts are not only readily explained by our theory, but are those whose existence follows from it as a matter of course.

Prof. Loomis makes the average storm travel due east in the direction of the arrow (*Fig.* 11), and divides it into four quadrants. Of these *a b c* is the "west quadrant" and *a d e* the "east quadrant," the first being in the rear and the other in front of the region of low barometer. Now, comparing his

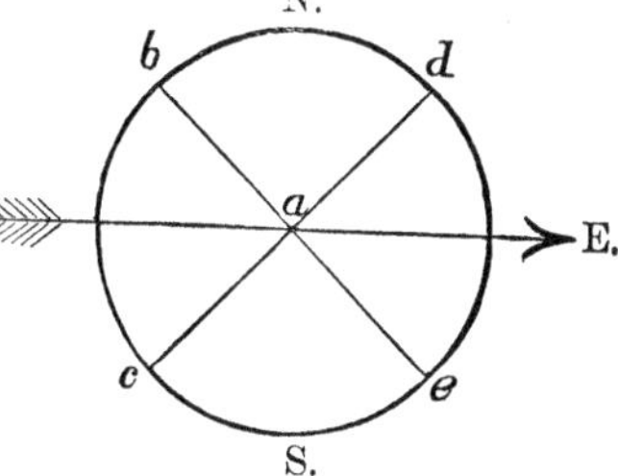

Fig. 11.

results with the laws of velocity we found in the consideration of north-east storms, the agreement is very apparent.

The progressive velocity of the north-east storm depends first on the amount of deficiency in the north which draws the equatorial current toward it, and second on the resistance the polar current offers to its displacement. This resistance, the pressure of the cold air toward warm regions, is least, of course, when the deficiency in the north is greatest, and increases as this deficiency is supplied.

As in the progress of the storm the deficiency in the north becomes supplied from above, the pressure of the cold air toward warmer regions—*i. e.*, the obstacle it presents to its displacement—increases; and from the consequent banking up of the polar current the plane of meeting becomes more vertical, and the equatorial air more quickly reaching cool regions, more condensation takes place, which liberates a greater amount of latent heat, and this in turn expands the air and causes it to rise from below more rapidly and in greater volume. Thus the velocity of the equatorial current—the "wind in the west quadrant"—is greater when the banking up of the polar current—the "wind in the east quadrant"—causes both its own velocity and that of the storm to grow less.

Prof. Loomis has been able to find a partially true law from averages of the Signal Service observations, because the Signal Service noted only north-east storms; but if he had been given the observations of south-east storms alone, he would have deduced a law just the reverse of the one he discovered. If, however, he had been given the observations of both north-east and south-east storms, averages would have brought him no result at all. His law is, after all, only applicable to a certain period of the north-east storms' development, as will be noticed by reference to our particular consideration of the subject.

The following is confirmatory of the elliptical form of the

region of calm as opposed to the form made necessary by the Cyclone theory:

"In fifty-five per cent. of the whole number of cases, the major axis of the isobar exceeded the minor axis by one-half of its whole length; in thirty per cent. of the cases, the major axis was more than double the minor axis; in nine per cent. of the cases, the major axis was more than three times the minor axis; and in four per cent. of the cases, the major axis was at least four times the minor axis.

"These results appear to me to prove that the centrifugal force arising from the circulation of the wind around the storm centre cannot be the principal cause of the fall of the barometer, for otherwise the shape of the storm would be more nearly circular."

## IV.

*Testimony from the Report of General Albert J. Myer, Chief Signal Officer of the United States Army for the year* 1873.

The United States Signal Service is so well organized and managed for purposes of observation that it has established the existence of important "meteors" that are entirely new to the Cyclone theory and are not provided for by it. The nomenclature and arrangement of these meteors is therefore somewhat indefinite, and to be useful in the present connection must be more clearly defined. We will endeavor to do so from particular instances.

In the Monthly Weather Review for March, 1874, the atmospheric disturbances are divided into two classes, "storms and cyclones" and "anti-cyclones." The storms and cyclones are to be understood as areas of barometric depression, since the twelve cases noted are spoken of as "twelve noticeable depressions;" while the anti-cyclones are spoken of as "areas of high barometer, around which the wind drew in a general direction with the hands of a watch," which is in the opposite direction to that assigned to the winds of a cyclone by the Cyclonic theory. The characteristics of these phenomena are further given as follows:

"Some of these anti-cyclonic areas have been very large, covering more than one-half of the country at the same time. The pressure of the atmosphere near their centres or crests has in some cases been as high as 30.58 and 30.73 inches. The general path pursued by these meteors has been from north-west to south-east. They have largely served to determine the temperature, wind and humidity conditions of the entire country. They have also exerted a marked and potent influence on the direction, intensity, etc., of all the cyclonic centres. Some of them remained stationary, or almost so, for several days in the north-west."

Areas of high barometer are not spoken of by the Signal Service as anti-cyclones except when to the north of the cyclonic areas. The areas of low barometer, or the "storms and cyclones," will be readily recognized as our region of meeting of the opposing currents. Now, the "anti-cyclones," it will be noted, are for this month "very large, covering more than one-half of the country at the same time;" the barometric pressure is very high; their general path is southerly; they largely serve to determine the temperature, wind and humidity of the whole country; and they exert a "marked and potent influence on the direction, intensity, etc., of all the cyclonic centres." It is further stated that the winds during this month were "characteristically from the north-west, the "only observable exception" being in "the Gulf of Mexico and the Western Gulf States." All these conditions indicate that the "anti-cyclonic areas" are nothing more than the area of high pressure of our *polar current*, moving southward either as the return oscillation of a north-east storm, or in an aggressive movement, displacing the equatorial current and producing south-east storms. It has been already explained that in our theory the changes of the wind in a forward movement of the polar current are in the reversed order to the changes in a forward movement of the equatorial current, and therefore the difference noted by the Signal Service in the winds of the cyclones and the anti-cyclones goes to corroborate the definitions we have given to these terms. The anti-cyclonic areas would be "very large" in March in the United States, since the polar current is then still the prevailing wind. Now, if the anti-cyclonic areas are the polar current moving southward, we must look for the area of depression, or region of meeting, in front of them, which will be more or less prominent as the movement of the polar current is an aggressive one or merely a return oscillation. This the March Weather Review does not give in direct connection with the anti-cyclones, since these are treated as independent phenomena, but under the head of "Storms and Cyclones" we find after an enumeration of the "twelve noticeable depressions" of the month, the following:

"Besides these storms, several depressions have apparently advanced from the vicinity of Hudson Bay, south-eastwardly, nearly to the Lower Lake region and St. Lawrence valley, but scarcely producing any marked effects in these sections, because their centres were moving eastward on higher parallels of latitude.

"Meteorological data, gathered from various sources, show that these storms have been very severe after passing off the American coasts, and have apparently become more violent as they penetrated the middle and eastern side of the North Atlantic.

"Without endeavoring to explain this last-named fact, it may be proper to notice that large masses of ice and icebergs were reported during March moving southward and eastward off the Newfoundland coast and banks."

These depressions moving in the same direction as the anti-cyclones are probably those we are in search of;* the Signal

*Since this was written the Signal Service Report for 1874 has come

Service, in default of observations from the North, infers that the centres of the depressions were in higher latitudes, but this is in all probability erroneous.

If, now, with the definition of terms we have given, we pass on to the consideration of the Signal Service reports of individual storms, we shall find I think that our theory and the phenomena as presented in these reports agree very well, and that a simple and rational explanation is furnished.

(*a*.) *The Nova Scotia and Newfoundland storm of August* 23, 24 *and* 25, 1873. (Chief Signal Officer's Report for 1873, page 1025, Appendix E.)

The account of this storm is given in an able report to the chief signal officer by Professor Cleveland Abbe of the Signal Service Bureau, with five maps showing the direction of the winds and the barometric pressure from August 23, at 4.35 P. M., to August 25, at the same hour.

Prof. Abbe considers that this storm probably originated near the coast of Senegambia, Africa, on August 13, moving north-westerly across the Atlantic until the 22d, when its course changed to a north-easterly direction, running up the coast of North America, gathering force meanwhile, until it culminated near the coast of Nova Scotia and Newfoundland, after which it continued its course, with diminishing force and increasing size, across the Atlantic, reaching the northern part of Great Britain on the 31st, and Norway on the 2d of September. He thinks its history (see *Fig.* 17) from the 18th to the 26th is clear, and believes "that the centre of the cyclone and its most terrific manifestation of power did not pass directly over Nova Scotia, but kept perhaps two hundred miles off its coast," but adds, "I am aware that discrepant observations may be adduced conflicting with this conclusion," and speaks of "the multiplicity of conflict-

into my hands; and from the consideration of it further on, the assumptions I have made here would seem to be confirmed.

ing accounts concerning the positions of vessels and the weather experienced by them on the 23d, 24th and 25th."

It is to be presumed that Prof. Abbe has, as is natural, attached the most importance to those observations which seem to corroborate his own theory, not recognizing the significance of those which conflict, and it would probably make the agreement of this storm with our theory more evident if we had the "discrepant observations" to which he alludes. We hope, however, to establish this agreement by means of the data which he has furnished. The maps used are reproduced from the ones given in the report.

That which Prof. Abbe treats as one and the same storm undoubtedly embraced, from August 23 to August 26, two separate and distinct storms, one of which, a north-east storm, travelled up the Atlantic coast in the track of Prof. Abbe's cyclone, and the other, a south-east, coming from the lake region in the north-west, struck its flank off the coast of New Jersey.* This south-east storm is not known as such by the Signal Service, although it was certainly the chief agent in the destruction on the Nova Scotian coast; but they have given the data by which to trace its course.

The Signal Service *Weather Review* for August, 1873, traces several "anti-cyclones" as follows:

"The paths of the centres of the several areas of high barometer are traced on map No. 1. (*Fig.* 12.)

"These areas, with but one exception, were first observed in British America, after which they moved with such uniformity and became so unusually well defined as to render it possible to locate their centres at each of the tri-daily reports of this office

*I was fully convinced that a similar collision of the north-east and the south-east storms frequently takes place on our sea-board long before I obtained any confirmation from the Signal Service investigations. My attention was first drawn to the subject from observing the occurrence of thunder and lightning when a north-east storm was in progress, which seemed to me abnormal.

Tracks of Areas of High Barometer for August, 1873.

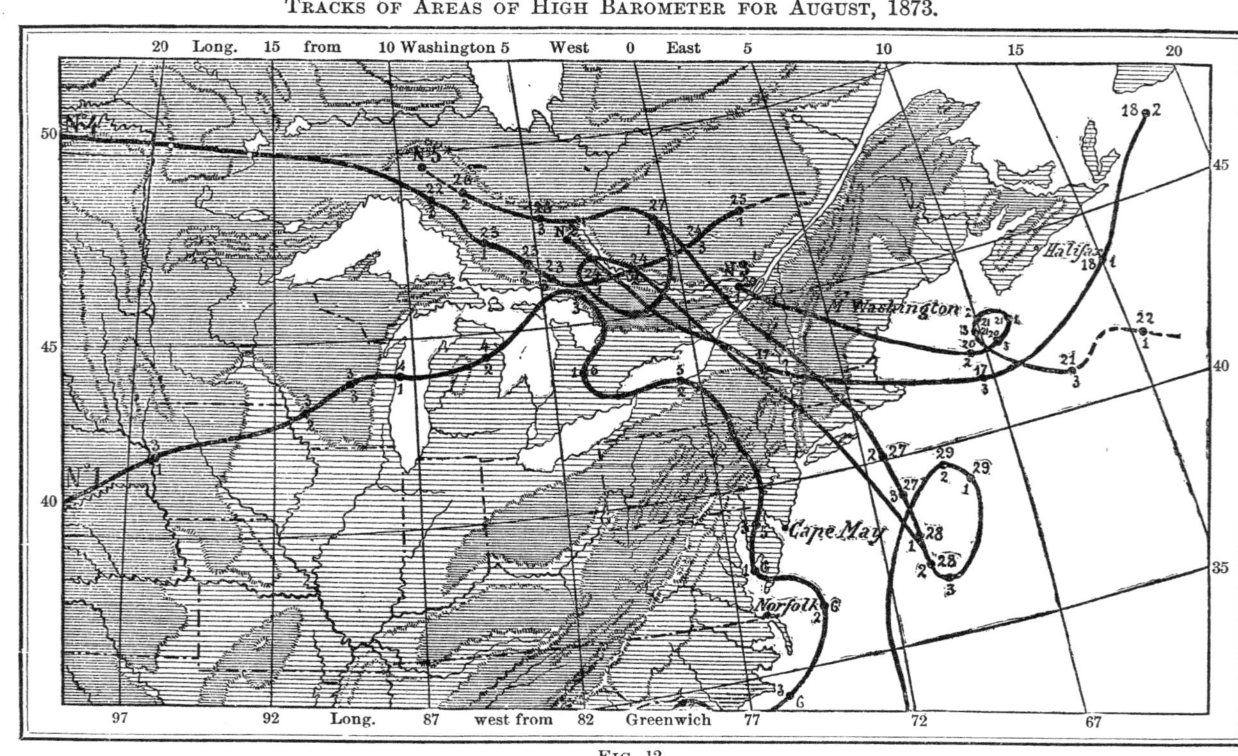


Fig. 12.

from the time of their first appearance until they finally passed beyond the limits of observations.

"The general direction of these paths while the areas remained central on the continent is approximately from the north-west to the south-east, but for want of more extended observations their final direction after passing off the coast remains as yet undetermined."

Now, by a reference to the map it will be seen that No. 4 of these areas of high barometer is first noticed at Manitoba in the afternoon of August 22, and at midnight of the same day the centre is placed north of Lake Superior. In the afternoon of the 23d the centre is placed north of Lake Huron, and by reference to *Fig.* 13, we find that at the same time the southern limit had reached the sea-coast. The polar current evidently divided north of Lake Huron, one branch following the valley of the St. Lawrence, the other keeping the original direction to the south-east. The cause of the division is readily found in the topography of the country, the heavy polar air being barred by mountain-ranges and flowing most rapidly over the lowlands. A glance at a general map of the United States will show that the current would thus flow across Lake Ontario, New York State, eastern Pennsylvania, Maryland, Delaware and central and southern New Jersey, avoiding the mountains of northern New Jersey and south-eastern New York, until the whole depth of the polar current had reached them. *Fig.* 12 will indicate the several paths between the mountains which the polar current may take in its south-easterly course. The area of depression in front of the advancing polar current has in all probability been considered by the Signal Service as a series of unconnected "local storms." Now, we are not given the local storms for August, but there is a map of their distribution for July; and making allowance for a slight shifting north with the further advance of the season, we find that the region of greatest frequency of local storms in

AUGUST 23, 1873. 4.35 P.M.

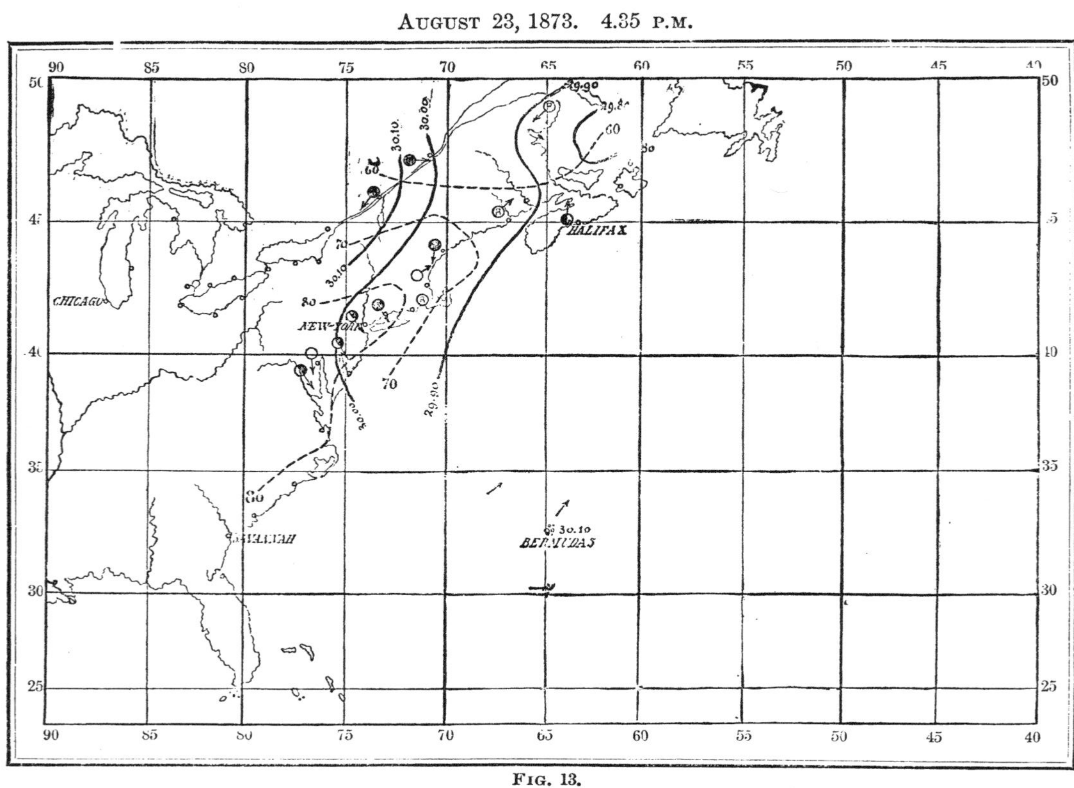


FIG. 13.

August will lie just in the path we have traced for the polar current. The *Weather Review* for July further says: "The numerous local storms that are experienced during the summer months have a certain relation to the large areas of high and low barometer, to the topography of the country, the position of the ocean and other bodies of water, etc.;" also, "as in former years during this month, so in the present year, with scarcely an exception, the areas of low pressure first became apparent in or beyond Dakota and Manitoba."

The polar current in its southerly course so far having been displacing equatorial air that offered little resistance, the continuous south-east storm marking its passage might readily be mistaken by the Signal Service for unconnected local storms. But when it reaches the Atlantic coast, and strikes the equatorial current of the north-east storm that is travelling over the ocean, the south-east storm assumes much greater magnitude than it had before; and here the Signal Service have observed it, although, the region of meeting being by this time out at sea, they note it merely as "indications of some atmospheric disturbance" which they attribute to the "cyclone," in reference to which the *Weather Review* for this month says:

"Although this storm did not occur within the limits of our stations, there were indications of some atmospheric disturbance off the middle Atlantic coast on the 23d which warranted the prediction made in the Probabilities written from the afternoon report of that date, viz.: 'For the New England and middle Atlantic coast, threatening weather,' and from the midnight report of the same date, 'For the New England and middle Atlantic coast, stormy weather,' with cautionary signals at Cape May, New York and New London."

The map, however (*Fig.* 13), shows the whole south-east storm extending from the coast of Virginia to the Gulf of St. Lawrence. The isobars will be noticed to show a regular increase of pressure to the north-west, indicating the inclination of the face of the current; by referring to *Plate VII., Fig.* 2, the position will be made clear. The isobar 29.80 of *Fig.* 13 probably represents part of the line $c''' \, d'''$ of the plate, but it will be noted to be drawn as a semicircle; it is, however, entirely on sea, where there are naturally no connected observations, otherwise it would in every probability have been drawn parallel to isobar 29.90, and extending almost as far to the south.

Such is the position of the south-east storm on the afternoon of August 23. Its right wing had arrived off the Atlantic coast earlier than its left wing; and had struck the north-east storm out at sea, when the left wing had probably just reached the Gulf of St. Lawrence. The middle was doubtless in the act of overtopping the northern branches of the Appalachian range, which had barred its advance, since Prof. Abbe reports at this time "continued north-westerly winds" from Mount Washington.

The north-east storm is also reported by Prof. Abbe as "at noon of August 23 in latitude 37° and longitude 67°, with south-westerly gales"—*the equatorial current*—"at the Bermudas. At this time the barometric depression attending the cyclone seems to have extended to a distance of at least five hundred miles north-west and northward of its centre, with falling barometer and cloudy weather reported in New England and Canada."*

The equatorial current, thus sweeping to the north-east, displacing the polar air in front of it, changes its position when the polar current of the south-east storm falls into its side. *Fig.* 14 shows what action has taken place during the following twenty-four hours. The north-east storm has doubled up the right wing of the south-east storm, and at the same time

* If this had been really a cyclone, it is not easy to see why the centre should be so much nearer the barometric pressure of 30.10 at the Bermudas than the corresponding pressure in the north.

AUGUST 24, 1873. 4.35 P.M.

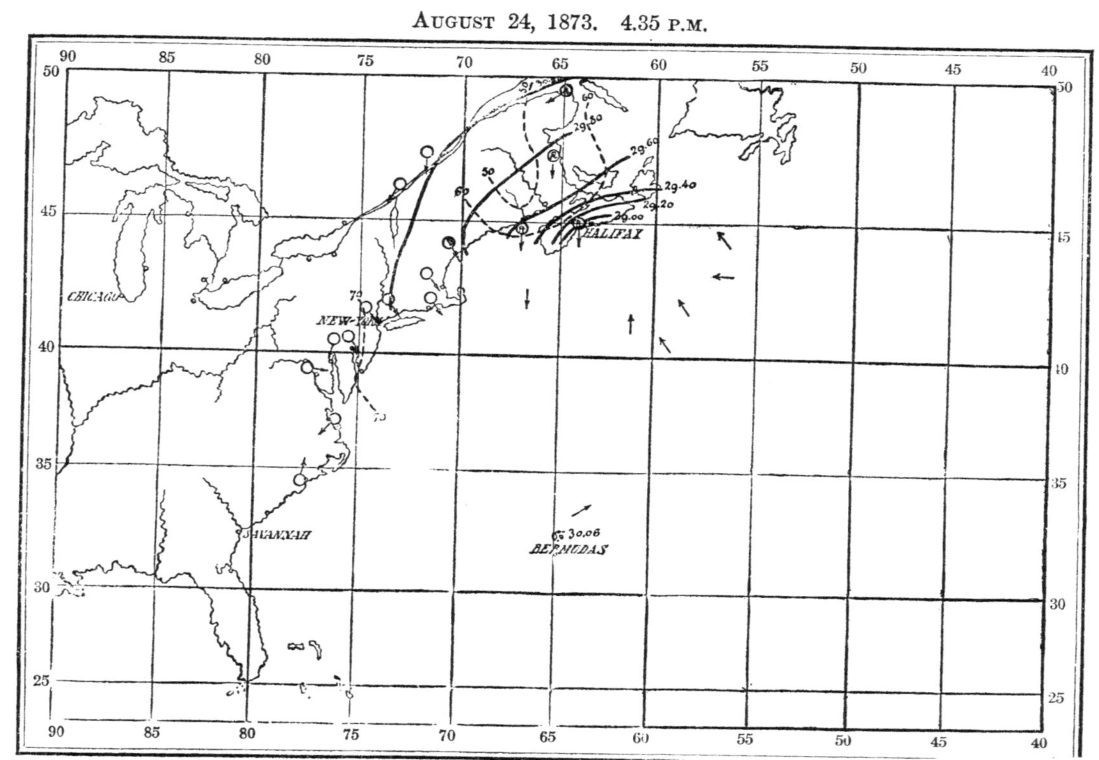

has advanced its own right wing to meet the left of the other, which has turned the high lands south of the St. Lawrence and comes down from the north; while in the middle the polar current has overtopped the mountains, and now advances with an unbroken front. The main conflict is shifted somewhat to the north, and has narrowed its area; the regions of low barometer of both storms have coalesced, and conform to the coast-line; the great fall in the barometer indicates great violence. The reason for great violence is manifest. The passive equatorial current of the south-east storm and the passive polar current of the north-east storm have disappeared, leaving in conflict the *active* and aggressive elements of both storms, and combining therefore the strength and fury of both.

This action is better developed by midnight of the same day (*Fig.* 15); and the isobars are more parallel, and have approached each other more closely. The plane of meeting has therefore become more vertical, and the rush of the equatorial current against it would be more destructive. Prof. Abbe says: "Between sunset and sunrise of this night occurred the greatest destruction of life and property in this region"—the Nova Scotia coast—" due to a terrific easterly wind, which within twenty-four hours backed from south-east to north-west." This shows that the polar current is advancing, but probably very slowly; and it is most likely that one or more tornadoes have occurred at the same time, which would travel along the coast toward the north-east.

The arrow in latitude 49°, longitude 47°, in connection with the arrow in latitude 44°, longitude 54°, *seems* to indicate a return oscillation of the polar current of the north-east storm, which would add another element to the conflict, and give the region of meeting probably a triangular shape. On the morning of August 25 (*Fig.* 16), the exhaustion of the storm begins to appear, the polar current of the south-east storm being seen by the isobars to have advanced, and the return oscillation of

AUGUST 24, 1873. 11 P.M.

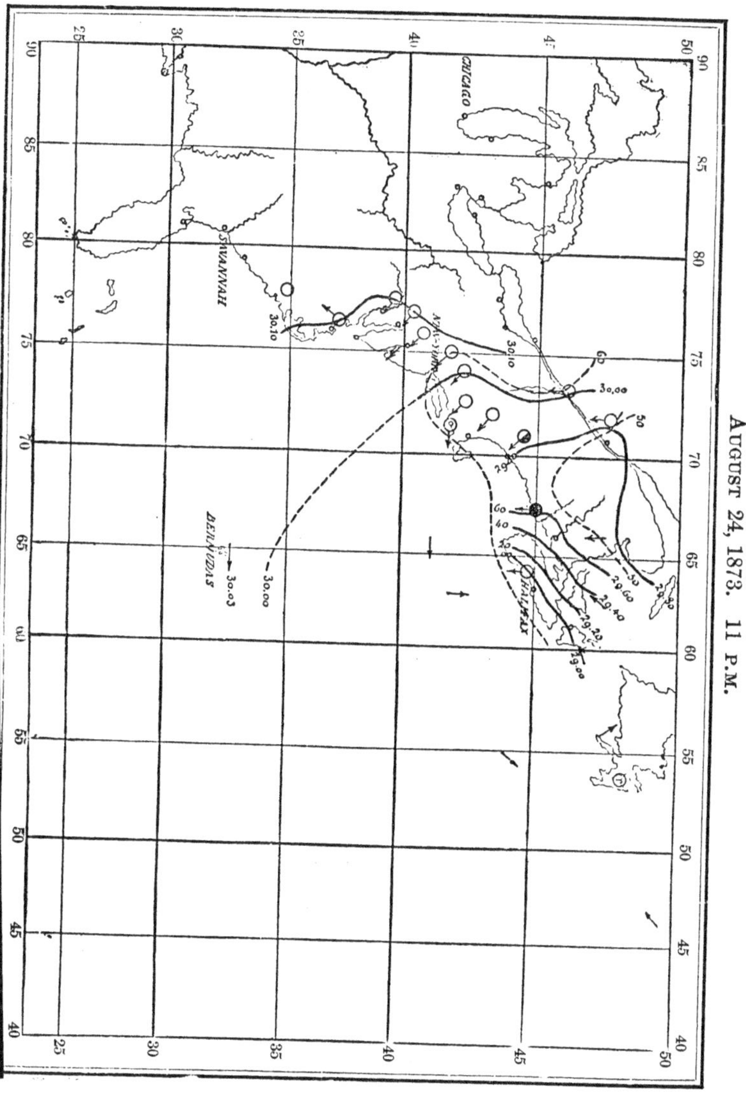

AUGUST 25, 1873. 7.35 A.M.

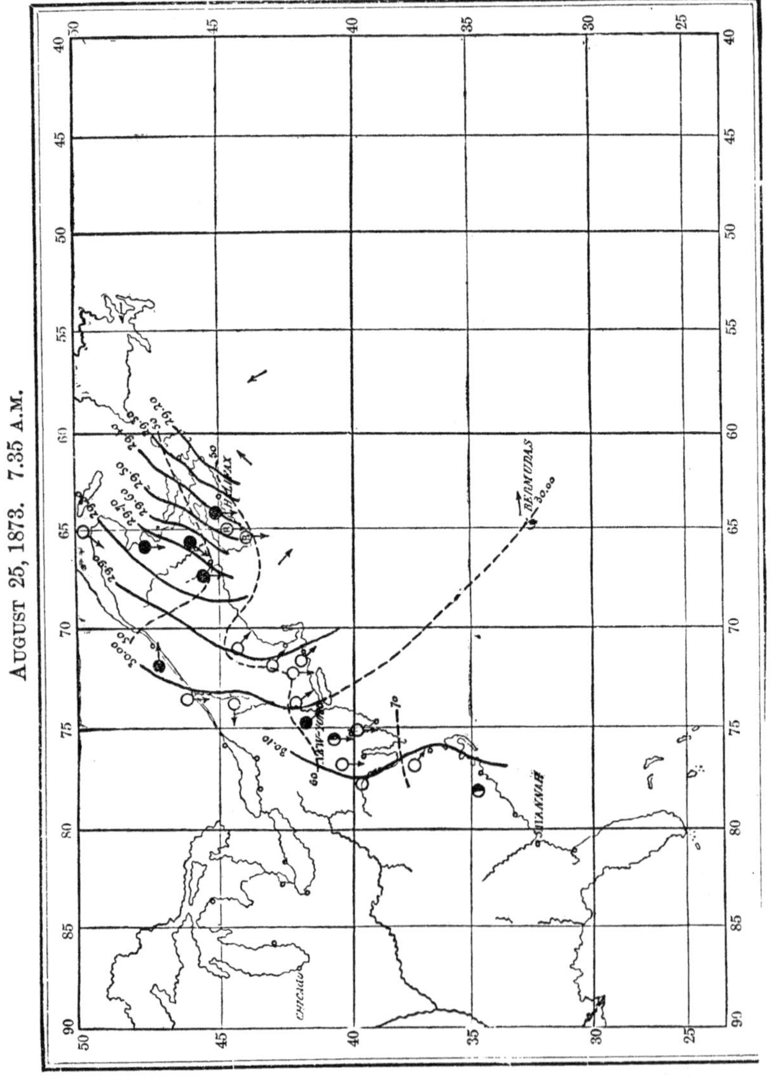

August 25, 1873. 4.35 p.m.

"Showing also the General Course of the Cyclone."

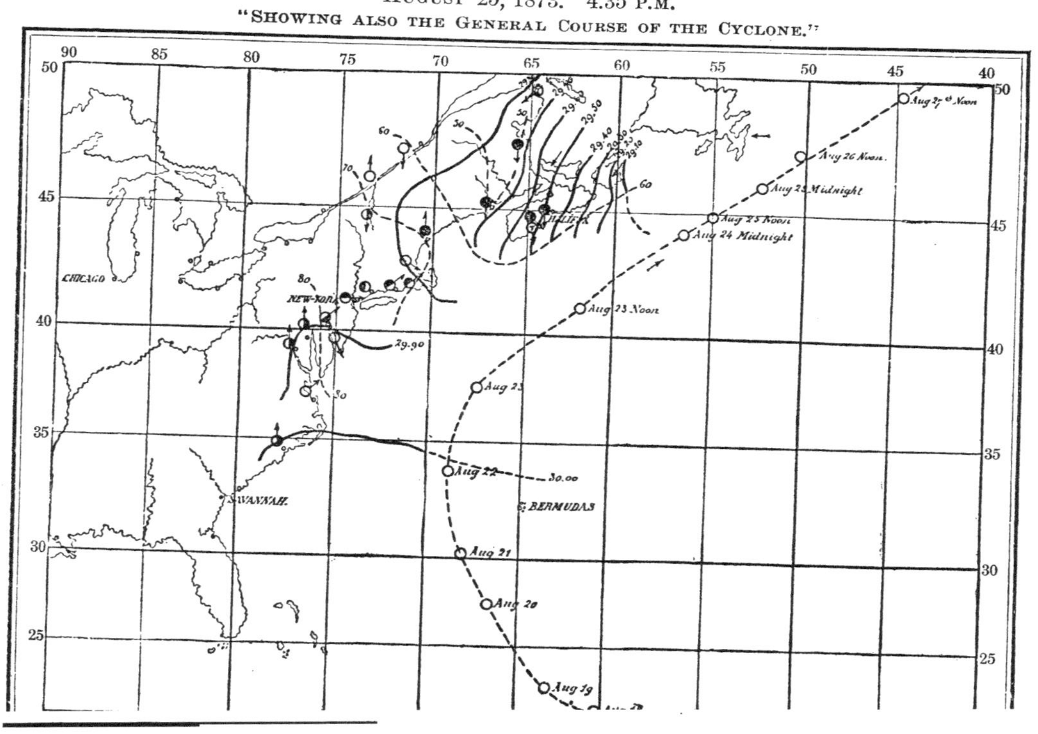

the north-east storm appearing by the arrow to have reached Newfoundland.

This indicates that the deficiency in the north toward which the equatorial current was moving has been supplied, and that this current is therefore weakened.

This is also shown by the meteorological conditions at the Bermudas, over which the tropical belt of high pressure seems to have been oscillating.

By referring to the maps it will be seen that on August 23, at 4.35 P. M., the descending tropical current, which supplied the equatorial current of the north-east storm, was sufficient to produce a pressure of 30.10, and, as shown by the arrow, after reaching the surface, travelled toward the north-east. During the next twenty-four hours the barometric pressure had fallen to 30.06, the direction of the wind being unchanged; at midnight of the 24th the pressure had fallen to 30.03, and the wind had materially changed its direction, indicating that the north-east storm had ceased to advance. On the morning of the 25th the barometer stood at 30.00.

The explanation of the whole atmospheric disturbance seems to be possible, although it could be wished that more data had been given.

Prof. Abbe states, "The highest pressure of the month was attained at the Bermudas on the 18th of August, and rainless weather continued in these islands from the 16th to the 21st of the month;" and at noon of the 18th there were "light north-east winds and falling barometer at the Bermudas." The inference from this is that the current *c* of *Plate V.* had joined the current *b* in a southerly movement to supply some deficiency in equatorial regions; which had probably caused a south-east—more strictly a south-west—storm in the torrid zone. The withdrawal of the current *c* from its ordinary course would originate not only the return oscillation of a north-east storm which had passed over the Atlantic on the 13th, 14th and 15th, and which will be considered farther on, but probably also the movement of the polar current in the Nova Scotia south-east storm. The winds at the Bermudas from the 16th to the 18th are not given, but their being light at noon of the latter day with falling barometer would seem to show that the south-east storm of the torrid zone had gone far south, that the deficiency had been supplied and a return oscillation northward was about to begin, the current *b'* of *Plate V.* displacing the current *b*, in a north-east storm which would, probably, begin in the neighborhood of the spot where Prof. Abbe first notes the "cyclone." (*Fig.* 17.) By the 21st we find the region of meeting of this storm is approaching the Bermudas, since there is reported at noon of this day at these islands "falling barometer and strong north-easterly winds veering to south-east." When the current *c* resumes its usual course, it will be in turn joined by the current *b*, and this will continue the return oscillation of the torrid south-east storm as a north-east storm up through the temperate zone. We find at noon of the 23d "south-westerly gales at the Bermudas," with barometric depression, "at least five hundred miles north-west and northward," and "falling barometer and cloudy weather reported in New England and Canada."

The entire phenomenon from our standpoint will thus be seen to consist of distinct individual storms, connected with each other, but differing in kind, and not, as Prof. Abbe thinks, one continuous storm from the coast of Senegambia to the British Islands.

It seems probable, however, that the gale experienced by the bark "Crest of the Wave" off the coast of Senegambia on August 13 might have been in connection with the storm of the 31st in Great Britain, and September 2 in Norway. It is not impossible that during this time occurrences took place on the eastern coast of the Atlantic similar to those we have described on the western; and it is highly probable that a definite north-east storm-track exists over Western Europe, into the side of which falls a south-east storm-track lying over the British Isles, Norway and Sweden.

(*b*.) *The storm on the coast of New Jersey during August* 13, 14 *and* 15, 1873. (Report, page 1026, Appendix E.)

Prof. Abbe speaks of this storm as preliminary to the one we have just considered, but does not seem to discover any definite connection between them. There are too few data to establish its manœuvres in detail, but such as we have indicate that it was of the same general character as the phenomena we have been considering, and part of a series of storm oscillations over accustomed tracks.

The north-east storm is indicated by "south-westerly winds and rain on the 13th, 14th and 15th," at the Bermudas, with steadily rising barometer, followed by lighter winds and pleasant weather on the 16th, and at the same time north-easterly winds and gales a hundred miles off the Middle Atlantic coast, "with northerly winds and clear weather" over New England and Nova Scotia. The south-east storm, although no "anti-cyclone" was observed, is to be seen in the "area of slight barometric depression" and variable winds west of the Alleghanies on the morning of the 12th, with "easterly winds, clouds and light rain" reported on the Middle Atlantic coast.

The middle part of the south-east storm seems to have first reached the coast while the wings were detained by the mountains north and south. The decided fall of the barometer by the morning of the 13th, "and north-easterly winds increasing about to high, with rain prevailing" throughout the Middle Atlantic States, indicates that the regions of low pressure of the north-east and the south-east storms had coalesced, as in the Nova Scotia storm. "The in-draft of air from the ocean" produced "increase of the disturbance," since it was the aggressive equatorial current of the north-east storm swung round to oppose the aggressive polar current of the other. It is significant that this "has been quite frequently noticed on other occasions." "In New England the pressure had slightly risen, it being apparently highest at that time over Maine and New Brunswick," showing the advance of the left wing of the polar current of the south-east storm. The advance of the right wing is seen in the "secondary barometric depression" appearing on the morning of the 14th to be "central over the peninsula lying between the Chesapeake and Delaware Bays." It bears the characteristics of a south-east storm, being accompanied by two or more tornadoes. The exhaustion of the storms and the re-establishment of equilibrium apparently took place on the New England coast.

(*c.*) *The storm of April* 14 *to* 18, 1873. (Report, page 1097.)

The full account given by the Signal Service of this series of storms is here reproduced; the nine excellent maps, however, which accompany the original cannot here be given.

"A storm-centre that was found to exist in Dakota on the morning of April 13 continued developing itself slowly over Nebraska and Kansas during the afternoon and night, with threatening weather and south-easterly winds in the Upper Mississippi and Missouri Valleys. Breckenridge, Minnesota, reported heavy snow the following morning, with high northerly winds. The storm now commenced moving eastward toward the lakes, where cautionary signals, ordered up on the previous day, heralded its advent. Central in Iowa on the afternoon of April 14, it appeared to be moving remarkably slow, while the pressure was diminishing very rapidly eastward to Lake Erie. After reaching Illinois, the midnight reports of April 15 showed that the storm-centre had divided itself into a number of small but very distinct areas of barometric depressions, extending eastward to the Alleghanies, with threatening and rainy weather in the Ohio Valley. The several small storm-centres united again during the following day, with the exception of one, which moved south-eastwardly into the Carolinas. The former storm-centre now changed its easterly course to a north-easterly direction, moving toward the lower lakes, but making very little progress—so much so that the centre remained almost stationary in Southern Michigan for sixteen consecutive hours.

"The small area that had moved into the Carolinas also changed its direction, and appeared as a well-developed storm on the coast of New Jersey on the afternoon of April 17. That area of low barometer which was over Illinois, Southern Michigan and the Ohio Valley on the 16th continued over nearly the same portion of country, with special storm-centres in Indiana and Lake Huron, up to the night of the 17th, when it moved north-east to Lake Ontario by the morning of the 18th, where it prevailed as a very large area of low pressure over the entire lake region on the afternoon of the 18th. The midnight reports of this date, however, showed the storm to be confined to the St. Lawrence valley, with rain and snow and brisk westerly winds over the lakes. Moving along the St. Lawrence, it again united over New Brunswick with that portion which had been moving along the Atlantic coast, and then disappeared beyond the limits of our stations. During the six days that this storm had been central in the United States, its frequent changes of direction, its dividing and reuniting, have made it, in many respects, one of the most remarkable storms traced by the Signal Service since its organization."

The phenomena which here appear so obscure find a natural explanation by the application of our principles. In the spring of the year, when the positions of the atmospheric belts begin to shift northward with the sun, the equatorial current displacing the polar and becoming the prevailing wind in our latitude for the season, the change is not effected without a severe conflict, especially at the commencement of the movement. This conflict, from the flexible and elastic character of the contending bodies, is a series of oscillations backward and forward. Over land the belt of polar air is in winter drawn farther to the south, as the belt of equatorial air is in summer farther to the north, than over sea. When the spring movement begins, therefore, in North America, the polar current lies farther to the south in the heart of the continent than upon the sea-board.

Prior to the phenomena which the Signal Service record, the equatorial current had undoubtedly gone to the north, and the depression seen first in Dakota was a south-east storm produced by the reaction of the polar current. The first map of the Signal Service (April 14, 7.35 A. M.) shows the advance of the equatorial current in a north-east storm, the isobars lying from south-east to north-west. It also shows an equatorial pressure from the south-east, the right wing of this current. The other maps show a series of oscillations: when one wing of the equatorial current swings forward, the other recedes; at times the one current prevails, at times the other. When the polar air advances, it conforms to the configuration of the surface; and where it strikes elevations too great to be surmounted, it is cut in two, and the regions of low barometer in front of its branches appear separate and unconnected. These branches may even take somewhat different courses. When the equatorial current advances, it surmounts the elevations, and the regions of depression again unite. The phenomena during these four days therefore consist of a succession of north-east and south-east storms changing into each other.

(*d.*) *Sergeant Frederick Meyer's Report on the North Polar Expedition*, 1871–'73. (Chief Signal Officer's Report, page 996.)

Sergeant Meyer accompanied Capt. Hall's north polar expedition by direction of the chief signal officer, Brig-Gen. Myer; we extract the following from his report referring to the meteorological conditions of arctic storms:

"The motion of the barometer-column was very marked, with

north-east and south-west winds; being very fluctuating and generally high, but falling with a north-east wind, and very low, but rising with a south-west wind."

"North-east gales showed different features, and, as it appears, these characteristics were very marked, if I distinguish two classes of north-east gales:

"1. Such as were the primary impulse of a violent commotion of atmosphere, inducing a south-west gale at an adjacent place.

"2. Such as were induced by a south-west gale in action at an adjacent place.

"It is evident that in the arctic regions, where sea channels and streaks of land follow in regular order, polar currents will always select their paths, either on land or on sea, in accordance with the greatest tension of atmosphere, dependent upon the season; they will induce a south-west wind, which, on the contrary, selects its path wherever the air is the most rarefied; a mutual displacement takes place, and two gales blow in opposite directions at adjacent places. This frequently was actually observed at Thank God Harbor and vicinity.

"Here are the characteristics of the two classes of north-east gales:

"When a primary impulse, a north-east wind was always preceded by high atmospheric pressure, low temperature and almost entire absence of moisture; veerings at the commencement and close of the gale were in accordance with the law of gyration. During the gale the barometer would fall, the thermometer would rise, and relative humidity increase.

"When a secondary action, a north-east wind was preceded by low atmospheric pressure, high temperature and low relative humidity; veerings before and after the gale took place contrary to the law of gyration. During the gale the barometer would rise slowly, temperature would almost remain stationary, and relative humidity would increase rapidly.

"South-west gales also had two different characteristics:

"1. Preceded by low barometer, high temperature and relative humidity; veerings before and after the gale, in accordance with the law of gyration; rise of barometer, fall of thermometer, and stationary relative humidity during the gale.

"2. Preceded by low atmospheric pressure, high temperature and low relative humidity; veering before and after the gale, contrary to the law of gyration; rise of barometer, fall of thermometer and rapid rise of relative humidity during the gale.

"Velocities above forty miles per hour were very frequent; light and pleasant winds were observed from all points of true bearing. . . . Observations on clouds were made at times of systematic observations; formations, similar to those known in our climates, were noted; strata were prevalent, and the cirrus cloud was seen in the region of cumuli."

"Precipitations in form of heavy snow or rain were rare, but very frequent in the form of fog, frost, smoke, haziness and light snow. It frequently was observed during the summer that when moisture was precipitated over an area consisting partly of land and partly of ice, it would take the form of rain on land, but the form of snow on the ice."

It will be remarked that Mr. Meyer particularly notes that "two gales blow in opposite directions at adjacent places," and that "a mutual displacement takes place," which is the basis of our whole system.

We have in his description also the north-east and the south-east storms—here really south-*west* storms, since the polar current is undeflected—with their characteristic meteorological changes in pressure, temperature and direction of the wind. There is not to be seen, however, in the frigid zone the distinguishing characteristics of the south-east storm regarding form of clouds, development of electricity and profuseness of precipitation, no thunder-clouds, lightning or "cloud-bursts" having ever been observed in arctic regions; and the south-east storm is therefore assimilated in these respects to the north-east. This is of course due to the fact that the plane of meeting of the two currents is here at a greater inclination than farther south. In fact, it is not to be doubted that there is a tendency of the plane of meeting in both kinds of displacements to approach more nearly a vertical position in equatorial regions, and to approach more nearly a horizontal position regularly as we advance toward the poles. The reason for this is manifest; the sun's rays falling more vertically at the equator, the equatorial current rises more vertically, being more heated, and as the poles are approached the equatorial current, being less heated, flows over the polar at a greater inclination. For simplicity it may be stated as a rule that the tendency of the plane of meeting to incline corresponds with the inclination of the sun's rays.

The features of the gales that Mr. Meyer has observed are here arranged in tabular form to make the changes more evident.

| | Barom. | Therm. | Relative Humidity. | Change of Wind as regards the Law of Gyration. |
|---|---|---|---|---|
| "North-east Gales." | | | | |
| "*Primary Impulse.*" | | | | |
| Before | High | Low | Very low | In accordance. |
| During | Falling | Rising | Increasing | |
| "*Secondary Action.*" | | | | |
| Before | Low | High | Low | Contrary to. |
| During | Rising | Stationary | Increasing | |
| "South-west Gales." | | | | |
| 1. | | | | |
| Before | Low | High | High | In accordance. |
| During | Rising | Falling | Stationary | |
| 2. | | | | |
| Before | Low | High | Low | Contrary to. |
| During | Rising | Falling | Increasing | |

The changes of pressure, temperature and direction of the

wind in a south-east storm are identical with those in the return oscillation of a north-east storm, the phenomena in these two movements differing only in the form of clouds, amount of precipitation and development of electricity; and as these characteristics of the south-east storm are wanting in the frigid zone, the storm system may be considered as merely backward and forward oscillations of the two currents, the polar current displacing the equatorial or the equatorial the polar, the difference between a return oscillation and an advancing storm of the other kind being merely one of degree. Mr. Meyer indicates the difference in dividing his gales into "primary impulses" and "secondary actions."

The first division of the north-east gales will be recognized as the displacement of the polar current by the equatorial; the change of wind being such as would be observed from a standpoint on the right side of the storm.

The second division of both kinds of gales is almost identical, and corresponds with the displacement of the equatorial current by the polar, the standpoint of observation being on the left side of the storm. The first division of south-west gales is the same movement as these last observed from the right side.

Mr. Meyer's observations of the clouds will be noted to accord with the theory that has been advanced regarding their formation.

The fact which he also observes that precipitations falling at the same time on land and ice took the form of rain over the former and snow over the latter is corroborative of the views advanced regarding the formation of snow.

(*e*) *The Iowa and Illinois tornado of May* 22, 1873. (Report, page 1047, see Appendix C.)

These tornadoes were investigated by Sergeant James Mackintosh, who was sent to the ground for the purpose with very thorough and excellent instructions. He was fortunate in the amount of testimony he was enabled to gather and the number of intelligent witnesses he found. The facts he reports are very valuable,* and he deserves credit for the labor he expended in discovering them, but the conclusions he draws and his method of reasoning are at times, to say the least, rather extraordinary; as for instance when he computes that the storm-cloud "must have been *sixteen miles* in height."

The facts in these tornadoes agree very markedly with those of the West Cambridge tornado, and show that they originated and developed under exactly the same circumstances. There were present in each instance a valley and a hill in the same relative position as Prospect Hill and the valley east of it; there is the south-west wind with a high temperature, and the north-west wind with a low temperature; there is the long black bank of cloud hanging in the north-west for a long time and advancing slowly south-east; there are the same movements of the vortex along its whole track; there are the triangular areas of destruction and those uninjured. (See *Fig.* 20, *Appendix C.*) There are also many other corroborations of the explanation given of the West Cambridge tornado, of which one of the most interesting is the *mud* manufactory doing its work this time on the body of a living witness, who "was wet and covered with mud," and who, in further explanation, says: "Felt very cold; felt warm soon afterward; seemed to be surrounded with a heavy mist." We find here realized several phenomena which the theory deduced from the West Cambridge tornado only indicated as possibilities; such as parallel and intermittent tornadoes and hail-storms (at Keokuk, Des Moines, Lincoln county, etc.), a water-spout, and vortices one immediately in front

* In my investigations in the West Cambridge tornado I had difficulty in finding sufficient witnesses, particularly as to the temperature and other conditions of the north-west wind. In this last particular especially Mr. Mackintosh's investigation admirably supplements mine.

of the main vortex, the other in its rear, manufacturing hailstones. (*Fig.* 22, *Appendix C.*) The witnesses all agree that there was a long black bank of cloud, cumulo-stratus, characteristic of the south-east storm, lying for hours along the northern horizon, stretched out from west to east. They agree that the cloud "rose"—*i. e.*, travelled to the south-east—but did not pass the zenith, the southern sky being clear, and that the tornado-cloud travelled beneath the cumulo-stratus and in the general direction of its line toward the east. They almost without exception saw the rotation of the tornado-cloud, and most of them are positive that the upper clouds, although in commotion, did not rotate. Some saw clouds from the south flying to the north, and from the north to the south, which without question is the zig-zag motion of the vortex as seen from a distance. The testimony is conclusive that there was a warm southerly wind followed by a cool northerly wind after "the storm"—*i. e.*, the tornado—had passed; and some witnesses even testify that the warm wind returned, indicating a beginning of the return oscillation of the south-east storm. One man says: "The wind before the storm came from the south quite strong. Then it grew calm. Then there came a very hard wind right from the north. It felt cool as the storm passed, but grew warm soon afterward."

The existence of a south-east storm extending over a large area seems to be unquestionably established, and any one who has comprehended the system set forth in this volume will readily recognize as the offspring of this storm all those tornadoes, hail-storms, "cloud-bursts," thunder-showers, "local storms," and kindred phenomena, which occurred over so extensive a region on the same day along the region of meeting of the two currents.

Recognizing the natural relation of all these phenomena to the south-east storm, and through it to each other, there is no difficulty in comprehending their occurrence in different latitudes and longitudes, and at different hours of the day; and it is easy to separate each one from those with which it is in connection, giving each its proper individuality. It will be seen that the path of each tornado is easterly, varying a little as the plane of meeting of the currents may have been bent one way or the other, or with the configuration of the ground; that each tornado originated at a noticeable depression in the face of the country; that in many instances, when nearly exhausted, it gathered fresh force upon striking a new depression, or in other words that another tornado originated here; that the country intervening between tornadoes was visited by high winds, heavy rains or hail-storms—all explained by our theory and otherwise virtually inexplicable.

Mr. Mackintosh, not knowing the south-east storm at all, has fallen into the error of thinking it a tornado, to which he thus gives gigantic proportions, making its diameter at least thirty miles, and considering it "somewhat probable that the tornado had a radius of one hundred and twenty miles." He calculates its force as *trillions* of horse-power—an amount simply inconceivable. After making his calculations toward this result he goes on to say, the italics being ours:

"These figures convey a better idea of the tremendous power of the tornado than any mere verbal description could do. They also show that the power evolved by the condensation of vapor, while enormous, is by no means sufficient to supply the whole energy developed by the tornado. We must therefore look for another source of power. This is no doubt to be found in the destruction of the atmospheric equilibrium by an abnormally-warm southerly current flowing *under* a much colder, and consequently specifically *heavier*, stratum of air. This brings us to the consideration of the general atmospheric conditions under which the tornado originated.

"An area of low barometer existed in the Mississippi and Missouri valleys on the 20th, 21st and 22d of May which moved very slowly northward. This induced a southerly current, abnormally warm for the season, over a large portion of the interior of the continent. The result was a series of violent local storms, or spasmodic atmospheric convulsions, along the whole southern declivity of low barometer. These storms were generally accompanied by hail, and always by lightning. They reached a climax in the tornado, which is the subject of this paper, and in that which simultaneously devastated a portion of Kansas. The circumstances under which these terrible meteors arise are, therefore, easy of comprehension. They are the same as those which produce the beneficent thunder-shower, only they exist in greater intensity. The warm southern current, drawn toward the centre of low barometer, passes *under* much colder and *heavier* air. So long as the *greater specific gravity* of a given volume of the upper stratum of air, which is due to a lower temperature, is balanced in the lower stratum by the *greater density* consequent upon greater pressure of the same volume of air, so long may the atmosphere remain in a state of unstable equilibrium. Any disturbing cause may, however, destroy this state of unstable equilibrium, because the moment the pressure upon the underlying warm air becomes equal to that upon the upper stratum it becomes the less dense, and therefore specifically lighter. Consequently, as soon as an opening is broken through the upper strata, the state of unstable equilibrium is immediately destroyed and a powerful ascending current formed. It is manifest that the state of unstable equilibrium may continue until the density arising from the lower temperature exceeds that arising from the greater pressure. The moment this occurs the unstable equilibrium is destroyed. The nearer the atmosphere approaches to this condition, the more intense will be the consequent convulsion. It seems probable that in the case of tornadoes this total destruction of equilibrium is a frequent, if not a constant, accompaniment."

I quote this passage because it contains the statement of a principle held by eminent authority, which is that a warm current can pass *under* much *heavier* air. To refute this it is only necessary to recall to mind the old Franklin experiment of the candle in the open window of a heated room. Light air can no more flow under heavy air than oil can flow under water. We all know that temperature diminishes in ascending from the surface of the earth, but we also know that the air grows *lighter* and the barometer falls. The theory that heavier air is in suspension above a region of low barometer toward which the southern current is drawn is manifestly erroneous, since the height of the barometer is governed solely by atmospheric pressure, which it is presumed no one will deny.

Upon Mr. Mackintosh's statement that of two strata of air one possesses the "greater *specific gravity*," and the other the "greater *density*," it is not necessary to comment.

## V.

*Testimony regarding a tornado at Winchendon, Massachusetts.*

The following letter from ex-Pres. Hill of Harvard was written in the latter part of 1851; the testimony it contains is the more valuable from the countenance he gives to it.

PROF. W. BLASIUS:

*Dear Sir:* On Saturday morning, after your lecture in Waltham, I chanced to meet Chauncey Newhall, Esq., of this town. I asked him if he took any interest in the tornado. "No," said he, "not much. I saw one twenty-eight years ago, when I was just twenty-one years old, and was so well convinced of the causes of it that I supposed no one could differ from me. When this one took place in Waltham, it was under such precisely similar circumstances that I could not doubt it was from the same causes, and so have thought nothing about it since." I asked him about the Winchendon tornado, and he replied that it was Sunday afternoon, about five or six o'clock; that there had been a strong south-west wind blowing all day, and was still blowing; that for some hours black clouds had been rising in the north-west horizon; that the north-west wind bearing these clouds, meeting the south-west wind in Pomeroy's Valley east of Northfield Mountain, produced an eddy or whirl that ran in a cycloidal path between the opposing winds for twenty miles or more eastward, till it struck Tully's Mountain; after crossing this the eddy did not descend again to earth, but went on whirling in the air, scattering down leaves, twigs, boards, etc., etc., the ruins of farm-houses, forests, etc., which it had destroyed.

I thought this testimony of great value to you, and hasten to transmit it. Yours, etc.,

THOS. HILL.

The following account may refer to the same tornado as that described by Mr. Newhall, although there would seem to be some discrepancy in the dates; if it does not, the evidence is still stronger, the locality being the same. The extract is taken from *The Collections of the New Hampshire Historical Society for the Year* 1824, vol. i., page 241. I have italicized the most salient points. "After the great rains of the 3d and 4th of September, 1821, the weather was generally calm and pleasant. The eighth and ninth were warm, the latter *sultry*. The wind in the afternoon blew from the *south-west* until about six o'clock, when a *dark cloud* was observed to rise rapidly in the *north* and *north-west*, and pass in a *south-easterly* direction, illumined in its course by incessant flashes of lightning. There was a most terrifying commotion in the cloud itself, and its appearance gave notice that irresistible power and desolation were its attendants. Few, however, apprehended the danger that was threatening, or that their dwellings which had long withstood the fury of the tempest were to be swept away like leaves before the winds of autumn. The tornado was felt, and it is said to have commenced, near Lake Champlain. Hail-storms and violent winds were also experienced in various parts of the United States at the same time, and nearly at the same period in the *West Indies*. The whirlwind entered the State at Cornish, and crossing the mountain gathered its strength as it passed through Croydon. Here the house of Deacon Cooper was shattered, his barn and its contents entirely swept away. Passing on in a direction east-south-east in its progress, collecting into a narrower compass its power, its path was along the lowlands, till it came to the farm and buildings of Harvey Huntoon, in Wendell, about eighty rods distant from the borders of the Sunapee Lake. The people in the house, eight in number, were frightened by the appearance of the cloud. They saw the air before it filled with birds and broken limbs of trees. In an instant the house and the two barns were prostrated to the ground, etc. . . . The village of Poughkeepsie, New York, was this day visited by a destructive hail-storm. Its duration was about ten minutes, during which an unusual quantity of hail fell, and in balls measuring from ten to fifteen inches in circumference, and weighing from three to fourteen ounces. A tornado which occurred in Massachusetts at the precise time with that here is thus described in a Worcester paper:

"'About six o'clock Sunday evening, September 9, a black and terrific cloud appeared a little south of the centre of Northfield, Franklin county, nearly in the form of a pyramid reversed, moving very rapidly and with a terrible noise. In its progress it swept away or prostrated all the trees, fences, stone walls and buildings which came within its vortex, which in some places was not more than twenty rods and in others forty or fifty. It passed from Northfield through Warwick and Orange, to the south-westerly part of Royalston, where its force was broken by Tully Mountain. Its path was strewed for a distance of twenty-five miles, through the towns of Royalston, Winchendon, Ashburnham and Fitchburg, with fragments of buildings, etc. The appearance presented by the track of the whirlwind indicated, as nearly as the writer can judge from actual inspection, that the form of the cloud and the body of air in motion was that of an inverted pyramid, drawing whatever came within its influence toward its centre of motion.'

"The extent of the whirlwind in New London was about four miles, varying in width as the column alternately rose and fell. From thence it passed up the north-west side of Kearsarge Mountain apparently in two columns, which closed again in one as it settled down the opposite side into Warner."

We see in the foregoing an extensive south-east storm travelling from the region of the great lakes to the Atlantic coast, accompanied by tornadoes, hail-storms and similar phenomena at various places.

## VI.

*Extracts from the answers of Prof. H. Mohn of Christiania, Norway, and C. Meldrum, M. A., of Mauritius, to questions propounded to a number of celebrated meteorologists, in accordance with a resolution of the Meteorological Conference at Leipzig in* 1872.

The object of the resolution of the Leipzig Conference was to obtain the opinions of celebrated meteorologists in various parts of the world as to the practicability and usefulness of weather-telegrams and storm-signals. A report embodying replies from some thirty gentlemen to the circular issued was made to the International Meteorological Congress at Vienna in 1873, and published in the following year at Berlin, edited by Dr. G. von Boguslawski. From this publication the following extracts are translated.

Prof. Mohn, in his article, which is marked by his usual ability, says:

"No small part of the storms which have visited Southern Norway have come without warning. The reason lies in the imperfection of the theory, in combination with the scarcity of telegrams and the inadequate number of observers for continuous observations. The changes in the atmosphere often take place with such rapidity that it is impossible to draw conclusions from the condition of the weather in the morning as to the storm on the next day. Several instances may be mentioned here: Storm-centres from north-west coming without affecting the barometer in Thurso (north-west storms on the west coast and in Southern Norway); storm-centres from the Arctic Sea coming over the Gulf of Bothnia (strong northerly winds in the eastern portion of the country); the rise of the gradient in consequence of the fact that the atmospheric pressure in the neighboring countries is sinking, while at the same time in Norway it is rising.

"Storms which we predicted from Christiania in the middle of the day, and which in the morning had not yet reached the cities on the coast, had often, according to observations, been completely developed at the lighthouse stations by the morning. Such warnings come too late. . . .

"Storms which we are so fortunate as to be able to signal early enough are those which belong to barometric minima that are well developed in the morning in the British Islands, especially in Ireland and the Hebrides; or storms from the north-west belonging to the rear of barometric minima which show themselves in the morning with low pressure in Southern Norway.

"Storms of which we can give a forewarning are those which belong to a barometric minimum. Nevertheless, there are cases in which we cannot give forewarning to the Norwegian coast of a storm, although tolerably low barometric minima show themselves in the British Islands; this is the case when the cold in Norway is continuous and strong. The best indication of a storm we have in the circumstances of the temperature at Dover, which lies two thousand feet above the level of the sea. The setting in of southerly winds and rise of temperature takes place at Dover from one to two days earlier than in Christiania.

In this case it may be taken for granted that a barometric minimum may extend over the country. But if the cold is severe and continuous, the barometric minima pass either south of Norway, the southern coast of which in that case experiences winds scarcely of the strength of a storm, or they pass to the north of the western coast toward the Arctic Sea.

"Storms which develop themselves in the limits between barometric minima and maxima, whose gradients assume sometimes considerable magnitude in consequence of the sinking of the atmospheric pressure in the minimum and its rising in the maximum, we cannot indicate, as the amount of variation of the atmospheric pressure at the different localities is proportionally small, and we are without knowledge of the conditions of the simultaneous occurrence of these phenomena."

In Prof. Mohn's description we may recognize the two kinds of progressive storms. Those which he describes as announcing themselves first at Dover, England, with a southerly wind and rising temperature, readily identify themselves with our north-east storms. The setting in of southerly winds, accompanied by rising thermometer at Dover, indicates that the region of meeting of the two currents is passing. Dover is about two thousand feet above the level of the sea, but the highest stratus, the characteristic advance cloud of a north-east storm, is ordinarily at a height of about six miles, and, therefore, when the change in the wind and temperature is observed at Dover, these advance clouds would probably in most cases be already in sight at Christiania.

These north-east storms, if the inclination of their plane of meeting does not vary materially from that in the north-east storms of America, should be visible in England and North-western Europe by their advance clouds from one to three days before the region of low barometer arrives. I have frequently in this country seen them three days in advance.

The storms which Prof. Mohn says cannot be predicted, and

which he describes as coming from the north-west or north-east and developing in the rear of the barometric minima, or the region of low barometer, agree with our south-east storms. They cannot of course be predicted by the barometer, because, when the barometer falls, the storm has already arrived; but their characteristic cloud, the cumulo-stratus, can ordinarily be seen at least several hours in advance, and severe storms almost invariably give sufficient warning to escape danger.

The observation regarding storms of this class, that their "gradients assume sometimes considerable magnitude in consequence of the sinking of the atmospheric pressure in the minimum and its rising in the maximum," agrees perfectly with our theory, since, as the plane of meeting toward the crisis of the storm assumes a more vertical position from the banking up of the polar current, the difference in pressure in the two currents is, of course, proportionately greater.

Prof. Mohn is the first eminent authority to corroborate my theory by drawing a distinction between these two kinds of storms, and his testimony seems also to warrant my assumption that there exists over the Eastern Atlantic and Western Europe a similar system of storm-tracks to that which I am convinced exists in America. (See *Plate X.*) There would then probably be also a similar coalescing of south-east and north-east storms as takes place on the Western Atlantic sea-board, which would explain the violence of the storms experienced.

This assumption is strengthened by Prof. Mohn's ability to predict at times storms coming from the north-west by a barometric depression in the south of Norway. This bears a resemblance to Prof. Abbe's observation on the Atlantic coast of America, connecting disturbances on the coast with others inland, of which, however, it seems to be the converse. The probabilities, it is to be supposed, are that the barometric depression on which Prof. Mohn bases his predictions belongs to an advancing north-east storm with which the south-east storm collides. This, however, in the absence of more data, is but speculation.

---

Mr. C. Meldrum, secretary of the Meteorological Society at Mauritius, says:

"Our storms have such a uniform character, as compared with those of Europe, that the determination of their centres, approximate distances and progress is at present well established, and this by observations at a single station, which are daily published till the danger is over. . . .

"Temperature, aqueous vapor, humidity and dew-point are of secondary importance to a judgment of the existence and the course of storms at Mauritius. As simultaneous indications they are sometimes quite useful, but the barometer, the direction and strength of the wind and the character of the clouds give the principal indications of a coming cyclone. Ordinarily, the temperature is high before the setting in of a hurricane, while the elasticity of vapor and the humidity are comparatively low. At the approach of the storm the weather becomes rainy and stormy, and the temperature begins to fall; the elasticity of vapor and the humidity begin to rise. But even when these indications are wanting, a falling barometer, an increasing wind from south-east and the appearance of high, white cirrus and cirro-stratus clouds, which gradually cover the sky, and at last change into a deep nimbus, are infallible prognostics of a distant hurricane. During the first part of the passage of a hurricane at Mauritius the wind is unchangeably polar, and during the last part equatorial. The elasticity of vapor and humidity are greatest with northerly and westerly winds—*i. e.*, in the equatorial current. At this time, however, the centre ordinarily has passed, and the danger is over; thus an increase of the elasticity of vapor comes ordinarily too late to serve as a warning. . . . In regard to the storms at Mauritius, our sole difficulty is the uncertainty as to when and where an approaching cyclone will return."

The last sentence would seem to indicate the oscillation of storms at Mauritius, which Mr. Meldrum states are of "a uniform character." It will be noted that in their beginning the wind in these storms is "unchangeably *polar*," and afterward is *equatorial*, and simultaneously with the change of wind there is a change in *temperature, moisture* and *atmospheric pressure.*

If these storms were cyclones, how would it be possible that at first the wind is "*unchangeably* polar," and after the "centre" has passed not only is it from the opposite direction, but has changed in its *temperature, moisture* and *pressure?* These changes would not be possible in the same current of air, which is necessary for the Cyclone theory. The "*infallible* prognostics" are observed to be "a falling barometer, an increasing wind and *the appearance of high, white cirrus* and *cirro-stratus clouds*" (our *stratus*), "*which gradually cover the sky, and at last change into a deep nimbus.*" This *exactly* agrees with my observations of the north-east storms of the temperate zone for the last twenty years.

These storms, however, seem to have assimilated to south-east storms in the same manner as the south-east storms of the frigid zone seem to have assimilated to north-east storms, and it will be remembered that in considering Sergeant Frederick Meyer's report it was shown that the cause of these assimilations is the different positions of the plane of meeting, which in the conflicts tends to assume a more vertical position as we go from the poles to the equator.

The distribution of the different kinds of storms over the surface of the earth from the equator to the poles is, then, in beautiful accord with the distribution of heat, their prime originator, and it follows that *local* storms are typical of the torrid zone, *progressive* storms of the frigid zone, and *both* of the temperate zone, according as the torrid climate of summer or the frigid climate of winter prevails. Thus the local storms are most gigantic in the torrid zone, are merely summer showers in the temperate, and are not observable in the frigid; the progressive storms assimilate to the south-east storm in the torrid, are distinctly both north-east and south-east in the temperate, and assimilate to the north-east in the frigid. The loco-progressive storms, occurring only in connection with south-east storms, are greatest in the torrid as hurricanes, typhoons, etc.; are on a smaller scale in the temperate in the shape of tornadoes, waterspouts, etc., and have never been known in the frigid.

In the same way it would follow that toward the equator the progressive velocity of storms becomes less and their destructiveness greater, while toward the poles these conditions are reversed.

Starting in our deductions from the acknowledged fact that the sun is the main source of all power and motion, we found in the ever-changing position of the earth toward it and in the inclination of the earth's axis to the ecliptic an explanation of the circulation of the atmosphere and its oscillation from north to south in coincidence with the seasons. In the disturbances of the regularity and extent of these oscillations, therefore, it seems that we should seek the causes of the irregularity of the seasons. Some winters are warmer than others, and some summers are cooler; and from experience it seems at least probable that these phenomena are always reversed at the same time on the opposite side of the globe—*i. e.*, that if the north temperate zone of the western hemisphere should experience a more than ordinarily warm season, the north temperate zone of the eastern hemisphere will experience at the same time a more than ordinarily cool season. We know from astronomy that in consequence of the effort of the sun to bring into coincidence the plane of the earth's equator and the plane of the ecliptic, the earth's axis, except at the equinoctial periods, acquires a sort of oscillatory motion like that of a top, and we also know that the orbit of the earth deviates somewhat from a perfect ellipse in consequence of the influence of the other planets. Is it, now, improbable that such a flexible fluid as the atmosphere should not coincide entirely with the earth in these perturbations, and that its belts of high and low pressure should therefore be at such times north or south of their normal position? If this is the case, when the tropical belts lie farther north than usual in the eastern hemisphere, the arctic belts would lie farther south in the western. This question, however, belongs rather to the province of astronomy than meteorology.

We have found in the unequal distribution of land and water over the face of the globe the causes of the disturbances in the circulation of the atmosphere, the origin of storms. As Prof. Virchow showed that disease is not something foreign, coming from the outside into the body, but only a local disturbance of the circulation of the blood, so may we look upon storms simply as local disturbances of the general circulation of the atmosphere.

## VII.

*Testimony from the report of the Chief Signal Officer of the United States Army for the year* 1874.*

The following extract is taken from a paper on "Relative Pressures, or Barometric Gradients," in the report for 1874 of Gen. Albert J. Myer, Chief Signal Officer. From it will be seen that meteorology is endeavoring to find in the "barometric gradient"—an imaginary line, and in most cases impossible at present truly to determine—that assistance only in reality to be found in *the plane of meeting*, which is not imaginary, but has an actual existence, and is in intimate connection with the life of storms.

* The Signal Service report for 1874 only came into my hands after this volume had already gone to press, but as it contained some valuable confirmatory evidence the publication of the book was delayed to include it. Nothing that precedes it has, however, been changed.

The extract will also be seen to be confirmatory of the velocity rules we have deduced.

"In all storm warnings the wind velocity is the most important element to predict. This can be calculated, not from the absolute amount of depression in a storm-centre, but from the relative depression. The greater the deficiency of pressure at any one point, as compared with the surrounding pressures, it is obvious the more powerful will be the indraught thither; and hence the greater the velocity and the danger of the cyclonic winds. It is very desirable to approximately determine in arithmetical terms what velocity the winds will attain at a station by the difference of synchronous barometer-readings at that and the neighboring station.* This is done by ascertaining 'the barometric gradient,' as it has been called. The barometric gradient numerically defines the storm's violence by dividing the distance between the two places given in nautical miles by the difference of the synchronous pressure observations.† For example, if the distance between New York and Washington be taken as one hundred and eighty-five miles, and the respective barometer readings be 30.40 and 29.90 inches, the barometric gradient will be one inch in three hundred and seventy miles. It has been ascertained by engineers that when the barometric gradients in storms are as great as one inch of mercury in one hundred and seventy miles, the wind is high enough to overturn many houses.‡ When the barometric gradient does not exceed one inch in six hundred miles, such danger is scarcely ever to be apprehended. In regard to vessels at sea, a gradient of one inch in six hundred miles will, however, sometimes produce

* See *Barometer Manual* of Board of Trade, London, by R. H. Scott, 1871, page 21, *et seq.*

† The "barometric gradient" was first proposed by Thomas Stevenson, Esq., C. E., in a paper read before the Scottish Meteorological Society, June, 1867. See society's *Journal* for January, 1868, New Series, No. XVII., p. 132.

‡ See paper of Mr. Stevenson, just referred to; also Buchan's *Meteorology*, p. 260.

dangerous winds. During the Bahama hurricane, in October, 1866, the gradient was at one time one inch in one hundred and fifty miles, with winds blowing from eighty to one hundred and twenty miles an hour.* The extremely steep gradients occur in nearly all the great tropical hurricanes and typhoons. The storm-disk is of small dimensions within the tropics, and the depression takes place so rapidly that the surrounding air has not time to come in and restore equilibrium gradually.

"It is of the utmost consequence, for the guidance of any one predicting a dangerous wind at any point or station, to obtain an arithmetical expression of what constitutes a dangerous barometric gradient.

"In the Mauritius gale of February 25, 1863, between that island and Réunion, the barometric gradient appears to have been about one inch in two hundred and ninety or three hundred miles, the wind blowing about sixty miles an hour. A very instructive record of the British storm of August 22, 1868, 6 P. M., shows, between Valencia and Liverpool, a gradient of one inch in three hundred or three hundred and fifty miles, with wind velocity rising from forty-five to sixty miles an hour.† On February 1, 1868, the readings were respectively 30.16 and 28.40 at Rochefort, France, and Aberdeen, Scotland (difference 1.76 of an inch), and the gradient one inch in three hundred and sixty miles. It was followed by a tremendous gale between the two points.

"'In the European tempest of January 7, 1839,' says Mr. Stevenson,‡ 'we find a mean gradient between Bara and Lismore of one inch in two hundred and eighty miles, and of one inch in two hundred and sixty-four miles between Lismore and Bell Rock—slopes steep enough to account for the damage done to buildings and other property.' No doubt, had interme-

* See Buchan, pp. 265–267.

† See pp. 9, 10, Non-official Report of Captain Toynbee.

‡ See paper in *Journal of Scottish Meteorological Society* for January, 1868, p. 132.

diate points of comparison been in existence, we should have found still steeper gradients. Tropical storms, from their greater violence, might be expected to occur in connection with very steep gradients, and such appears to be the case. Thus, on calculating that of the Bahama tempest in September, 1866, we get one inch in one hundred and forty-three miles, while during the hurricane on the Malabar coast recorded by Col. Sykes the observations indicate a gradient as steep as one inch in only fifty miles. In the great Scottish hurricane of January 23 and 24, 1868, the following invaluable observations and computations of barometric gradients were made at Aberdeen and Culloden, distant sixty-eight miles. On the 23d the following were the changes:*

| Time. | Gradient. | Wind Velocity. |
|---|---|---|
| 9 A. M. | 1 inch in 167 miles. | 70 miles an hour. |
| At noon | " 138 " | 91 " " |
| 1 P. M. | " 164 " | 80 " " |
| 3 P. M. | " 232 " | 60 " " |
| Midnight | " 521 " | 24 " " |

"These figures show in general that where the barometric gradient was about one inch in one hundred and seventy or two hundred miles, the velocity of the wind rose to more than ninety miles an hour, or the extreme hurricane rate. . . .

"In studying these data it is of course necessary to remember that the effect of a barometric gradient will be modified by the orography and relief features of the country.† Interposing hills and mountains will make the results very different from those produced by the same gradients in a level country. But from all these figures and facts we may roughly deduce some

* See *Journal of Scottish Meteorological Society*, January, 1868, page 132, *et seq.*

† See Ferrel *On Motions of Fluids and Solids relative to Earth's Surface*, p. 51.

useful approximate expressions as to what wind velocities will be likely to follow certain barometric gradients, and also what barometric gradients indicate peril to shipping.* The following results are tentative:

"1. When the barometric gradient amounts to one inch in seven hundred and fifty or eight hundred miles, a wind blowing about twenty or twenty-five miles per hour may be expected. Such a wind on the lakes is dangerous; especially is it to be apprehended in foggy, rainy or snowy weather. When the wind reaches even twenty miles an hour on the Atlantic coast, with a heavy snow-fall, it is then dangerous to navigation. Occasionally a gradient of one inch in eight hundred miles has been soon followed by a wind velocity of thirty or thirty-five miles an hour, but such instances seem to be rare. This gradient (one inch in seven hundred and fifty or eight hundred miles) may, therefore, be called the *danger gradient.*

"2. A barometric gradient of one inch in six hundred and fifty miles will generally produce a wind blowing about twenty-five or thirty miles or upward, except in a mountainous country.

"3. A barometric gradient of one inch in five hundred and fifty or six hundred miles will generally be followed by a wind blowing about thirty or thirty-five miles an hour, the results of course, as always, being modified by the topography of the country.

"4. If the barometric gradient is as much as one inch in four hundred and fifty or five hundred miles, the wind will probably blow about thirty-five or forty miles an hour.

"5. If the barometric gradient is one inch in three hundred and fifty miles, it will be followed by a gale blowing from forty-five to fifty miles an hour, though it may exceed that velocity.

"6. When the gradient is as steep as one inch in three hundred miles or less, almost a hurricane wind of say from fifty to

*See report of an inquiry into the connection between strong winds and barometric differences, by R. H. Scott, London, 1869, pp. 3 to 10.

seventy-five miles an hour may confidently be looked for, with still fiercer squalls.

"7. No gradient less than or about one inch in one thousand miles need be apprehended as a source of dangerous atmospheric disturbance.

"It should be mentioned that in computing the above gradients, as nearly as possible, the stations compared are those lying on the same line of cyclonic indraught—*i. e.*, in the path pursued by a particle of the air which rushes from the circumference inward to the centre of the storm.

"Owing to the present difficulty of applying the proper correction of barometers for elevation, it may be best not to use these approximate results with barometric gradients computed from readings taken from high mountain ranges or in regions rising more than twenty-five hundred feet above the sea. It may be instructive to add to the above observations the following remarks from M. Buys-Ballot, of Holland, speaking for his own country:*

"'On the 1st of January, 1870, pressure fell from Maestricht northward to Helder, the distance being one hundred and twenty-five miles and the difference in pressure 0.154 inch, thus giving a barometric gradient at the rate of one inch in eight hundred and twelve miles. The greatest force of the wind at Maestricht was forty-nine kilogrammes in the square metre, being equal to a pressure of about eleven pounds on the square foot. The direction of the arrow shows the wind was from south-west.

"'From a careful examination of a large mass of details collected in the Annuaires, the following results will appear:

"'1. As regards the relation of the wind to atmospheric pressure, the direction of the wind obeys the law of the relation better than the force does, nearly without exception, if pressure

*See *Scottish Meteorological Journal*, pp. 25, 26, New Series, No. XXVII. to XXVIII., for January and April, 1873.

be higher in the south than in the north, winds in such cases being westerly. On the other hand, easterly winds do not arise so easily as westerly winds; they not only do not follow the gradients so closely, but if the difference between the gradients be not considerable, they (the easterly winds) do not follow at all.

"'2. Polar winds have a different gradient from equatorial winds. Thus, if atmospheric pressure be higher in the north than in the south, a steeper gradient is required to give a pressure of six pounds to the square foot.

"'3. The east and north-east winds are not only weaker with respect to the steepness of the gradients which have to be formed, but they follow the formation of the gradients after a much longer interval of time than happens in the case of the north-west winds.

"'It indeed frequently occurs that after a pretty steep gradient has been formed, from which an easterly wind might be looked for, rain follows, and not a very strong easterly wind. In general, the north-west wind is a weak point in my predictions of weather, owing to the quickness and force with which these winds spring up after the barometric indications have appeared.

"'4. The converse of this does not appear to hold good, viz.: a strong wind does not arise when there has been neither a steep gradient preceding, nor a great difference between two consecutive gradients.

"'5. If there has been a strong wind after a steep barometric gradient, as for example on the occasion of the storm of the 28th of May, 1860, then the strong wind is not only preceded, but is also followed, by great steepness in the gradient. It often occurs after strong north-westerly winds that the gradient from Flushing to Helder or Gröningen continues to be great still, and is not followed by a continuance of the storm.'

"As has been already suggested when discussing the United States Signal Service gradients, it will always be necessary to consider the orographic and other features of the country for which high winds are computed. When the country is flat or littoral, and the wind has no retarding obstacle to overcome, the velocity will be higher than when the region considered is mountainous or hilly. In river valleys the descending wind will blow with unrestrained force. Generally, some hours must intervene between the formation of a steep barometric gradient and its normal consequence, a very high wind.

"It may finally be observed that, in general, the cyclonic winds will blow in a direction varying, as regards the isobaric curves, from the tangential to the centripetal. Sometimes the high wind will be nearly tangential, but the more rapidly and suddenly the barometer falls, the more nearly will its direction approach a radial line drawn from the circumference to the centre of the disturbance. If an average angle must be indicated, it is perhaps near the truth to say that the cyclonic winds will blow across the isobaric curves at an angle of about 40° in ordinary land-storms, and 60° in severe storms. But the topography of the regions so modifies, in each case, the direction as well as velocity of the wind that no *exact* arithmetical expressions can be rigidly applied. Thus, winds on the Atlantic sea-board, due to indraught from a storm-centre on the lower lakes, according to the law of storms ought to be east and south-east. But the diverting influence of the Alleghany Mountains will often make them more decidedly south or south-west winds.

"The meteorologist, however, by constant and close observation of the weather-map, will be enabled to predict very nearly the direction from a judicious comparison of all the conditions. In discussing this subject regard has been had solely to the calculation of the wind-velocity that will follow an *already existent* barometric gradient. During the progress of the cyclone, the gradients are, however, undergoing important changes. It will, therefore, often be as important to predict a future gradient as to ascertain that already formed.

"To predict the future gradient is very difficult, since it requires a study of the extent, direction and velocity of the movement of upper currents of the atmosphere. But, in general, it may be stated that the formation of new gradients during the progress of the storm will depend upon the amount, rapidity and area of the rain-fall or snow-fall accompanying the progressive depression. The greater the amount of precipitation in a given number of hours, the more marked will be the fall of mercury in the barometer* and the greater will be the indraught of cyclonic winds, and hence the greater the wind velocity.

"The telegraphic report of the rain-fall in the previous eight hours will, therefore, furnish the storm-warner the data for an approximate estimate of the future or following barometric gradient."

Modern meteorology evidently strives to solve its main problem—the determination of the law of the movements and violence of coming storms—by the study of "the barometric gradient."

It is hoped that the relation between the steepness of the gradient and the strength of the wind, taken in connection with Buys-Ballot's law—"The wind flows always from the place of highest pressure to that of lowest, turning by the rotation of the earth to the right on the northern hemisphere and to the left on the southern hemisphere"—will lead to the desired end, the ability to determine the direction and strength of the coming wind or storm from present meteorological conditions. The experience of the United States Signal Service and of Prof. Buys-Ballot himself, as exhibited in the above extract, does not, however, give much encouragement to this hope. The Signal Service finds "it advisable not to use approximate results with barometric gradients computed from readings taken from high mountain ranges or in regions rising more than twenty-five

* See W. C. Ley's *Laws of the Winds*, pp. 30–39.

hundred feet above the sea," and makes other reservations in the use of gradients; and Prof. Buys-Ballot, who has studied the relations between wind and pressure most closely, says that the winds from east and north-west—*i. e.*, from the northern semicircle—do not follow his law. He finds that the polar winds follow a different law in regard to the gradient from the equatorial; that "the direction of the wind obeys the law of the relation of the wind to atmospheric pressure better than the force does;" and that easterly winds "not only do not follow the gradients so closely as westerly winds, but if the difference between the gradients be not considerable do not follow at all." The reasons for these discrepancies are easily seen in the light of our theory.

Buys-Ballot's law contains a truth, but not the whole truth, since it gives us one force without another to counterbalance it; and in Nature wherever we find a force we find also its opposite. It assumes a movement of the wind from the highest pressure to the lowest—*i. e.*, from cool regions to warm—but it fails to recognize the compensating movement from warm regions to cool, which, in fact, is the mainspring of the whole mechanism. And since the law does not give any outlet to the wind after it has come from the highest to the lowest pressure, the law makes it of necessity *turn around* the place of lowest pressure. That this is a fundamental error is shown by the effects in the destruction caused by the West Cambridge tornado; wind, like other bodies, moves in *straight lines*, and varies from this only when forced to do so by obstacles in its path.* This also follows distinctly from the experience of the Signal Service, which says: "It may finally be observed that in general the cyclonic winds will blow in a direction varying, as regards the isobaric curves, from the tangential to the centripetal. Sometimes the

* The rotation of the earth, indeed, bends the main currents, but not more than through one quadrant; the equatorial current through that from south to west, and the polar current through that from north to east.

15

high wind will be nearly tangential; but *the more rapidly and suddenly the barometer falls*"—*i. e.*, in the middle of the storm, the line of the arrows *p* and *q*, *Plate VII.*—"*the more nearly will its direction approach a radial line from the circumference to the centre of disturbance.*"

As Buys-Ballot's law only recognizes the movement of *one* current of air, and as there are in fact *two* currents, the velocity and strength of each being dependent on that of the other, which opposes it, it could not be otherwise than that the winds of one semicircle should not agree with the law, and the winds of the other should agree with it only in direction, and not in force. Thus we see the difference of conditions in the two semicircles, which should not exist if the theory of a cyclonic movement of an air-current were true. And when the meteorological changes which by continuous observations are easily ascertained to take place as the region of low barometer of a storm passes are also taken into consideration, it must be evident that the cyclonic theory *cannot* be true.

As regards the gradient, Prof. Buys-Ballot's remarks prove clearly that it is not the desideratum that meteorologists are looking for, because it is artificial, and not in connection with the true nature of storms. It differs from the plane of meeting as much as the shadow from the reality.

Prof. Mohn* defines the gradient as follows: "By the direction of the gradient I understand the perpendicular (*normale*) drawn on the isobars from the place of higher to that of lower atmospheric pressure. By the size of the gradient I understand the number of millimetres by which the atmospheric pressure, reduced to the level of the sea, becomes less as we move forward over a certain distance, for instance over a geographical mile, in the direction of the gradient." He says further: "By the direction and size of the gradient the distribution of the atmo-

* *Bericht über Wetter-Telegraphie und Sturmwarnungen*, edited by Dr. Boguslawski.

spheric pressure at a place is fully determined. In a horizontal plane the change of pressure is the greatest along the gradient, and zero in the line at right angles to it"—*i. e.*, in the isobars. "For each direction between them, it is proportionate to the cosine of the angle the line of this direction makes with the gradient."

According to this definition, there are as many different gradients in a storm as there can be drawn lines from the higher to the lower pressure perpendicular to the elliptical isobars; and as the number of these lines is to all intent limitless, it is in most cases practically impossible to know exactly which gradient is determined. Those gradients which are to the south of the low pressure will have no significance at all, being in the equatorial current. Prof. Buys-Ballot, whose researches are so thorough and scientific, recognizes the difficulty when he says: "By the position of the aëroklinoskope I give a gradient exactly, but which one?"

The gradients of the plane of meeting alone have any significance, and it is for this reason that gradients have been found of some value in predicting the velocity and strength of the winds of an equatorial (a north-east) storm; but in the polar (the south-east) storm, which has mostly passed by before the plane of meeting arrives, the wind cannot be predicted by the gradient, because the only gradients that can be established in advance are those in the rear of the equatorial current, which have no definite relation to the storm at all.

This from our theory is a matter of course, and is testified to by Prof. Mohn also and by Mr. Gaster in the extracts we have elsewhere given. They all say they cannot determine the storms from the northern semicircle, and Mr. Gaster says, "Just the greatest gradients rather accompany the storms than precede them," which is easily understood, since the *greatest* gradients are those of the plane of meeting of a polar storm.

These differences of the gradients, which are perfectly in

accord with our theory, cannot at all be reconciled with the Cyclone theory.

The plane of meeting stands in the most natural and intimate connection with the action and progress of the storm, and with the relative velocity and direction of the wind of both currents; and from its angle of inclination to the earth's surface, in connection with the ascertained velocity of the prevailing current, the velocity and strength of the approaching current may be calculated. Its position relatively to the storm and to the places of observation may be determined by the clouds.

Although, however, the plane of meeting has great advantages over the gradient, it is in the prediction of polar storms or the winds from the northern semicircle almost as useless. Approximately we might, from the velocity of the prevailing equatorial current, draw conclusions as to the angle of inclination of the plane of meeting and the strength of the coming polar wind, but accurately we can do nothing, as the angle of inclination of the plane of meeting can only be definitely determined by observations north of the region of low barometer. The clouds are, however, safe guides, and, for practical purposes, of the highest importance, especially at sea, where all conclusions must be drawn from individual observations.

The Signal Service Bureau says, "the extremely steep gradients occur in nearly all the great tropical hurricanes and typhoons. The storm-disk is of small dimensions within the tropics." This directly corroborates our assertion that the storms in the tropics are similar to those of higher latitudes. (See chapter on "Storms of the torrid zone.")

The observation that "during the progress of the cyclone the gradients are, however, undergoing important changes," is corroborative of our theory of the changes of the plane of meeting during the oscillation of a storm. But the cause which is assigned for these changes is in itself more an effect than a cause. The Signal Service says, "In general it may be stated that the formation of new gradients during the progress of the storm will depend upon the amount, rapidity and area of the rain-fall or snow-fall accompanying the progressive depression. The greater the amount of precipitation in a given number of hours, the more marked will be the fall of the mercury in the barometer, and the greater will be the indraught of cyclonic winds, and hence the greater the wind velocity."

Now, this explanation is defective, because the rain-fall, itself left without a cause, is made the cause of the phenomena of which it is in the most part the effect. In the consideration of the changes of the plane of meeting during storm-oscillations, it was shown that the plane of meeting becomes more vertical—*i. e.*, "new" and greater "gradients" are formed—owing to the banking up of the polar current; and this causes the uprushing equatorial air—which produces the "depression" and "the fall of the mercury"—to reach more quickly the region at which condensation takes place, the rain-fall for this reason being more profuse. The increase of rain-fall in turn assists the operation by liberating latent heat, but it is not at all the original cause. Similar reasoning, of course, will apply to the converse proposition where the "new gradients" are found to be less, with a reduced precipitation.

---

The monthly weather reviews given in Gen. Myer's report contain much valuable and interesting matter corroborative of our theory; extracts are given in Appendix F from those for July, August and September, 1874.

Extended remarks on these extracts are unnecessary; any one who has followed us thus far will see their general bearing. A few points, however, may possibly escape attention.

The July review indicates distinctly the oscillation north and south of the *belts* of high and low pressure and the difference of their movement over sea and land. It says: "A comparison of the months of June and May shows that the area of mean low barometer" (the belt of low pressure of the temperate zone) "has moved slowly to the north-eastward, and that it now extends over the centre of the continent; in the mean time, the barometric pressure" (the tropical belt of high pressure) "has increased"—*i. e.*, gone farther north—"in the southern and south-eastern portions of the country, which is now within the limits of the increased area of high barometer, extending over the Atlantic between the twenty-fifth and fortieth degrees of latitude. During the last three months there has been a gradual increase of pressure in the region last named, the direction of increase being westward from the Atlantic, while during the same time there has been but little change in the mean barometric readings of the central depression."

The Signal Service in the report of 1874 has made a great advance from the report of the preceding year by recognizing an intimate connection between areas of high and of low barometer, although, since barometric observations are the chief reliance of meteorology, and the "depressions" are thought to be the *storms*, they have not been able to discover what the connection is, nor how the depressions differ from each other.

Among the July areas of low barometer, No. VII., which is evidently the region of low barometer of a north-east storm, is observed to move "almost directly east," displacing an area of high barometer—the polar current; which is noted as an exception to the rule that "generally it has been observed that the relative positions of the areas of high and low barometer materially affect the course of the latter, and that the former seem to deflect the latter from their mean tracks."

According to this, the Signal Service has found that in summer in our latitude the depressions generally are displaced by areas of high barometer—*i. e.*, that in the summer-storms the region of low barometer travels in front of the region of high barometer of the displacing polar current, and this sustains our position regarding the south-east storms. The exception, however, that they find is evidently a north-east storm, which is more or less unusual in midsummer in our latitude. The summer of 1874 was, however, unusually cool, and a northern wind mostly prevailed, indicating that the arctic belt of high pressure extended uncommonly far south over the continent of North America. The storms, therefore, were to a considerable extent the displacement of the polar current by the equatorial, and the frequency of these north-east storms during this summer induced me to change their title of "winter storms" in my former classification to the more general one of "equatorial storms;" for although they are characteristically winter storms, they also occur during the summer, and in this case the temperature is low. Whether we have in the temperate zone an equatorial winter or a polar summer depends on the location of the arctic belt of high pressure, the polar current, and the belt of low pressure, the equatorial current *c* of *Plate V.*

The south-east storm is fully shown in "area of high barometer No. IV." of the July review, of which it is said: "During the 28th, 29th, 30th and 31st this area moved from the north-west to the South Atlantic coast, succeeding the depression, which was attended by unusual rains in the Eastern and Middle States." Here we see the displacing polar current moving forward as an "area of high barometer," with its region of low barometer in advance, and producing the copious rain-fall characteristic of a south-east storm.

The "local storms" for the month show themselves to be of the same kind, since it is said: "Their occurrence seems to depend upon the relative distribution of barometric pressure considered in relation to the topography of the country. . . . From an examination of a large number of reports referring to these storms, it is shown that the regions of severity were limited in area, and that the storms uniformly approached from the north-west." These "local storms" will be noted as coming from the same quarter as the areas of high barometer; and were their dates definitely given, they would doubtless be seen to have travelled in front of areas of high barometer. Areas of high barometer Nos. II. and III. would thus with "local storms" be complete south-east storms.

Taking together area of high barometer No. I. and area of low barometer No. II., which the Signal Service notes as travelling in connection to the west, we have a fine example of a south-east storm (here south-west or west) of the torrid zone, produced by the currents *b* and *c* (*Plates V.* and *X.*) of the tropical belt of high pressure, which over the Atlantic seems to have lain to the east or north-east of this region. These two currents appear to have joined together to displace the current *b′* in the manner described when treating of the storms of the torrid zone. This movement seems at the same time to have started an advance of the polar current *N* of *Plate V.*, with area of low barometer No. III. in its front. The connection of these movements seems to have been recognized by the Signal Service, since they say that the "area of high barometer"—the tropical belt of high pressure—"which had previously extended over the districts on the Atlantic coast, . . . now moved to the south and westward, apparently drawing the depression"—No. III.—"toward the coast in the most direct line." The connection of the storms of the torrid and the temperate zones is here exhibited.

In considering the other storms given in the three weather reviews, it will be noted that those which we recognize as south-east storms are the most severe and destructive; as for instance area of low barometer No. X., for July, which destroyed many lives and much property at Pittsburg. This storm bears the south-east characteristics, even down to a dividing of the area of low barometer.

Similar interesting cases are to be found in the August and September reviews, including quite striking instances of colliding storms similar to those of New Jersey and Nova Scotia in August, 1873.

Nos. III. and IV. of the September areas of low barometer are valuable examples of parallel and simultaneous storms over the continental and the oceanic storm-tracks. (See *Plate X.*)

Possessing a complete system of storm-tracks over this continent, the Signal Service, having once recognized the intimate relation between the areas of high and low barometer and the guiding influence of the former on the latter, will soon find that they are organic parts of a storm, and not independent phenomena. It will be found that a "depression" or an area of low barometer is not a storm, but the *effect* of a storm—*i. e.*, the effect of a conflict of the two opposing aërial currents.

# CHAPTER X.

## *WEATHER PROGNOSTICS FROM THE CLOUDS, WITH SPECIAL HINTS FOR NAVIGATORS.*

THE changes and movements of the atmosphere are embodied so manifestly in the clouds that it requires only a little study of the different forms of these to be able to foreknow, for all practical purposes, approaching changes of the weather.

Those who understand the general laws of atmospheric disturbance will be able without difficulty to supply for themselves the guides for their observations, but the main rules are here given. They are particularly applicable to that portion of the United States lying on the Middle Atlantic coast, but with modifications easily supplied will apply to other localities.

### *NORTH-EAST STORMS.*

*Characteristic Cloud, Stratus.* (*Plate VI.*)

During winter the meteorological phenomena are the most simple, and therefore the easiest to comprehend. At this season that part of the aërial sea which mostly flows over the temperate zone comes from the arctic regions, and is, therefore, cold. It may come from any direction of the northern semicircle—west, north-west, north, north-east or east; in most places, however, it blows from the north-west or north-east.

If it comes over the sea from north-east or east, it is a moist, cold wind. If it comes from the west, or north-west, or north, it is a dry, cold wind. In Europe these circumstances are to some extent reversed.

The sky being serene and clear, the wind steady and northerly, no change of weather is to be expected until a long, hazy stripe of cloud appears above the horizon in the southern semicircle of the heavens, toward the south, south-west or west. Sometimes in the autumn these clouds also come from south-east, but in this case seldom mount very high and generally soon retire, so that the storm does not reach us. A little later in the season the stripes come from the south and are stretched out from west to east in the direction of *a b*. (*Fig.* 18.) During the middle of the winter and most of the season they come from the south-west, and are stretched out in the direction of *a′ b′*. During the spring, and sometimes also during the summer,* they come from the west, and are stretched out from north to south in the direction of *a″ b″*. Such a hazy, scarcely visible stripe of cloud is the herald of the coming north-east storm, which, in the middle of winter, will arrive in about two or three days from the first appearance of the cloud, and in spring and autumn in about one day. The time depends on season and place.

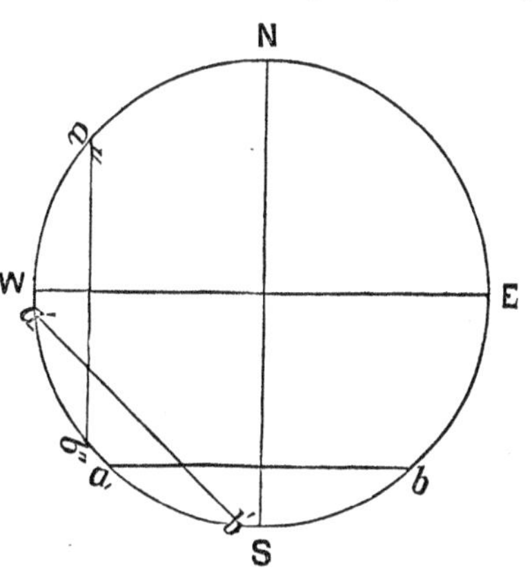

Fig. 18.

These storms are commonly called north-east storms, and occur mostly during the winter. They travel always against the prevailing wind.

The first stripe of cloud is soon followed by a second and more distinct one, which lies parallel with the first. These are followed by others, each one being always a little more distinct than the one before, and a little broader and closer to it. At last these stripes follow so closely and are so thick that they

* Notably in the summer of 1874.

form an unbroken screen of cloud, which mounts higher, following the stripes, until it covers the whole sky.

The first stripes disappear gradually and slowly below the north-eastern horizon in the same order as they rose in the south-west.

When they are about to sink below the horizon, and sometimes before this, the polar current which is then prevailing begins to freshen, and blows more strongly toward the coming storm, as if it would oppose its passage. It then generally begins slightly to snow or rain, and the snow-flakes are blown obliquely toward the storm. The fall of snow or rain increases and the wind becomes more violent as the crisis of the storm approaches. When this has arrived, the temperature begins to rise, and the wind dies away, the snow or rain falling vertically; we are then in the region of meeting of the two opposing currents—the area of lowest barometer. It is stretched out in the same direction as the stripes were.

As the region of calm passes the wind begins again to blow, but from a southerly direction, the opposite to that which it previously had. At the *edges* of the storm, however, it does not grow calm, but the change from northerly to southerly takes place gradually in the same direction as the motion of a fish's fins or the oars of a boat—that is, on the right margin (looking in the direction taken by the clouds) of the storm it will change in the direction in which the hands of a watch move, and on the left margin in the opposite direction; in the first instance from northerly to *easterly* to southerly, and in the second from northerly to *westerly* to southerly. This change occupies sometimes half an hour, sometimes half a day or longer. Frequently, when it is of short duration, it is interrupted by sudden gusts, and in all cases, when the change is finally effected, the wind blows more furiously than before, and its temperature has markedly risen. The storm is now near its end; and if its forward movement still continues, it will soon begin to clear somewhere in the southern semicircle of the sky, the clouds having all passed over.

As is generally the case, however, in winter storms in the latitude of Philadelphia, the most southerly limit of the storm does not pass over before a return oscillation takes place. The temperature in this case falls as the region of calm passes back again, and the wind changes to its original direction in the reverse order to that in which its first change took place. In the course of a few hours, or possibly half a day, the clouds will begin to rise from the horizon somewhere in the northern semicircle of the heavens, keeping more or less the stratified arrangement they had in their forward movement. The clouds thus dissolve until the whole heaven is clear, leaving us again in the prevailing polar current, with no change of weather to be expected until the long, hazy stripes again appear in the south.

Sometimes these stripes have not yet passed over us before the return oscillation begins, and then they are seen to sink below the southern horizon as they came above it. In the latitude of Philadelphia, however, they generally return the same or the following day; and there sometimes occur several of these forward and backward oscillations before the storm passes over and precipitation takes place.

It may happen during the continuance of a storm that several short oscillations take place in quick succession, and then the places over which the region of calm passes will experience successive rapid changes of wind and temperature.

The backward oscillation of a storm sometimes takes place with something of the motion of an eccentric wheel, so that if the left margin has passed over us in the forward movement, the right margin will pass over us in the backward movement, and the wind will then veer through the whole compass.

The direction that storms take in their backward oscillations is dependent on place and season, which also modifies other phenomena.

The moon shining through the hazy advance stripes of a north-east storm produces what is commonly called a *halo*. This is correctly considered an indication of coming stormy weather, but almost invariably the stripes themselves give the same indication before they rise high enough to produce this phenomenon.

### *South-East Storms.*

*Characteristic Cloud, Cumulo-Stratus.* (*Plate VIII.*)

The south-east or summer storms do not send their warning clouds—the cumulo-stratus—so far in advance as the north-east storms, but they do not extend over so large a territory, and travel much more slowly, especially when about to become destructive.

When, on a sultry, cloudless summer day, what wind is stirring comes from the southern semicircle of the horizon, mostly from south-west or south, a change is to be looked for from the northern semicircle, particularly from the north-west.

Any change in this direction announces itself by a long black bank of cloud called cumulo-stratus, in which globular masses of clouds are arranged in a long line, heaped upon each other and side by side, stretched out from west to east or from south-west to north-east. This bank of clouds rises slowly above the horizon, accompanied by lightning and continuously rolling thunder. As it rises higher a grayish sheet appears beneath, screening the sky between it and the horizon.

If the clouds rise rapidly, the storm will pass quickly and is not dangerous. In about a half hour after the first appearance of the cloud the prevailing wind rises and blows toward the storm; then follows a lull or calm, during which the dust is observed to rise and fly in sudden gusts, now toward the storm, and then in the opposite direction.

This calm does not last so long as in the north-east storm, and suddenly a colder air is felt coming from the direction of the storm-cloud. The wind has changed on the ground, but in higher regions, as is seen by the smoke from chimneys, is still blowing toward the storm, changing also, however, as the storm progresses. This change of wind takes place in the same order, relatively to the direction in which the storm travels, as in the north-east storm.

It now suddenly begins to rain or hail, generally quite copiously, and sometimes in such quantities that it is colloquially called "a cloud-burst."

The rain does not, however, last so long as in the north-east storm; frequently in an hour or two it slackens or stops entirely.

When the wind changes around again, the storm is retiring, and this change will now be seen first in higher regions. The clouds disappear or dissolve in the advancing more heated equatorial current, and soon the temperature of before the storm is re-established. If, however, the storm does not retire, but passes over us, it will clear in the north, and the temperature will be lower than before the storm.

If the storm is almost stationary for several hours before reaching us, it may not come at all; but if it should, a tornado may originate if the configuration of the ground is favorable. A whirling motion in the clouds on the western edge will announce a tornado or a hail-storm, which will travel in the direction in which the clouds extend laterally.

## *Local Storms.*

*Characteristic Cloud, Cumulus.* (*Plate III.*)

The local storms, the short summer showers of the temperate zone, develop themselves, when no lateral currents are present, around and above us, being the product of a vertically rising current. If lateral currents exist, they modify more or less the position of this rising column of air.

These storms are first seen in round specks of fleecy cloud, *cumuli* (*Plate III.*, *Fig.* 1), which grow gradually larger and unite into a mountainous mass, which, if undisturbed by lateral currents, soon precipitates its moisture in rain more or less copiously.

The temperature is not generally much affected, nor for long, and the change of the wind is only temporary, it blowing from all quarters toward the rising current.

When local storms originate in the polar current, they sometimes appear underneath the long, hazy stripes of a slowly-advancing north-east storm, producing a very picturesque effect.

These storms cannot be foreseen very long by the clouds, but are of little importance in the temperate zone. Principally in them is the barometer of use as a predicter, especially in the torrid zone, where they attain very great proportions, but the clouds will indicate them almost as early.

They are accompanied by lightning and short, quick explosions of thunder.

---

The movements of the atmosphere are much more simple on sea than on land, taking place over a much less variegated surface; the forms of the clouds are, therefore, more distinct and characteristic, and for the same reason the aërial currents are to be found mostly in their undeflected courses. The principal modifying influences are the warm ocean currents, icebergs or the proximity of land.

The embodiment of our principles in specific rules for navigation must of course be done by experienced navigators, but an attempt is here made to cover the general ground.

In the first place, it is deduced from our principles that the Rotary or Cyclone theory is radically wrong, and the rules for navigators which are based on it worse than useless.

These rules assume a circular area of low barometer in the centre of the storm, but my own investigations in 1851 convinced me that the area of lowest barometer is elongated, and sometimes bent into a curve; and recent investigations by the United States Signal Service Bureau, Prof. Loomis, Hildebrandsson, Ley, Meldrum and others have conclusively confirmed this. Mr. Meldrum "has published a treatise to prove that cyclones are not circular but elliptical in shape, formed between two opposing currents of air," and states that the rules based on its being circular frequently carry vessels into the dangerous section instead of around it. He cites the startling fact that "on February 25, 1860, forty-one vessels left the roadstead of Réunion with a south-easterly wind, which, according to the old law of storms, placed the vortex to the north-east, and these vessels sailed to the north-west to avoid it. The result demonstrated that the central vortex was really to the north-north-west, so that they ran directly into it, and only four of them, one a steamer, succeeded in crossing the storm-path. As for the remaining thirty-seven, only seven escaped total loss or very great injury." *

The existing rules divide the storm into a "dangerous semicircle" and a "manageable semicircle," which in *Fig.* 19 would be respectively *a b c d* and *a f e d*, the arrow-heads at these letters indicating the supposed course of the wind, and the small circle in the centre being the supposed region of calm, the *most* dangerous part of the storm. There is no question that some parts of the storm are more dangerous than others, but the Cyclone theory misplaces them.

It has been shown, particularly in the case of the West Cambridge tornado, that the equatorial current is destructive and the polar relatively protective, the tendency of the former being upward and lifting, of the latter downward and steady-

* I am obliged to rely for these quotations on a newspaper paragraph, having unsuccessfully endeavored to obtain Mr. Meldrum's treatise; the same facts can, however, be abundantly proved from other sources.

W. B.

ing. The dangerous region is, therefore, in the equatorial current, and the manageable region in the polar current. If, now, a vessel should happen to be placed just in front of the polar current, the equatorial wind would manifestly force her upper portion in one direction, while the pressure of the polar current on the water would force her hull in the opposite direction, both actions tending to throw the ship on her side; the

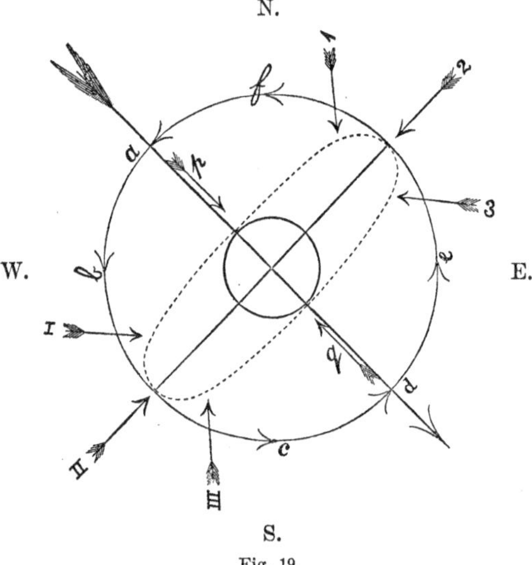


Fig. 19.

region between the two currents, which is the region of calm or of uprising air, is, therefore, the *most* dangerous part of the storm, and here the waves are highest, for reasons stated in treating of the subject previously. In the figure, whose direction is that of a south-east storm, the dangerous region is that over which the wind indicated by the arrows III *q* 3 blows, 90° from the location given to it by the Cyclone theory, which is the imaginary semicircle *a b c d*. The manageable region would be that over which the wind I *p* 1 blows, and *not* the imaginary semicircle *a f e d*. It will also be noted that the most dangerous region, enclosed by the dotted line, is much more extensive than the circle to which the Cyclone theory would confine it.

In the temperate zone, if the cumulo-stratus, indicating a south-east storm, is seen above the southern horizon, there is no danger, because the storm will go south. If it appears in the north, it will approach with the dangerous region in advance, and it is wisest to sail by the shortest course to the outside of the track, guided by the position of the cloud and its progressive direction. If the storm is yet distant, this will probably be easy. If, however, a vessel should find herself immediately in front of the middle of a south-east storm not yet fully developed, the wisest course is probably to sail straight through the region of calm into the polar current.

The direction in which the cumulo-stratus is outstretched, the velocity with which it rises above the horizon and the wind in which the vessel is give all needful information to avoid danger from the storm. The line where the uniformly gray screen meets the black cloud above is the region where the two currents meet in the upper atmosphere. The rising billows of water in front of the cloud is the region of calm ($c''' d'''$ of *Plate VII., Fig.* 2) where the two currents meet on the surface of the sea. If the cloud should become stationary, there may be danger also of a whirlwind, a water-spout or a hurricane, particularly near the region of warm ocean currents, or near islands or the coast. Such a rotary storm would travel through the region of calm of the main storm in the direction of the cumulo-stratus easterly.

North-east storms are, as has been previously said, not so dangerous as south-east storms, and in addition give warning by the hazy stripes of cloud much longer in advance; but on the other hand they are more extensive, and consequently more difficult to sail out of when once involved in one.

The position of the region of danger is reversed, lying to

the rear of the region of calm, which is of course the place of *greatest* danger, as in the south-east storm. If the storm develops not far to the south of your position, it will of course not give the usual length of warning, but as a compensation will not have gathered strength. Storms are, within certain limits at least, dangerous in proportion to the distance they travel.

It may frequently happen that the course of a vessel lies near and parallel to the region of low barometer of two currents which have not sufficient moisture or force to develop into a full storm, and short oscillations may then pass back and forth over the vessel's course, producing a regular succession of calms, followed in each case by a change of wind. I experienced this in coming from Europe to America in a Cunard steamer in the autumn of 1867, where the oscillations north or south took place once every day for the greater part of the voyage with almost the regularity of clockwork. A full storm did not develop at all, but the calms followed by a change of wind were very marked, necessitating daily changes of the ship's course.

The rolling of the vessel during the calm might have been avoided by keeping altogether in the polar or the equatorial current. It seems reasonable to suppose that these oscillations may frequently be made of service toward accelerating a ship's passage, especially on the middle and north Atlantic Ocean, where their direction is north-east and south-west. Thus by keeping in the equatorial current of a north-east storm in sailing from America to Europe, a rapid passage might be made, as also in sailing from Europe to America by keeping in the polar current of a return oscillation. The clouds will indicate when this is possible.

## CHAPTER XI.

### *METEOROLOGICAL OBSERVATION.*

WE have in the foregoing pages arrived at the conclusion that storms are local disturbances of the general circulation of the atmosphere, and we have characterized and classified the different species by their origin, direction, motion and clouds. It was clearly demonstrated in the destruction by the West Cambridge tornado and other storms that wind in general does not rotate, but flows in more or less straight lines, modified by local circumstances, and when in the case of loco-progressive storms it is forced into rotation, the rotary column is of very small extent. With these principles, and recognizing a storm as an individual and definite phenomenon developing itself around us, the method of investigation to be followed suggests itself.

Investigation must embrace, as far as possible, the *whole* of each individual storm from its very beginning, through all stages of its development, to the end, and the investigator must therefore be enabled to overlook at any moment the different meteorological changes over the whole extent of disturbance. This he can only do by means of assistants stationed at the most favorable points over the storm-track, and in telegraphic communication with him and under his control.

The necessity of such a course is now generally acknowledged, and clearly set forth by Prof. Mohn in his answer to the six questions of the Leipzig Conference, with the practical difficulties standing in the way of its execution. The importance of the subject, however, has induced several European countries and the United States to create government meteorological observatories, whose duty it is to determine and signal the rain areas and storms in advance to the different cities and harbors, and to investigate and establish the laws of meteorological phenomena.

From the principles we have enunciated, methods of foretelling rain areas and the position of storms are easily deduced.* For according to the state of moisture along the line *c d* (*Plate VII.*), and the difference of temperature north and south of it, condensations and precipitations must be formed around it and far to the north, where the two opposing currents overlap each other, particularly in north-east storms. It is then necessary to determine on the map the line *c d*, which may be described by uniting the localities at which the barometer stands lowest, since, as has before been explained, the line described on the earth's surface by the plane of meeting of the two currents is the line of lowest barometer. Having ascertained the position and direction of this line of lowest barometer, and the state of moisture and temperature surrounding it, we can without difficulty indicate on the map the area of rain. Knowing the velocity with which this line travels, which is easily obtained, its movements and positions can be calculated and the rain areas mapped out in advance.

Another more mechanical method can also be deduced. We know from those laws, that the area of cloud formation, or condensation and precipitation, is found above the region of calm, or the rising equatorial current along *c d* (*Plate VII.*), and extends over the inclined plane to the isobar of highest barometer in front and underneath the point *b*, and to the isobar of highest barometer in the rear of the rising equatorial current.

The rain area is to be found thus between the isobars of high-

* The principles, the application of which was evident, were given in the article published in the New York *Times*, in 1852 (see Appendix A), copies of which were furnished at the time to Prof. Henry and Lieut. Maury, in Washington.

est barometer surrounding the line of lowest barometer. The central observer, having telegraphic reports from his subordinates all over the country from three to eight times each day, giving the pressure, humidity, temperature, wind, etc., is able to establish on the map the isobars, and to foresee their movements, and consequently the areas of rain and cloud formation and the extent, character and movements of the storm.

Of all the governmental bureaus of meteorological observation that have yet been established, America is fortunate in possessing the most efficient for practical results. This is not alone due to the admirable organization of the United States Signal Service, but principally perhaps to the unequalled facilities it enjoys. It is more than all others favored by the extent, geographical position and configuration of the territory over which it is able to station observers. In connection with the British possessions and the West Indies, telegraphic reports may be had from all quarters of a territory extending from the torrid almost to the frigid zone, and in longitude over a sixth part of the earth's circumference, and embracing within its limits a system of storms of all kinds. Over this area storms develop and progress with great regularity, and there is not a north-east storm originates but that the Signal Service predicts its coming and its rain area. South-east storms, however, are not comprehended by the Cyclone theory, and the Signal Service, therefore, although it seems to have observed their parts separately, has mistaken them for *local* storms, or has classed their polar currents under the head of inexplicable "anti-cyclones."

The European Meteorological Institutions labor under great disadvantages, and owe their efficiency entirely to the ability and untiring exertions of eminent scientists like Dove, Mohn, Buys-Ballot, Toynbee or Scott, who, in spite of the great difficulties that exist, have nevertheless discovered some of the characteristics of the south-east storm. The limited area controlled by each institution affords it the means for observing only a part of each storm, and the diversity of language and custom obstructs ready international communication.

The results at which individual scientists have arrived thus seem, in many cases at least, to be the local expression of the general law. As instance it would appear that Buys-Ballot's law of the change of wind in a storm is probably the expression of the general law as applied to the right margin of north-east storms in their passage over North-western Europe. It is not unlikely that Holland lies in the right side of a regular north-east storm-track.

Prof. Buys-Ballot seems himself to feel that his law has no general application, as the following extract from his answers to the questions of the Leipzig Conference will show. He says:

"Although, since my communication to the Royal Academy at Amsterdam, in October, 1850, the latest French, English and American bulletins and maps have in general confirmed my opinion, advanced at that time, that the wind in the northern hemisphere takes such a direction as will place the region of lowest barometer to its left, and that it blows the stronger the greater the difference is, and that, however, the east wind does not become so strong in our latitude as the west wind, which may become very dangerous when the difference between Vlyssingen or Maestricht and Groningen and Helder amounts to 4 *mm.* or more; and although I have deduced theoretically in the year 1860 these results, which at first were only statistical, I do not any longer hold the practical significance of the same to be of so preponderant value. Formerly I thought that vessels should not sail out when there was a difference of 4 *mm.* in one hundred and fifty kilometres somewhere, and did not consider enough the loss of time by this delay; on the other hand, there is no sufficient guarantee that vessels which sail out when the wind inclines to the east will reach the end of the channel before this wind has been displaced again by westerly wind. I believe that the seaman himself is the only judge of the practical value of this rule."

After further remarks Prof. Buys-Ballot goes on to say:

"But if the above-mentioned rule should prove to be still the best, we would not have answered the very much more important question of Prof. Dove, which is: 'How many kinds of storms are there, how do the depressions of the air-column originate?' for of course these do not make their appearance independently, but are caused by former air-currents of the width of the polar and equatorial currents. To solve this problem a knowledge of the distribution of the winds and the pressure over the whole hemisphere and of the upper currents seems to be necessary. Nothing is so interesting in this regard as this question, but who will before long give the answer? There is besides also necessary the consideration of the direction of the mountain ranges, the outline of the continent, etc.; the whole problem is so complicated and the observations so insufficient, that we may congratulate ourselves if we contribute something to make the solution easier for posterity."

Prof. Mohn says in his answer, "*The chief problem in meteorology is, then, the law of the variation of atmospheric pressure.*"

Dove, Buys-Ballot and Mohn thus delineate the main problem of modern meteorology and indicate a path toward its solution, not concealing the great difficulties they foresee. If I presume to tread a different path, I must not be understood as slighting the advice of so able and experienced scientists; but my course of investigation, having fortunately been somewhat different from the ordinary, has led more quickly and easily to definite results.

It would seem not only reasonable, but necessary, to investigate the *individual* disturbances and their probable connection with each other from the equator to the arctic regions, by placing trained observers over what are ascertained to be the ordinary storm-tracks. They should particularly be placed at those points which seem to be most associated with the origin or development of storms, as for instance the Bermudas, West Indies, South America, and many other places, and especial attention should be given to the influence of localities. Storms being local disturbances, the position and configuration of continents, of large bodies of water or of islands in mid-ocean have most important effects.

Thus we should learn definitely the positions of the different belts of high and low pressure and the extent of their oscillations when locally disturbed in storms, or the distribution of the winds.

There should be international co-operation, and meteorological corps should be divided into two, a stationary division for the purpose of predicting and signalling the weather, and a movable division, composed of the most intelligent observers, for purposes of investigation.

Observations should be *continuous* during periods of disturbances; three observations in a day at definite periods, as formerly, or eight, as advised by the Vienna Congress, necessitate averages which I am convinced will never solve the main problem as to the different kinds of storms and their causes.

A single observer making continuous observations will come nearer the truth, for he has an opportunity to observe, during the precious moments of the passage of the region of low barometer, the meteorological contrasts and characteristics of a storm, which may escape notice during the interval between periodical observations. Storms do not accommodate us as to time and place. Mr. Wise during forty years made frequent balloon ascensions, and observed but twice the phenomena he relates, although they exist, I am certain, at all times, changing place only in the oscillations of the plane of meeting.

Mr. F. Gaster, of the London Meteorological Office, who seems to have considerable experience in storm-prognostics, in his answer to the six questions of the Leipzig Conference says: "My opinion is that the reports from many stations are capable of an improvement in regard to number as well as quality. I know of many instances in which after the observations at eight A. M. and two P. M. (at Valencia) the barometer at the last time began to rise, while an observation at twelve o'clock would have shown that the barometer, having risen up to that hour, began rapidly to fall, and that in this way storms have been overlooked which would doubtless have been noticed at the central office, where the weather is observed continuously."

It has been elsewhere shown that storms have in every probability been overlooked in the same way here in America, as in the case of the south-east storm in connection with our coast storms or with the tornado in Iowa and Illinois.

The different means for gathering information and meteorological instruments would appear to me to assume different values from those now assigned to them. Not where the storms are the most violent, and therefore the most complicated, as on the eastern coast of America, do we find the most valuable facts, but in the direction from which they come, the south-west or north-west. Places which have to storms a similar connection as Prospect Hill had to the West Cambridge tornado are important for investigations, and should decide the distribution of observers. Signal Service bureaus should also have one or two steamers and an experienced aëronaut at their disposal. Among the meteorological elements, the real direction of the wind is the most difficult to arrive at, especially at observatories above cities or near mountains and coasts, and wind observations are therefore in general the least reliable.

With regard to meteorological instruments, the thermometer, measuring a primary effect, is, with the hygrometer, at least as important as the barometer.

Since the year 1660, when Otto von Guerike, in Magdeburg, first predicted a storm by the sinking of his water barometer, this instrument has been in better repute as a storm indicator than it deserves. The weather-marks along the scale, once trusted, are not now much more relied on than the predictions of the almanacs, it is true, but to the navigator the barometer is still the only guide that science supplies.

We have shown that the barometer is valuable as an indicator chiefly in local storms alone, and that even then the formation of cumuli will tell the tale almost as soon. It is next of value as predicting north-east storms, but it is here generally a day at least behind the clouds. In the south-east and the loco-progressive storms it only begins to show the storm when it has already, to a great extent, passed by, and hours after it has been revealed by the clouds.

It is thus in only the most insignificant of the storms of the temperate zone that the barometer gives warning in advance of the clouds, and in the most dangerous and destructive it gives no warning at all.

Its shortcoming in the case of the south-east storms is acknowledged by Prof. Mohn, Mr. Gaster and others. Prof. Mohn says that he cannot indicate storms coming from north-west, and from north-east from the Arctic Sea, and storms in which the gradient becomes very great in consequence of the sinking of the barometer in the neighboring country, while in Norway it is rising. Mr. Gaster says: "Gradients are very useful, but just the greatest gradients rather accompany the storms than precede them, so that in telegraphing storm warnings the state of the weather may have essentially changed before the warning reaches its destination." Those storms in which the gradients—*i. e., the plane of meeting*—become greater—*i. e., more vertical*—and which come from the north-west or the north-east, are without the least doubt our south-east storms, and therefore cannot be predicted by the barometer, as is evident. These storms have escaped the vigilance of the United States Signal Service for the same reasons, and yet they are the most destructive of all and the most important to be predicted. Instruments are unquestionably very valuable in scientific research, but it does not do to depend exclusively on them, to the neglect of the visible phenomena that nature presents; and so it is that the clouds tell us much of which the barometer, useful as it is, gives no sign.

To give a practical illustration of their superiority over the barometer as a predicter alone, we may take the case of the storm of April 14 to 18, 1873, which we have already used in another connection. The maps of the Signal Service report show the isobars more or less parallel from north-west to south-east, diminishing in pressure gradually from the great lakes to Dakota. Now, connecting the gradual diminution of pressure shown in these isobars with the plane of meeting, the lowest isobar indicating the line *c d* of *Plate VII., Fig.* 1, and the highest the point *b*, it will be readily seen that the clouds would have been visible at the lakes before the barometer indicated any diminution of pressure, and at the same time that the lowest isobar made its appearance in Dakota.

The clouds not only tell us of the coming of the storm, but they tell us also from whence it comes, what position we are in toward its track, the winds to be expected, the changes of temperature, and many other things important to comfort and safety.

To the scientific investigator they can be of the greatest service. They give him information of the state of the atmosphere at heights which he cannot reach without a balloon, they tell him of the motion of the upper and lower currents of a storm while yet it is at a distance—the humidity conditions on both sides of the plane of meeting—approximately, at least, the temperature. More than all this, they give the means to establish exactly the difference in pressure over the storm-area, or the gradient, which seems to be the main problem of modern meteorology.

Prof. Buys-Ballot asks: "By the position of the aëroklinoskope I give exactly a gradient, but which one?" I answer that the clouds will tell whether it is the gradient of the main storm-producing current or that of the margin.

For in the *plane of meeting* we have the embodiment and realization of the true gradient, whose direction and position is made visible by the clouds, and whose inclination even is sometimes marked by the sheet of mist often existing in the region of meeting of the opposing currents. This sheet of mist is probably in existence more frequently than I am now prepared to affirm, but is mostly to be seen in south-east storms. Sometimes it is rolled up by the equatorial current into stripes running downward from the cumulo-stratus, giving the appearance, as described by one of the witnesses of the West Cambridge tornado, "as if the sun was drawing water."

Mr. Wise evidently came into this mist at a height of fifty-four hundred feet (see his description in the Appendix), and it will be noted that as he rose into it the temperature became higher.

This mist sometimes also becomes visible in a north-east storm, particularly when in the return oscillation a polar current comes from the north-west and rolls it up into long hazy stripes inclined toward the ground at the angle of the plane of meeting. The upper cloud, the stratus, is then seen extended from north-west to south-east, while the vapory stripes underneath in the plane of meeting are at an angle to it. If we could measure the heights of these clouds respectively, we should have data for calculating the depth of the two currents.

What fossils are to the geologist the *clouds* should be to the meteorologist. For practical purposes, however, it is only necessary to have a knowledge of their different forms and their transformations. To gain this knowledge is quite easy, needing only careful observation.

In the temperate zone the best time to begin the study is in January or February, when some of the irregularities of the earth's surface are obliterated by the snow, and when the horizontal air-currents, producing the progressive storms and their clouds, are less disturbed by upward currents. The phenomena presented at this time are therefore most simple and most typical. The experience gained in the repeated forward and backward oscillation of these currents will prepare the student for the more complicated influences and effects which the vertically rising currents, the originators of local storms, bring into the consideration as the season advances. A year's observation will acquaint him with the cycle of phenomena and make him a reliable weather-prophet, at least for every-day purposes.

Is it not beautiful that in the clouds are pictured all the workings of the atmosphere around us—that Nature gives thus unmistakable warnings of the storms which she is about to send? Meteorology should be the most popular and the most generally cultivated of the sciences. To observe and understand most of the phenomena that are presented we do not even need the apparatus of the scientist; Nature herself has provided us with instruments sufficient for the purpose. With practice our lungs will serve as a barometer, telling by easier or more difficult breathing whether there has been a change of pressure; our sensitiveness to heat and cold will suffice for a thermometer, and hygrometers are abundant.

Of course there is a large field left for the scientific investigator which cannot be occupied by the general observer; but for ordinary purposes the pursuit of the study by the means Nature gives us will be productive of much enjoyment and the greatest usefulness in the preservation of health and comfort.

# APPENDIX.

## APPENDIX A.

[*From the New York Daily Times, November* 18, 1852.]

### NEW THEORY OF STORMS, BY WM. BLASIUS.

THESE phenomena in our atmosphere, which sometimes prove a blessing, sometimes a calamity, and which constitute the weather, have in all ages and in all civilized nations attracted the attention of the intelligent, but never more so than at the present day. The importance of a knowledge of the true laws which regulate those destructive motions of the atmosphere which interfere so much with our comfort, and which are called storms, tempests, hurricanes, tornadoes, water-spouts, etc., increase in proportion to the increase of commerce and navigation. Who is not painfully affected in seeing that, according to Lloyd's list of shipwrecks, the average loss of ships at sea amounts to seven every day? If at one glance we could overlook the long lists of disasters that have occurred on our great lakes and on our extensive sea-coasts which are recorded every day in the newspapers, we would perhaps be still more surprised. A knowledge of the nature and laws which govern these phenomena becomes thus of more than a mere scientific interest, for it renders us independent of them, and accidents may be prevented by a sufficient attention to such knowledge.

Two theories, *entirely opposed to each other*, have been brought forward: one is called the *Rotary*, the other the *Centripetal*, theory; and from these, rules to guide the mariner have been derived. However, from the unsettled state of these two theories, these rules are rather calculated to mislead than to assist.

The very destructive tornado which last year, on August 22, passed over Middlesex County, Massachusetts, afforded me an opportunity to obtain information from Nature herself about a phenomenon which nowhere appears so frequently or with such characteristic accompaniments as it does in this country. A minute and unprejudiced survey of the destruction occasioned by this tornado, made during four months, and a subsequent study of the north-east storms, etc., have led me to the conclusion that the above-mentioned theories are based upon partial observations. I have reason to ascribe the unsatisfactory and contradictory conclusions that have been arrived at with regard to these phenomena principally to a wrong course of pursuit in the investigation of the subject. This error, however, is one so naturally committed by all persons that I also at first made the same mistakes and arrived at similar results. It will therefore be seen that these two theories could have both been defended from the facts with regard to this very phenomenon. In adopting a more philosophical course in my investigations, and analyzing the phenomenon from its first appearance throughout the whole course with regard to the state of the atmosphere and the places over which it passed before, during and after its occurrence, I became satisfied that different phenomena have been mistaken for one and the same, and that especially tornadoes are quite different in their nature from other storms. Hence the facts exhibited in the destruction caused by tornadoes cannot be used to prove and establish a theory of storms, as has been done.

I understand by storm only a violent motion of the air caused by a tendency to re-establish its disturbed equilibrium. The general and special causes of these disturbances may be found in the ever-changing position of the sun and moon toward our globe, and from the inequalities of the surface of the latter, producing differences of temperature and moisture in the air. A difference of temperature and moisture in different places produces an exchange and a motion of the air in the direction between those places. From the fact that we find the temperature and moisture of our atmosphere decreasing in two directions, perpendicularly and horizontally, and from other special causes, arise the following different kinds of storms:

I. *Local or Centripetal Storms.*—These are caused by a tendency of the air to re-establish its equilibrium, which has been destroyed in a *perpendicular* direction. Its characteristic cloud is the *cumulus*, which is the first elementary form of clouds. In our latitude the summer shower is an example of a centripetal storm.

II. *Progressive Storms* are caused by a tendency of the air to re-establish its equilibrium, which has been destroyed in a *horizontal* direction from the equator toward the poles. They may be subdivided for our latitude into—

(*A.*) *North-east or Winter Storms*, produced by a replacing of the polar current by the equatorial current. Its characteristic cloud is a long, narrow stripe, formerly called *cirrus-stratus*, which I consider as the second elementary form, and propose the simple name *stratus*.

(*B.*) *Squalls or Summer Storms*, produced by a replacing of the equatorial current by a polar current. The characteristic cloud is a combination of the *cumulus* and *stratus*, and therefore justly called *cumulo-stratus*.

III. *Both Local and Progressive or Rotary Storms*, caused by local and special causes, combined with those in I. and II. In our latitude, tornadoes, water-spouts and some hail-storms are examples.

1. *Then as to Centripetal or Local Storms.*—Wherever the air acquires a higher temperature or a higher dew-point than the air in surrounding places, it becomes lighter and rises upward. As it rises it becomes cooled, condenses its vapor, and forms a round globular cloud above the upward current, called *cumulus*. The air at the surface then rushes in from all sides toward the place left vacant by the upward current, and produces a centripetal storm proportional in severity and extending to the generating cause. It takes place in the largest scale during the whole year, in the region of calms or continual storms near the equator, where the sun never goes far enough away to allow any cooling of the atmosphere. The two trade-winds, which extend to 25° 30′ north and south latitude, may be considered the centripetal currents of this great and continual storm. The different effect of the sun's rays upon land and water calls forth special local phenomena of a similar nature, which considerably modify this general and continual storm. Thus dead calms alternate near the equator with terrific thunder-showers. The trade-winds, flowing to places where their capacity to contain aqueous vapor constantly increases, on account of a higher temperature, preserve a constant serenity and a cloudless atmosphere; this produces, in tropical regions, the dry season. As the region of calms or constant upward currents, following the sun in his course north and southward, passes over a part of the tropical regions, the rainy season is produced. Centripetal storms take place in the temperate zone during the summer season in the more harmless form of sudden showers above islands, volcanic eruptions, *great* fires, valleys surrounded by mountains, etc., and generally above places which produce a greater amount of heat than surrounding places. They only can be formed when there is no lateral or horizontal current stronger than the upward current. They are therefore local and unable to travel to great distances, like our north-east

storms. They occur never, or at least very seldom, in the arctic regions. This upward current was observed by Aristotle, explained first by De Saussure, and lately brought forward as the sole cause of all storms by Espy.

2. *As to Progressive Storms.*—The upward current near the equator spreads in the upper region like a mushroom toward the north and south, and gradually descends in 25° 30′ north and south latitude. One part returns toward the equator, forming the trade-winds. The other part flows toward the poles, and prevails during the summer in our latitude as a south-west wind. As it comes from the equator, it is called an equatorial current. As *only* one part of the upward current returns toward the equator, a deficiency of air in the equatorial regions will cause from time to time the air from the poles to flow over the temperate zone toward the equator. This true polar current appears on the northern hemisphere like the trade-wind, as a north-east or east wind, and prevails during the winter, at least in the northern part of the temperate zone. The meeting of these two currents in the temperate zone produces a calm on the surface of the earth. Here the equatorial current rises obliquely over the polar current, and descends at the pole the second time. In this region the atmospheric pressure will be found at its minimum, and therefore the barometer lowest on account of the upward motion of the equatorial current. On the northern side of this calm will be found a cold, heavy northern wind; on the southern side of it, a warmer, lighter southerly wind. Advancing toward the north, the barometer will rise, because the depth of the polar current increases, while that of the equatorial current diminishes. The region of calm will be found during the summer nearer the arctic region than during the winter. If it could be fixed for a whole season, as it is in the Indian Ocean, by a peculiar distribution of land and water, we would have during the winter a north-east, and during the summer a south-west, monsoon. A deficiency of air at the poles will cause the equatorial current to flow thither, and in displacing the region of calm and the prevailing polar current toward the north-east will produce the north-east storms. (*A.*) A deficiency of air at the equator will cause the polar current to flow thither, and in displacing the region of calm and the prevailing equatorial current toward the tropical region will produce the squalls. (*B.*) The exchange of air between the tropical and arctic regions would take place indifferently with regard to longitude if the surface of the earth were of the same nature. But the unequal temperature above the continents, and the oceans alternating with each

other, assists the progress of one or the other current to flow, according to the season, either over the continents or the ocean. The width of the storm seems, then, to depend somewhat upon the width of the continental or oceanic road over which the progressive current advances. The direction of mountains being different—viz., in the New World from north to south, and in the Old World from west to east—renders this exchange over the United States easier. Thus the region of calm, or the centre of the storm, oscillates during all seasons in our temperate zone from north to south and from south to north. This will explain the sudden changes of temperature for which this country particularly is known; for as this region of calm passes over a place, that place must experience the contrasts on the northern and southern side of it.

(*A.*) *The North-east Storms.*—The progressive motion of the equatorial current commences first in the upper region, and may be compared to tidal waves running up a river. The top of each wave, coming into colder regions, condenses its vapor and forms a long, narrow stripe of cloud, while in the trough between them the heavens remain clear. These stripes of cloud (stratus) lie about parallel with each other, but by an optical illusion they appear to converge to two points, in the north-west and in the south-east. The appearance of the first stripe over the horizon toward the south-west is a certain indication of the approaching equatorial current, or the north-east storms. The time which elapses between the first indication and the passing over of the centre of a storm depends upon the latitude and the season. In Boston it amounts to one or two, sometimes three, days. As the equatorial current advances from warmer to cooler regions it condenses more aqueous vapor, evolves more latent caloric, becomes thus lighter and increases in its upward motion, which in its turn increases the condensation still more. The equatorial current gains thus energy by its own action, particularly upward. The increasing upward motion deprives it sooner of its vapor, and its progressive energy on the surface. On account of this and its own increasing intensity toward the north, the polar current lifts it up in flowing in the opposite direction in its season bed. As it finds in its way air which has just before discharged its aqueous vapor, and as its own capacity for aqueous vapor increases, it brings clear weather, because the clouds become dissolved and vanish before it toward the south-west. An observing person will be able to determine the changes of the weather, and especially the veering of the wind, during that time beforehand. In order to understand this, let us suppose ourselves standing in the middle of the calm, and advancing with it toward the north-east. The wind at all places along the calm will be directed toward it. As we pass with the calm over a place the north-east wind before us will be replaced by the south-west wind behind us. On the left half of the calm or the storm it will veer over the left side through north-west, on the right half of the calm over the right side through south-east. Toward the borders it will veer through smaller angles than in the middle, where we stand. If in the backward motion of the calm, or the progress of the polar current, the borders pass over the same places over which they came in the forward motion, the veering occurs in all places in the same angle, but in an opposite direction. If, however, in the backward motion the north-western half passes over that part which in the forward motion the south-eastern half passed over, we will have a complete circulation in the sense of Dove's law. Such a motion may be compared to that of an eccentric wheel. It takes place in this country during the spring and fall, when the sun displaces the meteorological phenomena toward the north and south. It takes place in the Old World more frequently, probably on account of its more rounded form.

(*B.*) *Squalls.*—During the summer, when in the temperate zone the equatorial current prevails and becomes displaced by the polar current, the changes in the wind, in temperature and atmospheric pressure take place in a similar manner as in the backward motion of the north-east storms. The effects are, however, different, because here the colder polar current finds in its way an equatorial current nearly saturated with vapor. As it proceeds, shoving like a wedge over the surface beneath the equatorial current, it forces it upward. The equatorial current, growing cooler from below and above, commences to condense its vapor, to evolve heat, and increases, therefore, its upward motion by its own action. The characteristic clouds of an upward current—the *cumuli*—become thus arranged before and over the upper margin of the polar current, and form thus that combination of the two elementary forms of cloud, the *cumulo-stratus.* Such a black bank of cloud appears at first sight when it rises over the northern horizon like a gigantic locomotive passing suddenly from west to east. This long black bank advances continually, forming itself anew with the polar current. When the upper region of contact between the two currents where it lies rises over the horizon, a more equal gray appears beneath the black cloud. It is to some extent the remaining part of those black banks which were formed before, and which had precipitated their main water already in rain, and spread now like a nimbus over the polar current; partly it is the rain which falls down from the last-formed black bank. The progressive motion decreases gradually as the supply current produced by the upward motion of the equatorial current increases. At last it stops entirely, and becomes again replaced by the prevailing equatorial current. If, during the time of greater tension between the two currents, the equilibrium at one place becomes disturbed in the region of calms, the following kind of storms are generated.

3. *Local and Progressive or Rotary Storms.*—In order to understand these storms, let us suppose the region of calm arrived, in its march from north to south, nearly at the southern limits of a plateau. Let its direction be nearly or entirely parallel to the direction of the plateau, from west to east. A valley running from the top of the plateau to the general plain, in the direction from north-west to south-east, lies at the western half of the storm where the polar current comes from north-west and the equatorial current from south-west. That part of the polar current which comes over this valley sinks down and rushes forward more rapidly than those parts west and eastward from the valley. This produces a concavity in the upper region of the polar current like the valley below, but deeper. That part of the equatorial current balancing against the down-sunken part of the polar current will, on account of greater elasticity, rush through that concavity, and will rebound and produce a whirl in that region which is to be seen by the suddenly condensed blacker cloud. As the storm advances over the wider and deeper part of that valley the concavity in the upper region deepens even more and approaches the earth. Thus air from lower regions of the equatorial current rushes into the whirl and shares in it. The whirl gradually sinks downward. When the forward-rushing part of the polar current arrives above the plane where the full equatorial current at the surface of the earth can reach it, the whirl will touch the earth and the in-rushing part produce the first destruction in the direction from south-west. The whirl will travel then in the diagonal of the parallelogram of the two currents through the region of calm which is indicated by the direction of that long black bank of cloud. It moves first in a zigzag between the two currents, and gradually turns into a straight line. This mechanical formation of the whirl will doubtless be assisted by the increase of the rarefaction in its interior, produced partially mechanically, partially by the

increasing evolution of latent caloric, and perhaps by electricity, which, by friction of air of different qualities, may be generated. The greater speed of the equatorial current increases its rotary motion; the continual acting forces of both currents increase the progressive motion of the whirl. By the increase of the rotary motion, air around the whirl joins it and increases its diameter. The progressive velocity becomes first equal to, then greater than, the combined velocity of the two currents. The whirl is thus independent of the generating currents and of their diagonal of parallelogram; it goes, in virtue of inertia, with that acquired speed against the wind. The opposing forces soon diminish its rotary and progressive motion, and dissolve it.

Thus, in the first part of the tornado, I discovered only a destruction caused by the south-west wind, which rushed into the whirl when it touched the surface. No destruction from the north to the south or no left side was to be seen. I found then a combination of these two destructive forces, the whirl and the south-west wind, partially over the same place. The destruction of the whirl extended, however, over a very small space of about thirty feet, while the whole destruction extended already over a width of three hundred paces. Two miles farther in the track indications of the left side appeared, and the destruction of the whirl extended over a greater width. In West Cambridge, about six miles farther, the whirl extended almost over the whole width of six hundred paces. It seems to me that here the progressive motion of the whirl and that of the two currents were equal, so that there the rotary motion fully developed itself. It is here where the phenomena corresponded the most with the Rotary theory developed by Mr. Redfield. But from here over Medford the progressive motion seems to have increased in such a degree that the rotary motion was scarcely to be recognized. It seemed, as Rev. Mr. Brooks in the report of his investigations at that place says, as if a vacuum had travelled and drawn all objects in its course toward it. Over this part the Centripetal theory is best developed. But to the first half of the track neither of these two theories is to be applied. From these facts, and from other reasons, I am induced to believe that both of these theories were developed from analogous places.

What the valley produces over the land is produced over the sea by the more rarefied air above islands, the Gulf Stream, etc., and thus causes the water-spouts.

If a whirl has passed along the calm, the two currents balance as before, only at a place more southward. Similar conditions in other places of that calm will cause other whirls, which travel all in the same direction. This was the case in the above-mentioned storm, and has been observed with water-spouts.

The moist air of the equatorial current, being thrown over the polar current to great heights, produces, according to the number of whirls, one or more belts of rain or hail.

Only when the peculiar state of the atmosphere, as above described, coincides with such conditions at the surface, a whirlwind will be produced. Whirlwinds are therefore bound to localities; and this is known so well by insurance companies that they do not like to insure some farms because the crops are almost regularly destroyed by hail-storms.

Whether those violent progressive storms of the tropical regions, known under the name of hurricanes and typhoons, whose north-west direction has been so well traced by Redfield and Piddington, are storms of the second or third kind can only be decided when we are presented with some more of the results of the valuable investigations of Lieut. Maury. A want of space and diagrams prevents me from giving more here than the most general results of my investigations. Details and illustrations by diagrams I hope to present to the public in the form of popular lectures.

*New York, November* 16, 1852.

---

# APPENDIX B.

## ANALYSIS OF THE WEST CAMBRIDGE TORNADO.

*Giving the survey of the track of destruction, and the general and particular facts of this survey arranged with reference to their relation to each other.*

### DESCRIPTION OF THE GROUND OVER WHICH THE TORNADO PASSED.

The surface of the earth over the track of the tornado was quite diversified, being undulating, small hills alternating with shallow valleys. The track of destruction lies between the lines *A B* and *C D*. (*Plate I., Fig.* 1.) It began at the foot of Prospect Hill, in the neighborhood of Waltham, and ran from west to east over a gentle slope, where a plateau descends into a general plain.

The general plain south of the track extends to Boston, and is from forty to sixty feet above the level of the sea. Out of this plain, and in the track, rises the plateau to a height of from one hundred and fifty to two hundred feet near Waltham, and extends northward to Maine and New Hampshire, rising gradually.

The highest southern limit of this plateau runs in the curved line *E, A, R, S, T, U, V.* At the points *E, S, T, V* the descent of the plateau into the plain is somewhat more abrupt than along the rest of the line, where the slope is quite gradual, forming valleys which run from north-west to south-east into the plain. The track ran thus alternately over small elevations and shallow valleys.

At the very beginning of the track, and west of it, rose Prospect Hill, which is the highest point in the vicinity of Boston, and rises four hundred and eighty-two feet above the level of the sea, and about two hundred and eighty feet above the plateau, to the north-east. It is several times higher than any other of the projections of the plateau into the plain, which are severally at *S, T, V.* To the south and east Prospect Hill descends rapidly into the plain. The figures 150, 70, 60, 50, 40 indicate the respective heights in feet above sea-level.

East of Prospect Hill lies the valley *M*, the first and most important of those slopes which run from the plateau toward the south-east into the general plain. The second valley, *U*, lies between the projections *T* and *V*, and is wider and shallower than *M.* The third valley is east of Baldwin's Hill, *V*, and between it and Wellington Hill, just beyond.

The hills and slopes from *R* to *S* and from *S* to *b''* were at the time of the tornado thickly covered with trees, as well to the south of the line as to the north of it. At 50 was a little grove of pine trees; in the valley *M*, along Lincoln street, east of Prospect Hill, trees were only to be found here and there; near and around the house 35 was a corn-field. The hill *T*, on its crest and on its eastern slope, was bare of trees; on the western and southern slopes it was covered with pine trees about twelve feet high. As we follow the course toward the east, we descend from the hill *T* gently into the valley *U.* Here we find a slightly undulating ground, over which bare meadows and fields offered few objects for destruction. Going farther, we rise gradually and gently toward North street, on Baldwin's Hill, *V.*

Here the destroyed orchards and buildings offer again a good picture of the directions of the destroying forces.

At the eastern slope of this hill we descend rapidly into a meadow which is the eastern limit of the survey of the first section of the tornado's track. The length of this section, from Prospect Hill to Baldwin's Hill, is about two and a half miles. East of this meadow is Wellington Hill, the fourth projection of the plateau. The first projection, *S*, of the plateau reached only to the middle of the track; the second, *T*, crossed it entirely; the third, *V*, reached still farther south. On the south-easterly descent of Wellington Hill lies West Cambridge. West of West Cambridge, about three miles from the above-described section, lay the one which I surveyed first, and where the destruction was greatest. This represents the character of the second section of the track, which extended about to the Mystic River, between West Cambridge and Medford. The third section, from the Mystic River to the end of the track, is covered by the report of the Rev. Mr. Brooks, the important part of which is given farther on. This report is a conscientious and careful description of the general appearance of the destruction, made immediately after the occurrence, and when all disturbed objects were still in the positions in which the tornado had left them. These three sections cover the whole extent of the tornado.

### GENERAL APPEARANCE AND FACTS OF THE DESTRUCTION.

In all descriptions of tornadoes the position of the destruction is determined by reference to the axis. The adherents of the Rotary and Inblowing theory agree about the position of the axis generally, however much they differ in other respects.

By the axis is understood an imaginary line drawn somewhat over the middle of the course of the track, to which the destruction from both sides of the track points, and along which the effects of the destruction are the most visible. We find in the *American Journal of Science and Arts*, 1841, vol. xli., p. 76, the following definition by Redfield: "From the causes to which I have just alluded, the effects are usually more violent on and near the line passed over by the axis than in other portions of the track. This line of greatest violence is found to coincide nearly with the line which separates the inwardly inclined prostrations of the two opposite sides of the track. The latter line, or apparent axis of the track, is sometimes called the line of convergence."

There will be no difficulty in determining the position of the axis in this tornado over the section from West Cambridge to Medford; but over the first section, from Waltham to Baldwin's Hill, it is more difficult.

By analogy, and for the sake of simplicity in the plate, the line

*E F* is made the axis, although the real axis is not straight, but the zigzag red line. The line *A B* represents the left margin, and *C D* the right margin of the track, the course being in the direction N. 72° E.

For the sake of easy reference, the individual facts brought out by the survey are arranged in numbered paragraphs.

1. The destruction was, in quantity as well as in quality, different in different localities over the length and width of the track—that is, the destruction differed in different parts of the track in amount, kind and in degree of violence.

2. Over the right side of the track the destruction was fully developed over a width of three hundred and fifty yards; whilst over the left side there was no indication of destruction over the largest portion of this section. The first indication on the left side appeared in one tree near $b''$, a little more distinctly at $b'''$, and still more at $b''''$.

3. The destruction on the right side was not evenly developed. It was exhibited in a series of distinct facts of different kinds, which repeated themselves in regular order, distinctly limited areas of destruction of a well-defined geometrical form alternating regularly with areas where no destruction took place.

4. The first area of destruction is the triangle $a\ b\ c$. The point $a$ lies south of Prospect Hill—in reality, farther west than its position on this map. It contained forty destroyed objects, principally large trees. The second area of destruction is the triangle $a'\ b'\ c'$, containing twenty destroyed objects. The third area of destruction is the triangle $a''\ b''\ c''$, containing fifty destroyed objects. The fourth area of destruction is the triangle $a'''\ b'''\ c'''$, containing thirty destroyed objects. The fifth area of destruction is the triangle $a''''\ b''''\ c''''$, containing one hundred and fifty destroyed objects.*

5. The areas which were left uninjured are the triangles $b\ d\ b'$, $b'\ d'\ b''$, $b''\ d''\ b'''$, $b'''\ d'''\ b''''$ (paragraph 11).

6. In the triangles $a'\ c\ d$, $a''\ c'\ d'$, $a'''\ c''\ d''$, etc., there was little destruction, because the extreme margin was throughout less injured than the portions toward $b$, $b'$, $b''$, etc. But in $a''\ c'\ d'$ were found a few objects lying across each other, and those which, from their direction, belonged to the most western triangle, were lying underneath, showing that they had fallen first.

* The smaller objects destroyed—as grass, shrubberies, etc.—which assisted a great deal in determining the limits of the different areas, are, of course, not included in these numbers.

7. There is a remarkable change in the form and size of these triangles as we go over this section. The distances between the apexes increase with a striking regularity, viz.:

| | | | | | | |
|---|---|---|---|---|---|---|
| The distance from | $b$ | to $b'$ | is | 400 | yards. |
| " " | $b'$ | " $b''$ | " | 700 | " |
| " " | $b''$ | " $b'''$ | " | 950 | " |
| " " | $b'''$ | " $b''''$ | " | 1200 | " |

We thus find an increase in the distance between these points of two hundred and fifty yards.*

8. The angles which the lines $a' b'$, $a'' b''$, $a''' b'''$ and $a'''' b''''$ make with the axis $EF$ grow smaller. The angle $Eb' a'$ is smaller than the angle $Ebc$; the angle $Eb'' a''$ is smaller than the angle $Eb' a'$; the angle $Eb''' a'''$ is smaller than the angle $Eb'' a''$, etc.

9. The direction in which the destroyed objects pointed in the triangles $abc$, $a' b' c'$, $a'' b'' c''$, etc., is toward the respective apexes $b$, $b'$, $b''$, etc., as the arrows in those triangles indicate.

10. From the bases of those triangles $ac$, $a' c'$, $a'' c''$, etc., toward their apexes $b$, $b'$, $b''$, etc., the violence of the destruction increased —that is, while along the right margin of the track some trees were left uninjured, toward these apexes, all were blown down.

11. The areas $bdb'$, $b' d' b''$, etc., were not *totally* uninjured (paragraph 5); there was a certain destruction over these areas of a very different nature from the main destruction, and at first almost imperceptible, but more distinct in each triangle than in the one preceding. In the area $bdb'$ only two trees were destroyed, in $b' d' b''$ only four, in $b'' d'' b'''$ only nine, and in the area $b''' d''' b''''$, only twenty.

#### SPECIAL DESCRIPTIONS OF THE DESTRUCTION. THE FIRST AREA OF DESTRUCTION, $abc$.

12. About one mile west of Lexington Road, where a line drawn from $b$ over the house 2 would meet the line $CD$, the first destruction was to be seen in the breaking of an old, rotten apple tree, some broken limbs of trees and the overturning of an old well-cover. Those objects lay almost parallel with each other, and were turned toward $b$. From this point to the Lexington road no destruction was found, on account of a barrenness of objects, but the wind must

* The distance from $b$ to $b'$ is less proportionately than the others, probably because the first oscillation was not fully developed. See explanation of the tornado.

have blown toward *b* from all points of this area, from the fact that the carriage of a physician who happened at the time to be driving toward Waltham was seized by the wind south or south-west of Prospect Hill and pushed forcibly toward *b*. The principal destruction begins, however, east of the Lexington road.

13. The wind was so strong from the south-west at the house 2, where the principal of the high school at Waltham lived, that it broke the windows on the south-west side, and threw the supper which was on the table into an opposite corner of the room.

14. The northern and eastern sides of this house were covered with *mud*, but there was not a single spot on the southern or western sides. No rain fell in this place, and no water was near it.

15. The space around 50 was covered with about thirty pine trees. Five of them over the south-western edge of this grove were blown over or broken in the direction of the arrow 18. Some peach trees south of this grove were also blown over in the same direction. The destroyed trees turned a little more to the north, in following the line *CD* to the east. At 19 trees were broken in the direction of the lower part of the arrow, and the pieces broken off were blown away in the direction of the upper part of the arrow.

16. One remarkable fact is exhibited in the height of the breakage. The trees on the southern margin of this grove were broken near the ground, those more to the north a little higher, those in the middle quite high, and those on the most northern portion remained entirely uninjured. Between this grove and the projection *S* was a meadow and field which contained only a few small trees, and these were uninjured. The row of trees on Lincoln street was also uninjured. On the south side of the declivity of the projection *S* many branches and strong trees nine or ten inches in diameter were broken, and the pieces blown toward *b*. Here the ground was rocky.

17. On the top of *S*, ten yards south-west of the house 3 (Mr. Lyman's), were two small tuga trees bent over as the arrows indicate. Between these and the house were no trees, but a bare place. West of these trees, on the slope and farther to the north, the ground was thickly covered with trees, but all were left uninjured.

18. The leaves of the trees over the slope of the projection *S*, west of the line *b c*, appeared singed or withered, and the line of limit, which near *b* turned a little around to north-west, was so distinctly marked that the trees in this line had their leaves withered on the south and south-west side, while the leaves on the other side of the same trees remained uninjured.

19. Another very important fact is the following: The dots on both sides of Lyman's Road west of *b c* represent two rows of elm trees. The trunks of the row south-east of the road were on the S. S. E. side covered seven feet high with mud, the upper limit of which was distinctly marked. No spot of mud could be found above this limit or on the north or north-west sides. The elm trees on the other side of the road were entirely free from mud.

20. South-east of these rows of trees lay a field which had been ploughed some days before, and the surface of which had become quite dry.

21. No rain fell at that place at the time the tornado passed.

22. Farther south there was a ditch from two to three yards wide, the water in which was very low and at least three feet below the banks, which were perpendicular. This ditch lay one hundred and eighty yards away from the elm trees. It was called Lyman's Pond, although nothing more than a ditch.

23. Not one overturned tree in this area pointed toward *C D* or lay parallel with it, nor did the trees cross each other except in the instance described in paragraph 6.

### THE SECOND AREA OF DESTRUCTION, *a′ b′ c′*.

24. The second area of destruction was less favorable for thorough investigation, containing few objects exposed to the destruction. The grass, crops, etc., indicated, however, the course of the wind. Its southern portion comprised a meadow, field and garden, with only a few large trees here and there. Between Lyman's Pond, the ditch and Lyman's Road and the houses 4 and 33 lay a meadow. The dots from 4 to 33 represent uninjured trees. Between 4 and 35 lay a garden with a greenhouse. Between 33, 34 and 35 along the road is a field with crops. North of the road was the wood in which the destruction like a wedge was directed toward *b′*. In the orchard east of 4 all destroyed trees pointed to *b′*. The houses 4 and 35 are uninjured. The trees near *a′* point to *b′*, crossing those of the first area of destruction *a b c*.

25. A branch of a red beech tree south of the house 4 was blown over the house toward *b′*, and had fallen gently on square flower-pots without injuring them. These flower-pots stood in a half circle, turning from N. E. N. to N. W. They were overturned in the same order, the southernmost one lying on its neighbor to the north.

26. The house 4 was all wet on its south side, but not covered with mud. No rain had fallen here.

THE THIRD AREA OF DESTRUCTION, $a'' b'' c''$.

27. The third area of destruction exhibited on the whole the same phenomena as the two preceding ones, but much more characteristic and better developed. It was here that the remarkable arrangement in the direction of the destroyed trees first struck me, because it was so well marked that it could not be overlooked. All destroyed trees from the base $a'' c''$ and over the whole area pointed to $b''$. Those trees which lay nearest the line $a'' b''$ were more or less parallel with it; those nearer the line $b'' c''$ made a somewhat greater angle with $a'' b''$.

28. In the upper part of this triangle, toward $b''$, about twenty trees lay parallel with each other in the direction of the arrow 36, while another group, just as numerous, deviated about 4° from this direction, and inclined a little more to the line $a'' b''$, as indicated by the arrow 37. It appeared as if an oscillating force deviating about 4° in its direction passed over this field, throwing down now this group, and then the other. The deviation of this oscillating force appeared to grow smaller toward $b''$.

29. The leaves of the trees left standing in the lines $a'' b''$ and $c'' b''$ were withered on the south side, and those lines were so well marked by this that it would alone have been sufficient to determine these lines and the form of the area of destruction. The whole had the appearance as if a wedge with its base $a'' c''$ had been shot toward the point $b''$.

THE FOURTH AREA OF DESTRUCTION, $a''' b''' c'''$.

30. This area had the same general arrangement of destruction as the three preceding ones. It was, however, less visible, as the whole area consisted of meadows, fields and small elevations devoid of trees. In the corn and grass, however, the small oscillations in the general direction of destruction were more visible than in the triangle $a'' b'' c''$.

THE FIFTH AREA OF DESTRUCTION, $a'''' b'''' c''''$.

31. This area contained a great number of objects exposed to the destroying forces, and the general arrangement of destruction found in the preceding areas was here so well developed as to be typical of all the rest. But another destroying force of a new character seemed here to come into most prominence, and to the superficial observer might somewhat obliterate the general arrangement, which was, nevertheless, very clearly to be seen. The particular descrip-

tion of this area will be taken up farther on, after the development of this new force (the vortex) is described.

DESCRIPTION OF THE LEFT SIDE OF THE TRACK.

32. On the left side of the track, although the ground was thickly wooded and presented more objects than the right side, no destruction was to be found to any extent until approaching $b''''$.

33. The first indication of a destruction on the left side appeared at $b''$, in *one* tree lying toward S. S. W. Then it appeared between the lines $g f$ and $a''' b'''$, and farther on again between the lines $g' f'$ and $a'''' b''''$. The width of the first destruction on the left side of the axis was about one-fiftieth part of the whole width of the track, and of the second about one-thirtieth; while on the West Cambridge section it formed one-third, and at Medford one-half.

34. The destruction on the left side, too, appeared at first in narrow stripes indicated by dots at the arrows 39, 40, 41, 42, 43. The objects between these arrows were uninjured. At 39 two trees lay one behind the other; at 42, three trees, one in front, the others side by side behind it. The trees which lay the farthest from the line $a'''' b''''$ had more the direction of the arrow 44.

35. Besides these indications of a force on the left side, there were found at *m*, *n* and *o* stripes of withered leaves.

36. This destruction appeared at first to be from N. W.; farther on, from N.; and at West Cambridge, from N. E.

37. The quality of destruction on this side was essentially different from that on the right side—a fact very important in its application. No trees were uprooted or lifted up. The destroying force seems rather to press downward.

THE AREA OF THE DESTRUCTION CAUSED BY THE VORTEX.

38. The destruction described in the foregoing paragraphs was characterized by evidences that the forces acted in *straight* lines, the destruction on the right side of the track being directed toward N. or N. E., and the little on the left side to S. or S. E. The other destroying force, however, first *predominantly* exhibited in the fifth area of destruction, $a'''' b'''' c''''$, was rotary. It appeared first south-west of the house 3, near *b*. From here it ran in the red line from *b* to *e*, $b'$, $e'$, $b''$, $e''$, $b'''$, etc., the destruction changing in its direction as a rotary force would lay it, and as is indicated by the arrows *x*, *y*, *s*, *t*, *u*. The exact width of this zigzag belt could be determined only approximately. It appeared first indistinctly south-

west of *b*, and exhibited itself only in the crowns of the trees. It was estimated, from these exhibitions, to be about six yards wide. From *b* it increased rapidly. At *b''''* it appeared to be about one-tenth of the whole width of the track, and at West Cambridge it amounted to fully two-thirds.

39. Over this winding belt the destruction is the most violent and of a peculiar nature. It is over this area that trees were found robbed of their branches on all sides. Here were also found trees of from one to two and a half feet diameter split and twisted like a rope, torn out of the ground and carried far away. Houses were here unroofed and the roofs carried away forty or fifty paces; whole houses were torn from their foundations and carried off. This kind of destruction was not to be found elsewhere in the track.

40. The two tuga trees south-west of house 3, bent over in a half circle, were the first indication of this winding belt on the ground. From here to *e* it was only to be seen in the branches of the trees which stood on the eastern slope of the hill *S*. It was only over this path that there was any destruction in the triangles *b d b'*, *b' d' b''*, etc., which were otherwise left uninjured. (See paragraph 11.) The two trees destroyed in the triangle *b d b'* lay between the groups 12 and 13. The dots around 33 and 34 indicate trees around those farm-houses which were all left uninjured. North of the road were forest trees also untouched.

41. At *l*, in the triangle *b d b'*, were five trees in a row; the second and fourth from the road had withered leaves on the south side. In this triangle and the next, *b' d' b''*, the destruction was exclusively to be found in the tops of the trees. From *b''* to *e''* this kind of destruction took place between the woods 44 and 45 in single trees. The little wood 15 was uninjured.

42. At $\beta$ the ground was covered with shrubbery and a few tall oaks; 14 indicates a group of these oaks. The rotating force here took away the north-western trees of the group, then made a turn visible in the shrubbery, and assuming its original direction took away the south-western part of the group. The middle portion of these oak trees remained uninjured.

43. At the point *e'''* a man was lifted up, and set down fifty yards farther on to the east.

44. The houses 5, 46 and 47, on North street, were not injured.

45. The large barn 6 was twisted around somewhat to the north.

46. The building 7 was completely cut in two, and the upper half carried twenty yards away over the barn 6. The breakage was

nearer the ground on the south than on the north side. The houses 6 and 8 on either side of it were not destroyed.

47. The house of Mr. Lawrence, 8, was only slightly injured. One window on the south-east side and one on the west-north-west side were blown in.

48. A small building attached to it at the rear was carried four yards to 48, where it lay not much broken.

49. Half of the roof of the barn 9 was thrown to 49, the other half to 50.

50. The chimney on the house 10 was laid over on the roof toward the north, and one corner of a side building was turned a yard away from the house.

51. Mr. Baldwin was at that time in his barn 6, and states: "The wind rushed in from north-west and from south-east at the same time." The barn was turned in the same manner as the side building of 10. (Paragraph 45.) The door at the south-eastern side was carried toward the buildings 7 and 8. The barn had no wall under the southern foundation joists. The floor on which a cow stood was, therefore, lifted up, and the cow fell through.

52. Stacks of straw near $b''''$ were strewn in a semicircle, the convex side of which was turned to N. E.

53. At $\beta'$ and $\beta''$ the belt of this peculiar destruction seemed to have turned upon itself as at $\beta$. In the curve of $\beta''$ were four oaks about one foot thick, indicated by the letters *q p r*. They stood in a semicircle. The first was twisted, the three others were split, and then broken in a direction at an angle of 90° to the direction of the split. In the West Cambridge section were found several such turns, as at $\beta$, $\beta'$, $\beta''$, and in each instance the trees were found bereft of their limbs on all sides, and twisted.

54. In Cambridge, in one of these places, stood a house whose roof on the north side was thrown into the house, while the roof on the south side and the back building south of the house were completely blown away.

55. In another place analogous to *q* and 7 were two houses left uninjured, and the third between them carried away.

56. In the most northern of the two remaining houses a board one foot broad and one inch thick was driven through the wall. The part which penetrated the inside was broken off and had cut in half two consoles of a bureau. The sides of the wall were of boards, double, with an air-space between.

57. Another phenomenon was found in the same room which

many credited to electricity. In the glass door leading to the room opposite to the wall which the board had pierced was a circular hole about an inch and a half in diameter, which was surrounded by cracks radiating from it. The piece split out was larger on the inside of the door, showing that the blow came from the outside; on the inside hung a muslin curtain with a corresponding hole.

58. A granite gate-post seven feet high and one and a quarter feet square, planted three feet in the ground and standing between the destroyed house and one of those uninjured, was bent about four inches out of position.

59. A freight car which was standing upon the side track of the Lowell railroad near the dépôt was pushed along the track a hundred and sixty feet, and at this point men were taken up and carried sixty feet east, nearly at right angles to the track. (Brooks.)

### THE STATE OF THE ATMOSPHERE BEFORE, DURING AND AFTER THE TORNADO.

60. Some days previously, and on the very day the tornado took place, a south-west wind prevailed over this region of country.

61. About two o'clock P. M., on the day of the tornado, a long black bank of cloud appeared in the north-west above the horizon, rising slowly.

62. At the same time a great deal of rain fell at Lowell, about seventeen miles north of the track.

63. The cloud became stationary for nearly two hours and a half after it had reached a height of about 50°.

64. All those who observed it supposed a heavy storm was imminent, but this was delayed for several hours.

65. At four o'clock a south-west wind was still felt one mile north of Waltham.

66. From this time there was a very oppressive sultry calm. One man, coming home from the field to the house 47, said ten minutes before the tornado began that something extraordinary either had taken place or was about to do so, as he could scarcely breathe.

67. This calm was interrupted by violent gusts at several places north of the track, coming from north-west and north.

68. An occupant of the house 1 experienced toward a quarter of five o'clock a strong cold gust of wind from the north-west down the valley *M*, and saw at the same time a black cloud move in the same direction. This wind was so strong that a young lady who ascended immediately to the second story in order to shut the windows at the

N. W. side of the house was suddenly thrown back into the middle of the room by a violent gust of wind.

69. At Waltham the strength of the S. W. wind increased as the time when the tornado began approached. Ex-President Hill of Harvard College, living about one hundred yards south of the track, was obliged to close the windows on the S. W. side because of the great quantity of dust forced through the blinds. A short time before this he thought the wind too strong for rain. He was otherwise occupied at the time, however, and knew nothing of the tornado until the next day.

70. A Mr. Sanger, in the house 5, experienced a similar strong wind between his house and barn in the direction of the arrow 41 from north-west, blowing toward the tornado-cloud, which was at that time south of the house.

71. These sudden gusts occurred momentarily, and immediately after them the calm returned.

72. As soon as the tornado had passed violent showers of rain fell all along the track north of it. These rains were so unusually heavy that a lady two hundred yards north of $b''$ became thoroughly wet in making only one step out of her house. The rain fell in immense drops, and lasted only a few minutes.

73. Not one drop fell south of the track before night.

74. From information received, it appeared that the rain fell to the north of the track, nearer to it at Waltham than at Medford.

75. Between eight and nine P. M. the thunder and lightning was quite unusual—so much so that it attracted my attention; and I went up to the roof of my boarding-house, which was situated about three and a half miles S. S. W. of West Cambridge, to witness the spectacle. The bank of cloud at its western and north-eastern extremities had bent to the south, while in the north-west, in the direction of Waltham and West Cambridge, it seemed to be in the same position as in the afternoon. I was therefore surrounded with lightning on three sides. From these facts it follows that the cloud came from north-west and travelled to south-east.

76. This was confirmed by information received through Ex-President Hill, which showed that in the States of New Hampshire and Vermont a south-west wind had been replaced by a north-west wind, with low temperature and rain.

77. From a place north-east of house 1, and near to it, a great commotion in the clouds was observed above the first area of destruction *a b c*.

78. From the house 4 there was observed a cloud which came from the south-west and united with the main bank of cloud, which lay north of the house.

79. When the clouds moved from *b* toward the east, the vane on a spire in Waltham was seen to point north.

80. At a place north of house 1 several persons observed a cloud moving down the valley *M* toward S. E., and heard a noise similar to that made by a locomotive.

81. Mrs. Sanger, living in house 5, was so favored by circumstances as to witness a considerable part of the storm. Being unwell, she had lain down to sleep at two o'clock, but was awakened at three and a half o'clock by two very heavy claps of thunder. Looking from the window, she saw a dark cloud, and beneath it an appearance "as if the sun were drawing water," produced by parallel stripes of hazy cloud extending from the dark cloud to the surface of the earth. These stripes approached each other, and seemed to become denser and to form in a column. At four and three-quarters o'clock she saw a movement in the column from left to right, then from right to left, and at the same time upward, and the velocity forward increased as the column ascended. The cloud became lighter and advanced rapidly toward her. She became very much frightened, and ran up stairs to close the windows. Here she again looked out at the cloud, and found it descending the north-eastern slope of the hill *T*. She felt that the house would be swept away, and from fear sat down, unable to move. In a few moments she recovered, looked again from the window, and saw the cloud at $\beta$, where it seemed to be doing dreadful work.

---

The form of the tornado cloud was observed and described to me by scientific men. The assistant in the observatory at Cambridge who saw it pass the observatory window made a drawing of it. Dr. Gould of Boston observed that the lower part of the tornado cloud from time to time suddenly "exploded" and vanished. From all sources it appears that the cloud assumed different forms at different places, or looked differently from different positions.

Fig. 3 of Plate I. is drawn from descriptions furnished by witnesses at different points. Those who saw it from points in the track noticed its zigzag motion, and that it rose and fell; several in West

Cambridge described it as similar in appearance and motion to an elephant's trunk.

No one could be found who had made definite observations as to the changes of the barometer or thermometer, and the people were too much alarmed to observe the changes sufficiently to give more than very general impressions as to the state of the atmosphere, but the observation reported in paragraph 66 near the house 47 will indicate the state of atmospheric pressure.

Being convinced by the investigation of this tornado that it was originated by the configuration of the ground, I hurried to Waltham with instruments whenever during the next few months a similar bank of clouds rose above the horizon in this direction. On no occasion, however, did they become nearly stationary at this point, as before the tornado, and no tornado took place; but I frequently observed changes in the thermometer of from 15° to 30° F. in less than ten minutes, accompanied by changes in barometric pressure and direction of the wind. On such occasions singular oscillations appeared in the clouds as they came above the valley *M.*

### CONCLUSIONS FROM THE PRECEDING FACTS AS TO THE NATURE AND DIRECTION OF THE DESTROYING FORCE.

If I have succeeded in presenting, in the description of the surface, the state of the atmosphere and the destruction, a comprehensive picture of the tornado, the unprejudiced reader must be satisfied that neither the Rotary nor the Inblowing theory can explain this first section of the tornado track. Even Mr. Redfield, who accompanied me over the track from Waltham to West Cambridge, did not attempt it, but merely shook his head and said: "That is nothing; this section is imperfectly developed. The vortex was lying on one side;" but he could not explain *why* it should be lying on one side, or if it was how it could produce the destruction, nor, in fact, why the section should be imperfectly developed. When we came to West Cambridge, he grew more interested and said: "If you had taken twenty-five rods' length of the track in this part, it would be worth more than the two and a half miles near Waltham, for here the tornado is fully developed on both sides." And he was right as far as his own theory was concerned, for it was perfectly exhibited in West Cambridge, but it would not apply at all to either of the other sections.

In the same way Espy's theory was very well exhibited in the last section at Medford, but the absence of destruction on the left side of the track in the first section, and the evident rotary motion over two-thirds of the width of the track in the second section, proved an effectual bar to accounting for the whole phenomenon by the In-blowing theory.

The way was thus left clear to draw my own conclusions as follows:

1. From paragraphs 1, 2, 3, 4, we must conclude that the destroying force came from the south-west in a straight line.

2. It did not act all at once at every point of the line *C D*, but in separate successive movements, beginning at the most western end and travelling east. This appears from paragraph 6, for the trees in the triangles *a′ d c*, *a′′ d′ c′*, etc., belonging to the eastern sections, must have fallen later than those of the western, because the latter lay undermost.

3. The force was exerted over an area widest at the margin of the track (*a c*, *a′ c′*, *a′′ c′′*, etc.) and narrowing regularly in the direction of *b*, *b′*, *b′′*, etc., at which points its effects vanished suddenly. Its destruction was more violent as its limits contracted, and most so at the points *b*, *b′*, *b′′*, etc., beyond which it ceased to be found at all.

4. This force had a tendency obliquely upward.

5. As this force acted with increasing violence as it approached the points *b*, *b′*, *b′′*, etc., and then vanished suddenly, it must have been suddenly neutralized or directed upward by an opposing force, which acted thus protectingly over those areas left uninjured.

6. This protecting force was manifested on the ground toward the south, and only in higher regions toward the north; it must, therefore, have had an oblique position.

7. This protecting force from the north changes its character somewhat from a protective to a slightly destructive one as we advance in the track; but it is at long intervals, and then only over small, short streaks. Its direction is even then decidedly downward, while the force from the south is just as decidedly upward.

8. Between these two forces, of which one, from the south, acted aggressively and destructively, and the other, from the north, defensively and protectingly, a third of an entirely different character appeared at *b*.

9. This third force acted more violently and in a rotary direction, while the others acted in straight lines. It exhibited a still greater lifting power than the force from the south-west.

10. The diameter of this rotating force appeared at first to be only about six yards, but it increased rapidly in size as it travelled toward

the east, being greatest at West Cambridge. From this place it decreased again still more rapidly until it disappeared.

The following general principles seemed to be brought out by the investigation:

1. That the tornado grew out of the coincidence of the particular state of the atmosphere—*i. e.*, the particular condition of the storm —in connection with the peculiar configuration of the earth, but was not the storm itself, as until that time had been maintained and is even now maintained.

2. That the tornado follows entirely different laws in its motion and appearance from those of storms generally, and, therefore, cannot be made the base of universal storm theories, as has been done.

3. That there are different kinds of storms—different in their origin, motions, effects and appearances.

---

## REV. CHARLES BROOKS'S REPORT.

The state of the atmosphere from sunrise to the time of the tornado, on August 22, was peculiar. Many spoke of a dead closeness —a remarkable want of elasticity in the air. Many complained of lassitude from this cause. Clouds gathered, and there were appearances of wind approaching, but it did not come. For an hour before the tornado there was here almost a perfect calm, yet it was a calm prophetic of we knew not what. An old sea-captain told his wife, at four o'clock P. M., that "if he was at sea he should expect a water-spout."

*Direction.*—Coming from Waltham, the central line of march seemed to be from W. S. W. to E. N. E., till it reached the western edge of Medford at the Mystic River, near the "Wear Bridge." Here it changed its direction slightly, and moved from W. by S. to E. by N., keeping this line to the edge of Malden, beyond which I have not traced it. From a hill forty or fifty feet high, near Fulton street, I could take its centre on the hills of West Cambridge, and found it S. 60° W., or nearly W. S. W., while its centre from Fulton street to the hill in West Medford was W. by S. exactly, thus showing that it curved slightly toward the east at its passing of Mystic River. After taking the direction at Mystic River, Lowell Railroad dépôt, Miss Brooks's hill, Mr. Hall's hill, and at Fulton street, the result seems to be that its march was upon a straight line. . . .

*Form.*—All who saw the tornado speak of its "form." Whether the dust, water and other materials which it gathered into its bosom, in the air, gave it such visible shape, it is not important to inquire. To some who watched it closely its form resembled a tall, wide-spreading elm tree; to others it appeared like an inverted cone. Several represent it as a dense upright column, and a few as having some resemblance to an hour-glass. It might have had these forms at different places in its route, or it might have appeared differently at the same moment to persons looking at it from different angles. Some who watched it at right angles to its line of march, and some who saw it from elevated points, through four or five miles of its course, concur in saying that the conical point let down from the cloud moved about at short distances, now pushing down to the earth and now rising from it. Its side motions were compared to those of an elephant's trunk. This action was like the descending tube in a nearly-completed water-spout at sea.

*Width.*—Measuring on the line S. by E. and N. by W.—which is at right angles to the central line of motion—I took the outer southern and northern edges, where marks of violence were unequivocally left—such marks as the breaking of limbs of trees, bending of fences, prostrating of corn or unhinging of a window-blind. At Mystic River its width was seventy-one rods; at the Lowell Railroad dépôt, sixty rods. Between these places it moved over an almost perfect level. At Miss Brooks's it was fifty-four rods wide; and here it crossed the hill on which her house stands, which is perhaps fifty feet above the level of the river at low tide. At Messrs. Swan and Hall's land, at the "meeting-house brook," it was seventy-six rods. Here it moved over a small valley. In Mrs. Porter's wood-lot it was fifty-six rods; at Dr. Kidder's, on Andover turnpike, it was fifty-four rods. At Fulton street I could not ascertain its width with perfect accuracy, but think it was not much over forty rods.

Connected with the subject of width is this fact—that in several places the distance from the centre to the outer *southern* edge is from eighteen to twenty-five rods farther than from the centre to the *northern* edge. At one place the ravages on each side were nearly equidistant from the centre; but in all the other cases of measurement the statement above was verified.

Another fact connected with the subject of width is this—that it seemed to dart off on each side at unusual distances and do violence in a narrow-pathed excursion; or rather, to speak more intelligibly, there seemed to be some strata of air on its outer borders more ready to rush in toward the central line of march than contiguous strata. This is shown many times in orchards, where rows of trees stood at right angles, or nearly so, to the central line; some entire rows were prostrated, while their nearest neighbors on each side remained unmoved. The violence in these narrow pencils of wind seems to have been as great twenty rods from the centre as it was within two or three rods. This rush of wind in veins, from the outer edges to the centre, is marked over the whole route. It reminds one of flashing pencils of electricity.

*Speed.*—The agitation of mind in those persons who were within reach of the tornado and felt its power was too great and lasting to enable them to measure its velocity with reliable precision. If an individual on "Prospect Hill" had seen it through five or ten miles of its march, such an individual might guess at the speed with the best chance of accuracy; but, after all, it could be only a guess. A few facts may help us in guessing. Mr. West, who was building a house for Mr. Haskins, saw it coming from West Cambridge, and watched it with anxiety. As soon as he saw it destroy the new house west of the Lowell railroad dépôt he sprang out of the house where he was, and ran, as he says, "for his life," to shelter himself behind a wall only five rods distant from the place where he started. He had scarcely got to his shelter when the house he had left was entirely destroyed. He thinks there could not have been over five or six seconds between the falling of the two buildings. I was in my sister's house at the time; saw it but an instant before it struck the house. I rushed to lock the front door, and at the moment we felt the first shock I cried out violently to the family that "all was over." I opened the door and sprang upon the bank over which its centre had just passed and looked for it. It had gone at least a mile before I could reach the place, though the distance from the house was not three rods. It seemed to me but a breath of time; and now, after reviewing the facts, I cannot persuade myself that its speed at that place was less than fifty miles per hour.

*Power.*—They who, like us, were in it, and have seen its terrible ravages, need not be told that it exhibited a power in the elements never witnessed by the oldest inhabitant of this region. Houses strongly built were demolished as if they had been made of paper. Oak and walnut and cedar trees of the largest growth were entirely uprooted, some of them snatched out of the ground and carried through long distances, roofs of buildings taken up as by sudden suction, and carried into the embrace of the cloud and transported for miles. The roof of Miss Brooks's house was seen to go thus; and although every beam and rafter went with it, we have not yet been able to find even a shingle of it, though we have searched through three miles. Its action upon the grass and corn was remarkable. It not only prostrated them, but partly buried them in the earth. The fields in this respect looked as if a heavy roller had passed over them.

Its action upward was yet more remarkable. No one saw any object driven *downward* by it, but all testify to its taking things *up*. To name a few instances. Shingles and boards and rafters and slates which are known to have belonged to certain houses were found two or three miles from the places. A tree of very large size in Miss Brooks's orchard was decapitated; the trunk now stands erect, but the top was taken up and carried off, and never has been found. So there are instances, in every locality, of objects taken up and transported through great distances. One witness says she saw the large barn owned by Miss Brooks rise in the air, and then fall in ruins. There is evidence yet remaining that this large barn, built of heavy timber and plank, was taken up and then carried fifteen feet before it was torn to pieces. Many buildings were moved in a similar manner. A freight car which was standing upon the side track of the Lowell railroad, near the dépôt, was driven upon that track one hundred and sixty-five feet, and then taken up and carried sixty feet east nearly at right angles to the track. At Doctor Kidder's a thick, strong brick wall was thrown down ten feet from its foundation; some of the bricks carried to a great distance. A pine tree ten inches in diameter was broken off, then carried some hundred feet into the air, and then thrown through the roof and window of Doctor Kidder's house. His lightning-rods were much bent.

Another trace of power left behind by the tornado is seen in the small fragments into which it shattered every fragile thing. It seemed to act upon a building as a mill grinds whatever is put into it. If every square foot of atmosphere in the column had been armed with a steel tooth, and the buildings and trees which went into it could have passed through it, it could not have shivered them to smaller pieces. I leave to poets to describe the powers and terrors of this phenomenon, while to me it seems like a large storm intensified. The winds which, if spread over two hundred miles, would have made a severe storm throughout that extent, seemed concentrated within as many yards.

*Direction in which trees and vegetables were thrown.*—With regard to this part of the subject, I would state *as the general fact* that there was uniformity in the directions in which objects were thrown. Under similar circumstances similar appearances exhibit themselves. For example, with respect to trees; they which were standing in the centre of the line of march, supposing that centre to be a line running W. by S. and E. by N., lie coincident with that line. They which were nearest to this line on each side of it lie nearly parallel with it, but not exactly. They on the north side of the centre point to spaces between E. by N. and E., while they on the south side point to spaces between E. by N. and E. N. E. They on the north side, which are farther yet from the centre, and next to those last mentioned, point to spaces between E. and E. S. E., while the corresponding ones on the south side point to spaces between E. N. E. and N. E. They which are farther still from the centre, on the north side, lie pointing to spaces between E. S. E. and S. E. by S., while they in corresponding distances, on the south side, lie pointing to spaces between N. E. and N. by E. They on the north side which are farthest from the centre lie pointing to spaces between S. E. by S. and S. by E., while they at similar distances from the centre on the south side lie pointing to spaces between N. by E. and N. by W. Those trees which lie pointing S. by E. and N. by W. lie at right angles to the central line of march, and of course lie pointing in exactly opposite directions. Nine-tenths of the trees prostrated by the tornado lie in the positions above designated. They which are not directly upon the central line lie pointing to that line. This is true of the trees and shrubs and corn and grass up to 90° distant from the point E. by N. on each side; and there, at 90° from that point, they stop, all being included within E. by N. and S. by E. on one side, and within E. by N. and N. by W. on the other.

The above statements record the *general* facts respecting the directions in which trees and other vegetables were thrown by the tornado. It seems as if a vacuum had travelled (if we can say so) fifteen or twenty miles from W. by S. to E. by N., and the wind had rushed in with violence, not only behind it, but on each side toward its central line of motion, prostrating the trees in the manner above stated.

Of the remaining one-tenth part of the trees and objects thrown about by the tornado, a very different statement must be made. The following facts, carefully verified, as the others were, by personal examination, seem to contradict them all. . . .

*Miscellaneous Items.*—There were many who thought that the apples lying upon the ground at the time were baked on their south side by the heat in the wind. That most apples so situated among us were found so baked is true; but whether the sun had not previously done this, according to his usual action in a midsummer drought, is what we leave others to decide. No one who was in the wind felt any baking heat during its passage. If there had been heat sufficient to bake apples to the extent asserted, that heat must have scorched the leaves and grass, and would probably have set fire to hay or shavings.

*Whirl.*—I find but one tree twisted by the wind, and that is a large cedar, five and three quarter rods south of centre, and it lies pointing N. N. E. It was south of a large wall, in contact with which it stood and across which it fell. It is twisted just half a revolution. Whether the falling of trees next it or trees thrown out of the tornado, or any such cause, could have given it the whirling motion, it is impossible to say. No evidence of any such forcible action upon it is discoverable. It was a tall tree, but not so tall as the buttonwoods three or four rods east of it, which stood equally exposed. Throughout the track in Medford I find no evidence of a rotary motion in the force which prostrated the buildings, trees, etc. There may have been in the moving cloud a swift and constant motion round a perpendicular centre, but this revolving whirlwind did not blow down the trees and corn. If it had done so, the trees and corn would have lain in curves and circles corresponding to the direction of the force, whereas they all lie straight. Large fields of corn, through every part, showed the motion of a force acting in straight lines. I could not find any trace of a curve. The ground and grass were definitely marked in extensive, open fields, and no sign of curvilinear motion could be detected. All showed straight lines of march toward the central line. Upon the central line, where the apex of the inverted cone just touched the earth, there we should expect to find trees twisted off, but I find not one. All on this line lie thrown down, without any trace of a whirl in the power that prostrated them. In most of them the bark upon the west side is scraped lengthwise, up and down, with no mark of circular motion. Two facts more may be added here. Large trees which were broken off from five to ten feet from the ground exhibit uniform testimony. The sap-wood on the west side did not break so readily as the interior layers, and therefore it was peeled off in strings; these strings remain erect as they grew, and show no trace of twist or revolution. Twenty-eight rods north of centre stands erect the trunk of a large apple tree in Miss Brooks's orchard, before mentioned. The top of this tree was taken up, perpendicularly I presume, for the shreds and layers of the sap-wood stand pointing upward as they grew, showing no vestige of bending or contortion.

The inverted cone of wind and cloud, as it travelled through its course, may have revolved round a perpendicular axis, as many assert it did. I know not why it should or why it should not. Having no theory to patronize or decry, I readily accede to the testimony in this particular, leaving disputants to classify the facts as they may. But I would suggest this idea: if a beholder should see such a tornado coming toward him or going from him, he would see objects projected into it from both sides of it; and these opposite motions would give the appearance of a whirl or rotation, although the objects may be moving in straight lines. The inverted cone, whatever may have been its composition, form or motion, left behind it a vacuum of such a character as to force the wind, after it and on each side of it, with a violence sufficient to uproot the strongest oaks; and the motion of these in-rushing columns of air was in straight lines, and they were generally toward the centre of the line of march.

In Mr. Hastings's orchard, S. of his house, on the banks of the Mystic River, stood a large old apple tree. This tree was seventy-four and a half rods S. S. E. of what seemed to be the outer southern edge of the tornado; nevertheless, it was beheaded, split, and lies pointing exactly E. A hundred trees in its immediate vicinity were equally exposed, yet remain untouched.

The effect on some trees is worthy of record. A large horse-chestnut tree, near the brook in Mr. Usher's land, was decapitated, leaving only a few small limbs attached to the lower part of the trunk. Within a week after the tornado the buds on these limbs began to swell, new leaves soon appeared, and then blossoms; so that on the 16th of September, twenty-five days after its decapitation, it displayed ten or twelve full-grown blossoms. I regret that some of these blossoms were not allowed to remain, in order to see how soon a perfect nut would have been formed under these extraordinary circumstances.

The action of the wind was searching indeed, and many strange movements were its result. In a small room four rods S. of centre was an engraved likeness of President Fillmore pasted strongly upon a rough plastered wall; around it were many other engravings of like size. This room was so situated that the wind came in at a west door and went out at an east window. The wind selected His Excellency's head, took it from the wall without tearing it or soiling it in the least, and having carried it through an open window transported it more than a quarter of a mile and deposited it in the garden of a friend, who returned it safely, to be again fastened in its place. Political prophets may tell us what this foreshadows.

In the middle of Mr. H. Whittemore's house, in West Cambridge, in the second story, there is a door in whose top are six small panes of glass. This door is exactly opposite the front window, which was blown in during the tornado. Before the six panes of glass hung a white cloth curtain; through this curtain was perforated a small ragged hole not larger than a pea; directly behind this hole the pane of glass is perforated, and a hole is left almost as large as a half-dollar. This hole in the glass was nearly round, and its edges, instead of being sharp as broken glass is, seem melted into roundness. Moreover, for a quarter of an inch round the edges of this hole there is a thin wavy layer of apparently melted glass. A few cracks in the glass ray off from the centre of the hole. Since the tornado a piece of glass which was loose has been taken out, thus destroying so far the circular form of the hole and the wavy layers which bounded it. We hope that many will examine this singular fact, especially in connection with electricity, and show us how the glass could have been melted and the cloth remain unscorched.

To enumerate all the strange facts connected with the tornado would fill pages, but I must leave them. I cannot, however, omit the mention of the sympathy shown for the sufferers. Five or six individuals were more or less injured in body. Mrs. Caldwell was taken up by the wind and carried over fences and trees, through a distance of one hundred and fifty feet, and safely deposited by the side of a neighbor's barn. Strange to say, she was only bruised a little. Such was the suddenness and force of the motion that she can give but an imperfect account of her aërial excursion. Two men at work upon a new house were thrown several rods, and one was injured considerably. The son of Mr. Sanford was thrown upon the ground, and while there his father's house, which was moved seventeen feet from its foundation, came down upon his legs, and so crushed both feet as to render their amputation necessary. . . .

# APPENDIX C.

(*From the U. S. Signal Service Report for* 1873.)

## THE IOWA AND ILLINOIS TORNADO OF MAY 22, 1873.*

### STATEMENT OF THE FACTS.

THIS tornado could not by its destructive effects upon trees, buildings, etc., be traced farther back than section 35, Warren Township, Keokuk county, Iowa. *At the point where the destruction commenced, the South Skunk River bends southward and then again to the east, thus half enclosing a low level area of about one mile in length by half a mile in breadth. This bottom-land is surrounded by bluffs about* 70 *feet in height on nearly all sides, the river flowing close to the bluff on the south-west. It was at the north-east edge of this natural amphitheatre that the tornado first attained force sufficient to demolish fences. These fences were thrown down by a south-west wind for a space forty rods wide.* The buildings of W. W. Morrow, situated halfway up the bluff, were partly destroyed. But although its first destructive efforts were here manifested, it by no means follows that this was the starting-point of the tornado. On the other side of South Skunk River, directly opposite, there was a strong wind, accompanied with some hail and rain, while to the north and west a tremendous rain fell, preceded and accompanied by large hail. The storm evidently arrived at Morrow's farm a wellnigh full-formed tornado. To trace it backward over a country where its phenomena were only those of a violent thunder-storm I found to be difficult and deemed unnecessary.

The attempt to prove a connection between this tornado and the thunder-storm near Des Moines of May 22, 4 A. M., has not been

* From the abundant testimony of witnesses in Mr. Mackintosh's report, which almost all corroborate my views, I select some of the most prominent, and indicate by italics some points bearing most strikingly on my theory. Mr. Mackintosh's explanations are given in some cases, although I do not indorse them.

The similarity between the tornadoes here reported and the West Cambridge tornado is so striking that the reader will find no difficulty in applying the same principles and supplying an explanation of anything that at first sight may appear obscure. The numbered *sections* refer to the Government surveys.—W. B.

successful. For although the Des Moines storm exhibited tornado-like power, since the distance between Des Moines and Morrow's farm is only seventy miles, and since the Des Moines storm occurred ten hours previously, its rate of motion, if it is identical with the Keokuk county tornado, cannot have exceeded seven miles per hour in a straight line. But as will afterward be shown, the tornado travelled more than twenty-nine miles per hour. This objection is by no means insuperable when viewed in the light cast upon the subject by the general modes of movement of storm-centres across the continent. These tornadoes, however, exist as something independent and automatic within the limits of areas of low barometer; and since their motion is governed by laws peculiar to themselves, it must meanwhile be accepted as valid. Besides, a hail-storm traversed Keokuk and Washington counties May 22, at 6 or 7 A. M. There is much more probability of a connection between this hail-storm and the Des Moines storm of 4 A. M. than between the latter and the tornado, which occurred eight hours subsequently.

In the Neosho County *Journal*, of May 24, is an account of a highly destructive tornado which desolated a portion of Lincoln county six miles long by one-half mile wide. This tornado was apparently every whit as violent as that in Iowa. The time at which it occurred is given as about 3 P. M. It cannot, therefore, be identical with the subject of this paper.

The conclusion follows that, wherever this tornado may have originated, it first attained to desolating violence on Morrow's farm, Its previous history was only that of a thunder-storm accompanied, perhaps, by an unusual tumult and whirling of the clouds. In tracing its development and progress, therefore, I probably labor under no disadvantages which do not necessarily attach to the history of all such meteors except those arising from the circumstance that the tornado was not at any point of its progress witnessed by a skilful meteorologist.

Mr. Morrow testified that neither he nor any of his people noticed any funnel-shaped appearance or tongue of cloud approaching the earth. There was a strong wind for a minute, but the destructive gust appeared to be instantaneous. A smart shower of hail followed the gust. *A whirling of the clouds was observed several minutes before the wind.* A little lightning was seen. The storm travelled *east-north-east* over Andrew Surber's farm, blowing down fences, with a *south-west* wind. He saw the clouds whirling like a great wheel 35° in width before the storm, but did not notice any funnel appearance. A few hail fell with the wind, and a considerable shower of rain after it.

The same phenomena were repeated on J. E. Storer's farm. A steady roar was heard as it approached. No lightning seen.

About forty rods *north of the line of destruction* on these farms resides William P. Liske. He saw two clouds, one in the south-west and the other in the north-west, which appeared to rush together in the west. As the tornado came up, and about twenty minutes before it arrived, the wind *changed to the north, and blew so strongly* that the door had to be held to prevent it from being blown in. Saw no lightning and heard but little thunder. Saw no funnel appearance.

Elleot Utterback was sixty rods *south* of the tornado at this place. He saw the clouds come whirling. The height of the whirling clouds was about 60°, and the width about 30°. Saw lightning and heard thunder once or twice. Hail followed the wind in small quantity, and rain fell in considerable amount three-quarters of an hour later. During the day the direction of the wind was *southerly.*

John Malcum, section 30, Lancaster township, testified: "Was one mile south of tornado when it occurred. Heard a roaring like steady thunder in the west about a quarter of an hour before the storm came. Saw no lightning. A cloud covered the western, the northern and the north-eastern portion of the sky. It extended somewhat beyond the zenith. The rest of the sky was clear. Saw a whirling mass of clouds. Could distinctly see them whirl contrary to the hands of a watch. The whirling mass appeared to be about 60° high when directly opposite. A smart shower fell some time after the tornado."

On Malcum's farm the roof of a stable was blown to the south-east. This was the first damage done by a north-west wind. Two hundred yards south of the stable a fence was blown toward the north-west and north. This was the first evidence of a destructive south-east and south wind. The storm *after becoming destructive had travelled one and a half miles before it developed force sufficient to commit destruction by a north-west and south-east wind.*

T. Dawson, section 31, Lancaster township: "The tornado passed directly over the farm buildings." He testified: "Saw tornado approaching like two dark clouds with an intervening lighter-colored space between them. These two clouds together presented a funnel-shaped appearance; the upper end of the funnel entered the overhanging mass of cloud, which covered the half of the sky and extended to the south-east a little beyond the zenith. Its lower end did not touch the earth. It whirled contrary to the hands of a watch. Its elevation appeared to be about 60°, and its width at summit 40°. Heard some thunder previous to tornado. Did not see any lightning. After the tornado there fell a few small hail and a little rain."

The breadth of fences thrown down on this farm was about sixty rods. The out-houses, etc., were damaged. A cultivator weighing about two hundred pounds was carried or dragged thirty feet. It presented to the wind a surface of not more than three square feet. If it was carried, the lifting force of the wind must have been between sixty and seventy pounds per square foot. The ground showed no signs of its having been dragged.

M. Williams, lawyer, section 32, Lancaster township, testified: "Time, probably 2.10 P. M.; it was a few minutes after 2 P. M. Watched the storm as it approached for about one hour. A cloud rose in the west, which, stretching to the north-west, presented the appearance of heavy rain. Previous to the approach of this cloud the sky was nearly clear. The wind during the day was southerly. About twenty-five minutes after the tornado the wind was again from the south-west. The storm-cloud did not extend far past the zenith to the south. Saw the funnel distinctly. It alternately lengthened and contracted, rose and fell. When it contracted, it appeared as if the narrow point next the earth was cut off, leaving the lower end broader. At times the upper end appeared to reach the overhanging clouds, and at times to be *not so high*. It was of a dark blue color when two hundred and fifty yards distant. When three hundred yards distant, it subtended an angle of about 75°. The angle subtended by the top of it at that distance was about 55°. It had a zigzag motion. Half an hour previous to the tornado there was incessant lightning in the north-west. Heard no thunder. There was no lightning in the tornado. A little rain and hail fell just before the tornado, and a smart rain-shower about twenty minutes after it. Have heard that to the northward there was a terrific storm of rain and hail, accompanied with thunder and lightning. The wind was south generally during the day. As the tornado approached the wind changed to a little east of south. Saw the dark funnel strike the ground on my farm. Saw it whirling contrary to the hands of a watch."

This witness was stationed about twenty-five yards south of the funnel when nearest to it. The fences were generally thrown toward the centre on either side; but where the dark cloud touched they were carried away for a space sixty yards wide. We have here the first evidence of the dark cloud touching the earth in perfect funnel form. But its touch is yet only temporary; like a child learning to walk, its footsteps are yet uncertain. *It proceeds with a wavy, zigzag, circular pendulum motion.* By and by its tread will make the earth tremble.

The storm traversed Jones's farm, throwing down fences, until it struck the Wolfden schoolhouse, which lay near its centre. The school was in session when the tornado struck it.

Richard Weller, teacher, testified that this occurred at a quarter past two P. M. precisely. This time is valuable, and I have adopted it as one of the data for calculating the velocity of the storm. The schoolhouse was moved, with the children and teacher in it, to the east, the north end thirty feet, the south end twenty feet. It was not overturned. The windows, roof, etc., were much damaged, but there were no evidences of explosive forces. The weight of the building was given by Mr. Williams as probably thirty thousand pounds. The surface exposed was three hundred and sixty square feet, besides the slanting roof. The slant of the roof was about 45°. The foundation was stone. It became very dark as the tornado struck. After leaving the schoolhouse, which is situated in a slight ravine-like depression, the fury of the tornado abated somewhat. Hence, although it was nearly central over the hamlet of Hayesville, the frail houses were scarcely touched.

S. U. Alford, who lives a quarter of a mile south of Hayesville, saw the tornado-cloud swinging round in a circle like a flock of birds, and every now and again making a dip to the ground and darting up again as high as the top of a tree. Its color was very dark, inclining to green. *The wind, which was south before the tornado, changed to north after it.* A little hail fell as the tornado passed. . . .

A. N. Bucher, one mile east of Hayesville, and about ten rods south of the tornado: Saw a funnel shape, large at top, small at bottom, of a dark green color. It looked like a kettle of soup boiling over. The funnel ended in a large cloud, which did not extend much south of the zenith. The bottom of the funnel kept bulging up and down. *Wind was from the south previously. It changed to the north-west* as it passed, and it *grew cooler.* At this place only a few fences were thrown down. . . .

The storm up to this point had been travelling east-north-east. Since leaving South Skunk River, it had been traversing a rolling prairie, with numerous sloughs, as they are called, but nothing like a watercourse. A little to the east of the last witness it struck Troublesome Creek, the banks of which are well wooded. No sooner did it do so than it increased greatly in power, changed its path temporarily to due east, and developed the phenomena of two or more funnels or branches of a funnel. Down in the hollow, among the trees, stood the house of widow Jacobs. It was completely demolished, but without signs of explosion. The storm-traces were already in great part obliterated, and a new house rebuilt. The path of destruction was two hundred yards wide at this point, and the general aspect of the fallen trees within this limit presented all the appearances of a complete cyclone, revolving contrary to the hands of a watch, although nothing particularly worthy of notice presented itself. About a quarter of a mile from the main track to the south, a *swath* about fifty yards wide was cut through the fences by a *south-west wind.* This swath appeared to curve toward the main storm-path, but it was not possible to follow it until it reached it, because of the sparseness of the fences, and because there had everywhere on that side of the storm been a strong *south-west* wind, and this swath was merely exceptionally strong.

The storm-centre next traversed the Grout farm, now occupied by Samuel Brunt, and passed about one hundred yards to the north of the village of Lancaster. Here its operations became more interesting.

Samuel Brunt testified: Heard it roaring a long time before it arrived; as it approached saw *two* funnels distinctly; their summits were lost in the overhanging mass of dark cloud. Saw funnel on the south side, which was the smaller, swing around in a half circle and join the larger one. The funnel had a pendulum motion. When it struck the ground, it seemed to smoke, the smoke surging up like spray upon a wave-beaten rock. The wind felt *cold* as it passed. Saw lightning during tornado. The breadth of the dark apex of the main tornado when it touched the ground appeared to be about one hundred feet. There the wheat was mown as with a scythe.

The breadth of the path of the storm of sufficient power to throw down fences was here two hundred yards. The fences on the north side were blown south, those on the south side north, while along the centre everything was carried east with the storm. . . .

J. B. Jacobs, Lancaster village, witness: Saw distinctly *two* whirls, the north one being the largest.

William Davis, Lancaster village, witness: Watched it for perhaps an hour previous to its arrival. Heard it for half an hour. Saw funnel when half a mile distant. The summit of it was lost in very dense clouds. It was funnel-shaped. The elevation of its summit was about 15°. It appeared to be about as high as the summit was broad. The top was twice or thrice as broad as the base. The clouds above it did *not* appear to whirl. Saw lightning during the tornado and heard thunder above the roar of the tornado. Previously the wind blew from the *south-east* strongly. After it passed, it blew from the *north-west*. Saw boards whirling round in the funnel. . . .

L. W. Low, Lancaster village: Mr. Low's house stood south of the principal portion of the village, and near the centre of the tornado. Testimony: Was in the house when the tornado came. The south-west corner was lifted off the ground. The floor was then driven in toward the roof, and the house went to pieces. Was severely injured. *Was wet and covered with mud. Felt very cold. Felt warm soon afterward. Seemed to be surrounded with a heavy mist.* Saw only one funnel. Saw lightning on both sides of it.

The last witness has weak eyesight.

This completes the evidence for the village of Lancaster. It is somewhat discordant, or, rather, various. Some saw only one funnel, some two funnels side by side, and others two funnels superimposed, with the small ends together. The discrepancies are, however, easily accounted for. As the cloud approached it grew very dark. The tornado doubtless changed its form rapidly. The observers took a glimpse at it and ran to attend to their houses, or, as in the case of Follman, had to watch it under difficulties. Those who saw two funnels appear to have seen through the centre of what appeared to those at a greater distance as only one funnel with the larger end down. The evidence afforded by the ruins in the path of the storm gives no support whatever to the belief that there were two distinct whirlwinds. The two dark clouds touching the ground worked together in the strictest harmony in producing such effects as would be produced by one tornado whirling contrary to the hands of a watch; but as already instanced, *streaks of wind of unusual power curved in half circles toward the centre at certain places.* One of these streaks passed in a *north-easterly* direction through the town of Lancaster, while the main whirl was one hundred yards to the north of it. This streak was at first only a few yards broad, but rapidly increased in width as it proceeded. It first unroofed a frail stable, without injuring the house beside it. It then increased in force, throwing down four or five houses, and unroofing as many more. The following shows the position of the houses and the directions in which they were blown. (*Fig.* 20.)

The long arrow denotes the main track, the curved arrow the streak mentioned, the short arrows show the direction of the destructive wind which threw down the various buildings. *Between the building a and the main storm-path there is a space of fifty yards comparatively uninjured.** The sketch does not pretend to be strictly accurate as to distances, but to give the relative positions of the houses.

Leaving Lancaster, the whirlwind travelled down the declivity toward North Skunk River in a direction somewhat east of north-

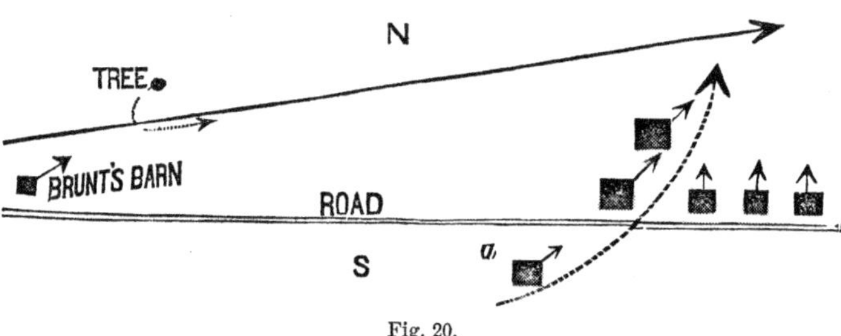


Fig. 20.

east. It levelled the fences in its path in the way already described, and never varied from its commencement to its end. The house of widow Dogget, situated about a quarter of a mile south of the river, stands a little to the north-west of the storm-centre, at the commencement of the level bottom-lands. Here two deep ravines, one from the south and one from the east, meet. In these ravines the storm developed enormous power, smashing up the timber terribly. The roofs of the house and barn were carried south and somewhat west. The trees on the north side of the centre were thrown down toward the centre, some pointing south-west and south, but the majority south-east. On the south side of the centre they lay pointing north-east, north and north-west. An oak tree twelve feet in circumference at the base was broken across twelve feet from the ground. At the bottom of the narrow, steep ravine, running east

* The triangular area of destruction is here very marked, all the arrows of the houses to the right of the figure pointing to the same point, and the areas "comparatively uninjured," immediately adjoining, would, I am sure, have been found to be also triangular.

That the "streaks" of destruction by a south-west wind were at first narrow, but increased in width, is unquestionably an error, as the cut shows, unless, indeed, Mr. Mackintosh means that the streaks were narrow near the track of the vortex, and increased in width as they progressed away from it.—W. B.

and west, trees were lying just as they fell, some pointing east and some west.

Mrs. Wimar testified: That difficulty was experienced in preventing the wind from bursting in the door and windows; that it felt *cool* as the storm was passing; that a few hail as large as hens' eggs fell before the hurricane, and a great deal of rain afterward; and that the point of the lightning-rod upon the barn was partially melted by a flash of lightning.

One quarter mile beyond Mrs. Dogget's house the tornado reached Skunk River, which it then followed for over two miles in a south-easterly direction until it came to the southerly bend of the river, opposite Kohlhaus's saw-mill, when it suddenly turned to the north-east. . . .

The house of Joseph Ash, situated on the face of the bluff, and distant from the river about half a mile, was blown to the south-south-west. Large trees were at this distance blown down in the ravines running to the river. Mr. Ash testified that the wind lasted a few minutes, and that it changed to the *north-west after* the passage of the tornado. A little hail fell before the storm, and a small shower of rain after it. Saw lightning and heard thunder. It grew *cool* as the storm passed.

Matthias Gengler's house stands on the summit of the bluff, one mile distant from the river. Due north of this farm was the saw-mill of Joseph Kohlhaus, where the tornado turned to the north-east. Mr. Gengler testified that it presented the appearance of a column rising from the river to the clouds. Its width at the top was twice as great as at the bottom. It was perfectly round and perpendicular. *It moved steadily along, without jumping up and down and from side to side.*

Matthias Hotel's house is a quarter of a mile east of Gengler's, and at the same distance from the river. He testified that it appeared to him like a big tower. Sometimes it was wider at the top than the bottom, and sometimes at the bottom than the top. *All afternoon previous to the storm it was very dark in the north.* As the tornado approached, *the wind grew very high from the south*, endangering the buildings. . . .

The Black Hawk mills are situated about one and a half miles farther down the river than the point where the tornado left it.

Eli Walker, proprietor, testified that he heard a roaring for perhaps an hour previous to the arrival of the tornado. Saw it approaching apparently in a straight line for witness. It seemed to move slowly, and was perfectly steady, without any oscillating motion. Could not in the column itself recognize a whirling motion, but the light clouds around the summit of it were whirling. The top of the column had an elevation of about 30° when nearest. Saw it suddenly bend to the north-east at Kohlhaus's. Before the tornado approached, *the northern sky was black with clouds*, which extended eastward. The *south was generally clear*. A hail-stone or two fell as the tornado came up, and a light shower of rain afterward. Saw no lightning. Heard thunder previous to the tornado. *While the whirlwind was on the river, the water ceased to flow over the dam, although the river at the time was high.*

E. Stout was at Black Hawk mills. He testified: Saw it distinctly in funnel shape. Could see it as far as Lancaster from the summit of the mill-buildings. The top of it appeared, when one and a half miles distant, to be 15° in height. Saw two funnels come together and form one. The smaller one came from the south and joined the other. The top of the funnel looked like a solid body of water. Saw flashes of lightning from top of funnel, apparently northward. The small end of the funnel was up, but there was not much difference in size. The clouds above the funnel appeared to be whirling and approaching the centre. The funnel which came from the south was of a lighter color than the other. The wind changed as the tornado advanced, and blew strongly toward it. The clouds above the narrow top of the funnel appeared to whirl in funnel form, with the wide end upward.

The following represents the apparent direction of motion of the two funnels as they approached each other.* (*Fig.* 21) . . .

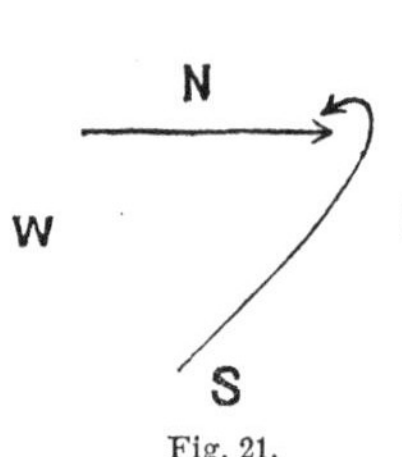

Fig. 21.

The house and steam saw-mill of Joseph Kohlhaus stood directly in the path of the meteor, at the distance of a quarter of a mile from the river, on the north side.

Mr. Kohlhaus testified as follows: The tornado appeared to stand *still* for several moments at the *bend of the river*, and then all at once bounded forward to the house. While standing still, it seemed to shoot or grasp out first on the one side and then on the other, as if discharges of artillery were taking place on these

* The explanation of this seems to be that at this point there was a protuberance of the polar current through which the main vortex cut, while one of the lesser vortices accompanying it, having less force, was turned out of its course by the polar air, and skirted it, joining the main vortex again.—W. B.

sides. The roaring was terrific. It resembled the sounds of machinery magnified a million times. It was a combined woo-oo-oo and whirr-r-r-r. Watched the column as it approached. It was funnel-shaped, but changed its appearance. It twisted around and up like a screw. Could not recognize bodies in the column; it was too black; and when the funnel came near, it grew as dark as midnight. *All the clouds were very low.* They did *not all* revolve. Saw lightning before the storm.

The building stood upon the summit of a rising ground, about thirty feet high. Between it and the river is a half pool, half marsh. It was completely emptied of water. The breadth of the path of wholesale destruction was, upon the summit of the hill, two hundred and seventy yards. The house stood one hundred yards from the eastern and one hundred and seventy yards from the western extremity of this path. The timbers and contents of this house were carried in a half circle first to the north-west, then to the west, then south-west, then south, and finally to the north-east, the heavier articles being generally sifted out first, thus marking the way the ruins went.

On the eastern edge of the path was an orchard, and on the western a wood. The trees in the orchard were blown down from the south-east and south; the trees in the wood from the north and north-west. Portions of the clothing from the house and shingles from the roof lay among the trees in the wood or stuck among the branches. There were no signs of explosion, the doors and windows having been blown in. The inmates were all more or less injured. The width over which fences were blown down was here about three-quarters of a mile. An iron plough, weighing two hundred pounds, was carried forty yards. The sheet-iron chimney was carried two miles to the north-east. An iron sausage-machine, six inches by eight, and weighing fifteen pounds, was blown away. Part of it was found twelve hundred yards distant. The wheels of wagons were smashed and the tires twisted.

After leaving the mill, the storm ascended a hill some two hundred feet in height, levelling the fences, but with evidently diminished violence. . . .

Passing over the top of the hill in a north-east direction, it struck Rock Creek, which here runs south, with a little easting. Immediately altering its course, it went straight up the creek for about half a mile, developing prodigious power. The large trees which lined the banks were torn and peeled and overthrown in promiscuous ruin. At a point where there is a small circular island, and a considerable amount of stagnant water around, the storm would appear to have stood still for a moment.

There were no trees on the island itself. There was no evidence whatsoever that the barking of the trees had been effected by electrical action or sudden evaporation. Everything tended to prove that the bark had been loosened and broken by the excessive bending of the trees and by flying missiles. One of the steers killed at this creek had an oak rail driven completely through its shoulders.

On reaching a slough which enters Rock Creek from the north-east, the tornado followed it. Beside this slough and close to the creek was a small grove of young trees belonging to John Stein. This grove was completely carried away, nothing remaining except a few barkless twigs. At no point in its course did the storm develop greater energy than at this grove. Generally young saplings, over which the centre of the storm passed, were, although stripped of bark and twigs, left standing. Here the ground was whipped as bare as though the grove had been lashed with a whirlwind of fire. The tornado then passed between the houses of William Goeldern and John Stein, sweeping the fields, within the narrow path of its greatest violence, clean of grass, wheat and corn-stumps, while the ground was torn and furrowed by flying rails and trees. The rails and broken timber had been gathered from the fields; but John Stein assured me that they lay thickest along the centre of the storm. Along the sides of the paths of greatest violence many rails were driven deeply into the soil, end foremost.

While the main whirlwind thus pursued the path described, there were smaller offshoots or arms which played havoc on its south-east side. Such an arm cut a swath about twelve yards wide through Schild's orchard from *south-west to north-east,* the swath widening as it went. . . . The relative positions favor such a surmise. This streak of strong south-west wind was a quarter of a mile distant from the centre of the main tornado.

*A similar streak levelled the fences close to the house of John Stein for a width of fifty yards, while nearer the main tornado the fences remained standing.* This streak, I surmise, joined the main storm at the grove above mentioned. A similar arm tore down the new barn of F. A. Latz, about a quarter of a mile farther on, without injuring weaker buildings close beside it. The path of this streak is said to have been very distinct among the fences until it joined the whirlwind near the house of Peter Marsh. The fences were, however, already restored.

George Starr, three-quarters of a mile south-east of the tornado, witness: About one P. M. it commenced to thunder and lightning in the north-west. The storm advanced along the northern sky, and it lightened terribly there previously to the arrival of the tornado. A big cloud extended from *south-west to north-east.* It cleared up immediately after the tornado, both here and in the north.

John Marsh's house stood a little to the north-west of the centre of the storm. His testimony: Watched it as it came directly toward me. It deflected a little from side to side, with a zigzag motion. It turned and twisted like a screw in revolution. All the family were in the house, the house having no cellar. It became as dark as midnight. . . .

The corn-stalks in a contiguous corn-field were thus disposed: Those on the south-east side of the centre curved around from pointing nearly due north to nearly due west. Those on the north-west side curved around from pointing nearly due south to nearly due east. Along the centre all pointed with the storm. This shows the direction of the last wind, strong enough to alter the position of the stalks.

Matthias Linen, a quarter of a mile north-west of the edge of the storm, testified that it presented the appearance of a great column, reaching from the ground to the clouds, and whirling contrary to the sun. It seemed to *remain almost still* at some places, and then would dart forward. Hail four inches in diameter fell as the storm passed. They were very irregular in form.

Paul Ritter, Clear Creek township, section 9, testified that the tornado looked like a big tree, only it was five times greater at the top than at the bottom. It turned like a wheel in a mill. Its direction of evolution was against the hands of a watch. At the distance of a mile its top, when it entered the cloud, made an angle of about 60°. Hail as large as pigeon's eggs fell before the storm, and it rained very hard after it. Saw lightning in the west previously.

Mr. Ritter's house stands about seventy yards to the north-west of the storm-centre. Its path is here about two hundred yards wide. The arrangement of stalks in a corn-field was the same as that already given. The roof of the house was carried south. A stump-cutter, which was standing by the house, was carried—the iron portion fifty yards south, the wooden portion half a mile to east-south-east. Wheels which came within the reach of the storm were dashed to pieces, and the tires twisted into all sorts of shapes. An oak tree three inches in diameter, and which stood exactly in the storm-centre, was split by a fragment of a board one inch thick. The board was originally probably six inches broad and eight feet long. Of the two small fragments remaining in the tree, the longer was only seventeen inches in length. The board was driven into the tree from the south-west. The path of extreme violence, about fifty yards wide, was strongly marked in the grove of young oaks. They looked as if they had first been lashed against a pile of stones, and then trailed in the mud. Portions of bark were struck off and the smaller branches shattered and peeled. This grove stands upon the edge of a steep declivity about one hundred feet in height, at the bottom of which flows Clear Creek. Here is a circular hollow nearly enclosed by high bluffs, and within it the storm raged with demoniac fury, smashing trees of four feet in diameter to pieces. . . .

The storm now turned somewhat more to the northward, traversed several fields, demolishing the fences, until it struck the house of R. F. Campbell, Lafayette township, on the borders of Clear Creek township. The exact position of this and the two immediately preceding houses was difficult to determine upon the map, because of its very defective condition, and because their owners could not tell me what section they were in.

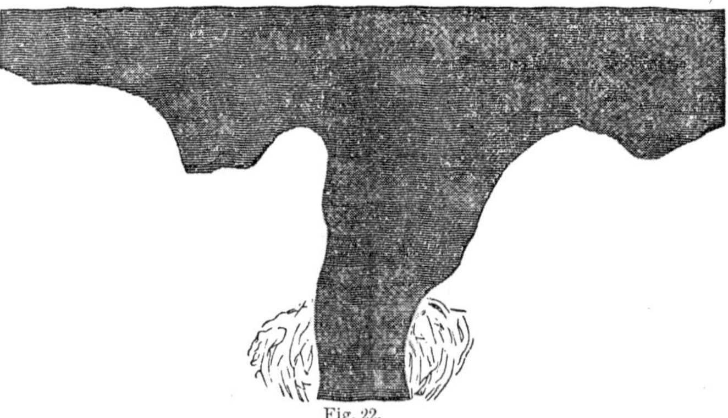

Fig. 22.

Mr. Campbell testified: That previous to the tornado he observed several currents above one another among the clouds. The wind was from the south-east. The lowest current of clouds from the south-west, the next from the north-west, and the highest from the north-east. It commenced hailing about fifteen minutes before the storm. The hail was, in some instances, three inches in diameter, and fell in considerable quantity. *It was calm when the hail fell.* The hail was very cold. When two were put together, they immediately froze. The north was full of black clouds previous to the tornado, in which the lightning flashed incessantly. Heard a dull, thundering noise in the north-west previous to the tornado as of *falling hail.* There appeared to be *rain or hail falling on both sides of the vortex* as it approached.

The preceding cut shows the appearance it presented at the distance of seventy yards. There appear to be *two* incipient funnels, one on each side. . . .

This was the last destruction in Keokuk county. The tornado ceased to touch the earth on Mr. Campbell's farm. It drew itself up into the cloud from which it had come down. *Hitherto it had traversed a country full of deep and well-wooded ravines.* Here it entered upon a flat, bare country—in fact, a watershed. It continues much the same for the seven miles which the tornado here skipped.

J. Yeats, Brockway's farm, Lafayette township, witness: Saw whirling in the clouds, after the tornado lifted, contrary to the hands of a watch. Watched it for ten minutes at least afterward, and it continued to whirl. The whirling portion of the clouds did not appear to be wide.

Mrs. Fobes, who resides about one mile north-west of the line of the tornado, witness: Saw the funnel. It seemed to stand still. Then it took a bend to the east. Then it grew so dark she could not see it. It grew lighter, and she could see it distinctly to the north-east of Campbell's house. It vanished suddenly, and she saw it whirling at a furious rate in the clouds contrary to the hands of a watch. *Did not notice any more roaring after the tornado lifted.* . . .

Joseph Charlton, Keota, witness: Saw the funnel distinctly reaching from the earth to the clouds. The clouds were *very low.* Saw the tornado disappear. It had only to rise a little way when nothing except the low cloud was visible. The dense low clouds continued the same, and the funnel only disappeared. *The southern sky was clear.* . . .

G. W. Erwin, Keota, witness: Remembers that when the tornado lifted the sound ceased.

W. R. Charlton, Keota, witness: Did not notice the noise after the tornado lifted. Heard it long and loudly before. . . .

The storm having ceased to act as a tornado upon the surface of the earth, I proceeded to Westchester, Washington county, where it was reported to have struck. . . .

G. W. James, station agent, Westchester, witness: Saw the main cloud whirling rapidly contrary to the hands of a watch. *Saw an arm come down* and strike the ploughed field. Could hear roaring overhead. The roaring was louder before the storm arrived than when it was here. A few large hail fell, and a little rain. . . .

Mrs. Thomas Gavin, Westchester, witness: The wind blew down the blacksmith's shop in the rear of our house. The house itself was shaking. Hail fell as large as hen's eggs. It grew quite dark when the house was struck. Everything was blown toward the *north-east*. . . .

Rev. J. P. Coffman, Cedar township, section 33, witness: The tornado arrived about three P. M. Heard the noise for more than one hour previously. *When it was hailing, heard the sound just as distinct as before.* Did not hear roaring after the storm passed. The wind before the storm was nearly *due south.* After the storm, and with the rain, the wind came from the *north and north-west.* Have learned that *two or three miles to the north the rain was tremendous.* There was lightning in the north-west previous to the tornado. As it approached saw light, fog-like clouds rushing, with the greatest rapidity, from the north. Its form was not so distinct before as after it passed, when it presented a decided funnel appearance. It was nearly clear in the south. When the funnel was distant about one mile, it appeared to subtend an angle of about 25°. The funnel might have entered the dark, overhanging clouds, but it appeared to be wholly in view. There seemed at one time as if there had been a violent explosion in the revolving mass, as it was somewhat broken up. Hail larger than pigeon's eggs fell with the south wind before the storm.

The tornado passed over Mr. Coffman's house, blowing down fences about a quarter of a mile in width, and damaging buildings. *It was all done by a south-west wind.*

Calvin Craven, Cedar township, section 33, witness: Previous to the storm the wind blew briskly toward it from the east. The cloud as it approached extended from *south-west to north-east,* covering the whole northern sky. Heard the roaring of the tornado like several trains in motion about thirty minutes previous. Saw white, foggy clouds darting through one another with frightful velocity as it came near. *Above these whirling clouds* was a dense black cloud. A few hail fell before the tornado, and a little rain after. Have heard that a most tremendous rain fell about one mile and a half to the north. *It was extremely warm before the storm.*

J. C. Brown, Jackson township, witness: Was on the north-east of Calvin Craven's. Noticed the tornado first as it was tearing his fences, etc. At this time there was one whirl which reached the earth. It was not a jet black, but the color of coal-smoke. There was a big cloud directly over; but although in commotion, it did not whirl. Went into a ditch to escape the hurricane. *I then saw other two funnels, one on the south side and the other on the north side of the main one.* All three moved forward toward me; but the outside ones also moved toward the central one. In a short time they joined the central one, which then appeared to stand still, and whirl around and around for a moment. The side ones did not whirl. They were bent forward at their lower ends where they touched the ground. The middle one did not whirl. It moved due east and then north-east, and then due east again. The tops of all these were several times wider than the lower portions. Saw no lightning. A little hail fell before, and a little rain after. The wind blew from the south-east before and from the north-north-east after the tornado. . . .

R. H. Craven, Cedar township, section 27, witness: A little hail fell before the tornado, and a little rain after it. The wind was north-west when the rain was falling. It cleared up about half an hour after the rain. In two places on the road east of Scranton's house *ten to fifteen rods of fence were blown down, leaving the intervening fence standing.* The fences on this farm were blown as usual.

W. H. Burham, Cedar township, witness: Was on the edge of Scranton's farm. Heard the storm a long time before it came. Saw it about twenty minutes. *The wind before the storm came from the south quite strong. Then it grew calm. Then there came a very hard wind right from the north.* An intensely black cloud, apparently about four feet wide at the bottom and swelling out like a large haystack, passed three hundred yards to the south. The top of it, when it entered the clouds, appeared to be about 45° high. *It moved up and down, now striking the ground and now passing over it.* When it struck the ground, it tore up everything. Saw it whirling contrary to the sun. Hail as large as walnuts fell before the storm, and a hard rain-shower after it, and then it cleared up immediately. Heard there was a heavy rain two miles to the north, washing away culverts and bridges. *It felt cool as the storm passed, but grew very warm afterward.* Saw rails flying out from the summit. An average rail weighs about forty pounds.

Frank Brown, Cedar township, section 26, witness: Distinctly saw the funnel revolving contrary to the hands of a watch. Its height at one and a half miles' distance was about 15°. Its top was five times broader than the lower end. Saw it strike the ground after it passed. Dark clouds appeared to strike the ground and rebound like spray. Saw only one funnel. The cloud extended from *south-west to north-east,* covering the whole northern sky. Observed sheet lightning in the tornado several times. It grew slightly *cold* as the storm passed. When the tornado had passed about one and a half miles, it appeared to stand still, and a strong gale with rain blew directly from it, so that I thought the storm was coming back. Almost everything on the farm which was blown down *was blown toward the north-east.* The breadth of path is a quarter of a mile.

Mr. Brown's house stands on the south-east edge of the storm. . . .

W. W. Cook, Cedar township, section 25, witness (house four hundred yards south-east of the edge of the storm-path): About twenty minutes before the storm came up the wind blew briskly from the south. When the tornado was passing, it blew a strong gale from the south-west. It rained after the tornado, and during the rain the wind blew from the west. . . .

J. W. Plumber, Cedar township, section 25 (house on south-east edge of the storm): When the tornado was several miles off, saw a mass of clouds come from the north-west and another from the south-west, and rush together. The angle between the southern limit of the south-west clouds and the northern limit of the north-west clouds, when several miles distant, was about 45°. The angle of elevation was about 35°. Besides these under-clouds, there were overhanging masses of cloud. Saw the funnel form distinctly after the storm passed. It appeared to be twice as broad at the top as the bottom. It looked like a screw turning contrary to the hands of a watch. When three-quarters of a mile distant, it subtended an angle of 25°. Hail fell about half an hour before the storm, with a gentle east wind. When the storm had approached within half a mile, *the wind came so strongly from the south as to blow a man off his feet.* It rained a little some few minutes after it passed, with a west wind. About twenty minutes after the tornado a light shower fell, accompanied with a *north-west* wind of about twenty-five miles per hour. Saw lightning in the north-west before the storm. . . .

R. M. Stevenson, Jackson township, section 25, witness: The wind blew from the south-east as the storm came up, changing to north as it passed. The rain came with the *north wind.* Saw the funnel make two dips and touch the ground. The top of the tornado, when seven hundred yards distant, appeared at an angle of 35°.

The house of this witness stood a quarter of a mile south-east from the centre of the storm. The outbuildings were somewhat damaged. . . .

A. Booth, Cedar township, half a mile north-west of storm: Saw it twenty or thirty rods north-east of Frank Brown's. Saw it whirling against the sun. The wind came from the east before the storm, and from the north-west after it. . . .

Thomas Waters, Jackson township, section 19, witness: Saw the tornado coming rolling on the ground like a wave. Went to the cave, and called upon Mrs. Waters to follow. She would not. Stood in the mouth of the cave, which was eight yards south from the house and facing it, and saw the house blown away. It was struck from the *south-west.* First, a portion of the roof was blown off, then the house went bodily like lightning. When the house had gone, I came out of the cave, and was blown to the *east-south-east.*

Mr. Waters's house was 30 by 16 by 11 feet without the roof. It was carried, sill and all, twenty-four yards down a declivity without being turned round or tilted over. When it struck the ground, it at first merely shaved it with the foremost sill, gradually going deeper, until the resistance became so great as to cause the house to turn over, when it went to pieces. The ground was ploughed up about two feet at the deepest point. The house had fallen three feet in travelling twenty-four yards. Its weight was at least ten tons.

Between the cave, which was only about four feet above the surface, and the house, but nearer the cave, stood a small tree. Against it a spade was leaning. Mr. Waters testified that it was *not* blown down. Two yards east of the tree stood a bucket containing a small quantity of lime, and weighing ten pounds. It was *not* disturbed. To the south-west of the cave the trees were *comparatively uninjured over a triangular space, while on either side they exhibited signs of the greatest violence.* An oak sill which had evidently been carried with the house until it struck, and then hurled due east, was driven four feet into the soil at an angle of 45°. Its dimensions are 16 feet by 8 inches by 8 inches, and its estimated weight three hundred pounds. It was found eighteen yards east of where the house struck. . . .

J. K. Marbourg, Jackson township, section 17, witness (house eighty yards from storm-centre, with an excellent view of Gibson's house): Watched the storm a long time before it came. The west was first filled with clouds which extended until they covered all the western and northern heavens, reaching a little beyond the zenith. The tornado first appeared as two clouds, one from the south-west and the other from the west, rushing to one point. Together they presented somewhat the appearance of an arrow. The whirl was seen forming when they met. Above them were dark, heavy clouds. When the tornado came nearer, it presented the appearance of one funnel, revolving contrary to the hands of a watch, and drawing everything up.

When at Gibson's house, where I had the best view of it, and where it was one hundred and twenty rods distant, it presented the appearance of two funnels uniting in one, at the height of forty or fifty feet. The bases of the two funnels were about two hundred feet apart. They presented somewhat like the following appearance.*

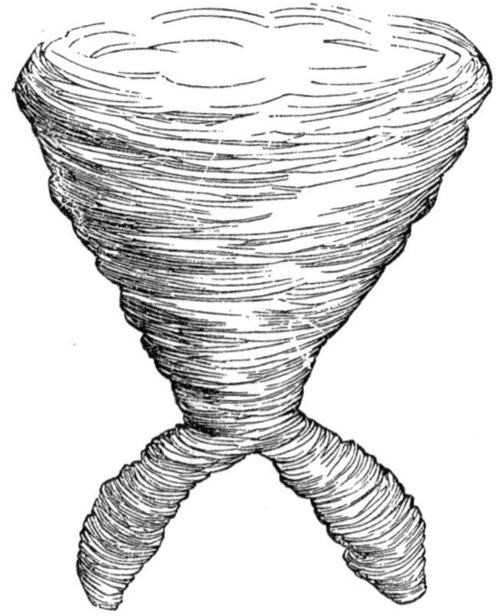

Fig. 23.

The *two funnels did not appear to revolve around each other.* The first came to the east of Gibson's house, took his stable, and then turned

* The explanation seems to be that of the lower branches, one was the dust of the in-rushing equatorial air and the other the dust of the in-rushing polar air, a certain quantity of which would be drawn into the vortex, especially at its point of greater violence.—W. B.

back to his house. The two then appeared to unite. Could not see the two afterward. The tornado disappeared behind a building. It grew very dark. The funnels were of a dark blue. Everything in them was rising. The timbers from Gibson's house flew up. Did not see clear sky through the open space between the two funnels, but a bright yellowish hue. The upper funnel extended to the clouds above. Hail, or rather chunks of ice from a pigeon's to a hen's egg in size, fell before the tornado column came in sight. The wind then blew gently from the east. After the tornado had destroyed the schoolhouse, there came a violent gust of wind from the *north-west*, which considerably damaged my outbuildings. I had started to go to the schoolhouse, and it carried me several yards before it. Immediately there fell a torrent of rain, with *cold wind* from the *north.* Was near where the school had been, but could not see anything. Suddenly saw the teacher and children, as if they had sprung out of the earth. They were coming toward me. They were *shivering.* They could give no account of what had befallen them. Never saw such miserable-looking beings in my life. I had four children there, and did not recognize them. *The mud was pelted into their skins,* so that it could not be washed out. It is not all washed out yet. A dead child was found forty yards north-west of the schoolhouse. The storm opposite my house was a mile wide. An oak post four inches in diameter was perforated by an oak board four and a half feet by four inches by one inch. (It had been thrown among the other rubbish, and was not to be found.)

James Clancey, residing with J. K. Marbourg, testified that he viewed the tornado from the same position as Mr. Marbourg, and saw only one funnel. I do not, however, estimate his observing powers so highly as those of his employer. . . .

J. H. Laughhead, Jackson township, section 16, witness: A little hail fell before the storm. It rained awfully for half an hour after it. *Wind during the rain* was from the *north-west.* It was very dark. Saw no lightning.

The house of this witness stands on the north-west side of the storm-centre, about one-third of a mile distant from it. The fences were blown the usual way.

Levi Moothart, Cedar township, about two miles north of the path of storm, witness: There fell the heaviest rain I ever saw; also hail as large as hen's eggs. The rain lasted about an hour, and the whole country was under water. The wind during the rain-storm changed from *south to west and north*, and at times it was very strong . . .

D. T. Carringer, Jackson township, section 15: The house stood on the south edge of the storm. It was carried to the *north-east* seventeen feet, going deeper into the soil as it went. It then turned over, and was blown away in fragments. The straw among the trees showed that *the last gust came from the north-west.*

Josiah Condit, Jackson township, section 11, witness: No hail fell before the tornado. It rained terribly right after it. The wind was blowing from *north-west* as the rain fell. Saw no lightning.

Mr. Condit's house stands upon the south-east edge of the storm, which here travelled nearly due north-east. There seems to have been a streak of exceptionally strong *north-west* wind, which struck the barn and corn-crib, and cut its way through the garden fences. The centre passed along the fields, producing upon fences and hedges the same effects as those already described. . . .

J. H. Lyttle, Highland township, section 12, witness: Had nearly half a mile of fence thrown down. The east and west fences were blown south; the north and south fences east. Heard roaring an hour before the storm came. The roaring was louder before it came than after it was here. Did not hear it after it passed. Saw the funnel until it came within three miles' distance. The whole northern portion of the sky was covered. Saw a cloud rushing from the south, and another rushing to meet it from the north. The clouds rushing north appeared to be the lowest. After the clouds came overhead could see the lowest clouds rushing rapidly from the south. These were broken clouds. Through them could see a higher current rushing from the north. A little hail and rain fell. The wind changed from the *south to the west and north-west* as the storm passed. The width of fence blown down was about one hundred and fifty yards.

Michael McGuire, Highland township, section 12: One-half mile of fence on the farm was blown down. The chimney was blown off and some trees levelled. All was done by a north-west wind. It hailed a little, and rained very heavily.

The storm now passed out of Washington county into Louisa county, travelling south-east.

Joshua Luckey, Louisa county, Union township, section 17, witness: The path of fences blown down on my farm was about six hundred yards wide. The fences on the west of the centre were thrown north; those on the east were thrown south. A few hail fell, and a smart shower of rain. Heard no roaring after it passed.

Charles Crim, Union township, section 20, witness: Fences two hundred yards wide thrown down to the south-east. The roaring was very loud for an hour previous to its arrival. Did not hear it after it passed. Saw no lightning. Saw a tongue of cloud shaped like a funnel hanging from the clouds. It did not reach the earth. At first it was hanging perpendicular. Then it commenced whirling like the tail of a suspended snake.

At this point I lost track of the tornado, and could not recover it, although I spared neither time nor pains. Only now and again could one find a man who could give any information even of what happened on his neighbors' farms a week or two before.

John Colton, Columbus Junction, witness: There was some hail, a brisk wind and a tremendous rain.

Mrs. Snyder, Oakland township, section 9: Heard roaring distinctly. There fell a very heavy rain, which continued until nearly dark.

Peter Attig, Johnson county, Tremont township, section 22, witness: About four P. M. there was a terrific rain-storm, with hail as large as hickory-nuts, and accompanied with thunder and lightning. My barn was struck by lightning. Perkins's barn was also struck.

Lone Tree Station: About four P. M. there was a violent storm of rain, hail, thunder and lightning.

Nichols Station: There was here a high wind, with heavy rain and hail, and accompanied with thunder and lightning.

At this point I gave up the search and took train for Illinois. Previous to describing its effects there, the following testimony may find a place.

H. C. Vittitoe, Warren township, Keokuk county, about three miles north-west of the tornado, witness: Saw a little south of the zenith the white under-clouds rushing in circles to a centre. The gyration was contrary to the hands of a watch. The funnel had not yet touched the earth. The wind came from the *north-west* pretty strong *after* the passage of the tornado, bringing with it a little rain and hail.

Dr. W. D. Hoffman, Sigourney, witness: Mrs. A. T. Page collected a number of the largest hail-stones. When melted, it was found that they had contained a quantity of *twigs, leaves, dry grass and mud, all reduced to fine proportions.* Hail weighing from four to eight ounces were common. One hail-stone, which was shaped like an apple, measured four and a half inches in diameter. The roaring was heard about twenty minutes before the hail began. It rose and fell like the cannonading in a battle. During the hail the wind came from the north-east, but it was very light. Sigourney is four miles north of the storm. . . .

A. H. Swan, editor of the Monmouth *Review*, witness: There was an exceedingly heavy rain, a little hail, and a great deal of lightning about five P. M. The atmosphere smelt as of brimstone previously. It was oppressively hot; perhaps 95°.

The temperature and pressure on May 22, 1873, at places near the tornado:

| | Davenport. | | Keokuk. | | West Union. | |
|---|---|---|---|---|---|---|
| | Bar. | Ther. | Bar. | Ther. | Bar. | Ther. |
| 7 A. M. | 29.73 | 64 | 29.64 | 69 | 29.49 | 61 |
| 2 P. M. | 29.60 | 77 | 29.51 | 85 | 29.46 | 65 |
| 9 P. M. | 29.69 | 66 | 29.71 | 72 | 29.53 | 64 |

The condition of the barometer and thermometer at West Union* was obtained from Frank McClintock, correspondent of the Smithsonian Institution, who also furnishes the following noteworthy fact: "Wind changed from the south to the west rapidly at 3.45 P. M. It worked back to the south before nine P. M." The relative humidity at—

| | Davenport. | Keokuk. |
|---|---|---|
| 7 A. M. | 94 | 85 |
| 2 P. M. | 77 | 54 |
| 9 P. M. | 94 | 85 |

We do not, therefore, overrate the relative humidity when we estimate it at sixty-five per cent. at two P. M. The average temperature at the earth's surface in the line of the tornado at two P. M. was, from the above, probably 76°, but in the wooded hollows much greater.

Mr. Jay, however, of Harper, Keokuk county, states that the temperature was 92° half an hour after the storm. The day was generally described as being very warm.

Having arrived at Prairie City, Ill., I endeavored to find out the exact locality where the tornado first began to overthrow fences, damage buildings, etc. On the farm of James Williams, Point Pleasant township, Warren county, there was a strong wind, but not sufficiently so to prostrate fences. About one mile to the east is the farm of Israel Jared, Point Pleasant township, section 24. Mr. Jared testified as follows: Saw streaks of cloud moving from the north and

* West Union is more than one hundred miles to the north of the tornado, and, therefore, too far off to furnish important data.—W. B.

south toward each other before anything touched the earth. Saw a cloud in the form and about the size of a haystack strike the ground on my farm. A few minutes before, hail of moderate size and in small quantity fell, followed, as the whirlwind was passing, by a smart shower of rain. The wind, which had been south-east, changed to the west after the tornado passed. *It was pretty warm before and cool after it.* Heard roaring some five minutes previous to the arrival of the storm. Fences were blown down for two hundred yards wide. They were blown toward the east. Saw some lightning. There was a heavy cloud to the north as the storm approached.

Mr. Jared's house stands about two hundred yards north of the storm-path. The tornado was here travelling a little to the north of east.

John F. Tatman, Israel Jared's farm, testified that he saw the funnel strike the farm, and that he heard the roaring for a long time previous.

Before leaving this farm the storm had developed all the characteristics of a tornado, except that the *east wind was not yet powerful enough to destroy*. . . .

*Streaks of unusually strong wind seemed to come now and again from the south side and run into the main whirl.* The wind on the north side was not nearly so strong as on the south side. Twice as much fence was blown down on the south as on the north side. Its noise resembled that of machinery, only very loud. . . .

B. A. Reid, Sr., Swan township, section 25, witness: Saw two clouds, one in the north-west and one in the south-west, rushing together with great rapidity. A whirling commenced right where they met, assuming the form of a funnel. Saw it whirling with the hands of a watch at the distance of about two miles. These low clouds were overhung by a heavy mass of clouds. The funnel reached up to this mass. There was a little hail and a little rain. My house is less than half a mile south of the centre. . . .

John Van Winkle, Union township, Fulton county, section 30, witness: The storm-centre passed thirty rods to the north of the house. Remained out of doors all the time. Saw the funnel appearance touching the ground a half mile distant. The roaring was so loud that I could not hear the breaking of the buildings. There was no crashing, but a whirring like that of a thousand threshing-machines. Everything on the south side was thrown toward the centre. Most of the wood was deposited along the centre. The storm *lay in the north-west a long time*, and during that time the wind was steady from the *south-east.* There seemed to be a dark cloud to the south-west, another in the north-west and a clearer space between. The wind blew from the *north-west* as the storm passed. . . .

J. B. Hatch, Union township, section 29, twenty rods to the south of the storm-centre, witness: The storm struck us a little before six P. M. As the cloud and darkness came over, everything appeared to be enveloped in a white mist. *There were no drops, but it wet everything.* The carpets in the house had to be taken up and dried. The paper on the walls was covered with *mud and fine-ground leaves.* The strongest wind came from the *south-west.* Everything was collected to the centre of the storm-path. Did not feel any choking sensation when surrounded by the mist. Did not feel cold. Boy felt chilly. It had been a very warm day. Saw lightning right in the storm. . . .

Cornelius Ackerman, Union township, a half mile east of Hatch's house and five rods south of the storm-centre, witness: Saw storm gathering in the north-west and south-west for some time. Hail nearly the size of hen's eggs fell before the storm. A *south* wind took the roof off the house. A *north-west* wind then still further demolished it. The wind took me off my feet. My hired hand, Cornelius Rice, was thrown down by the wind, and then pushed along the ground for several rods. He leaned on his elbow as he went. He *first travelled north, and then in a curve round to the east,* when he stopped his farther progress by clinging to the branches of a tree. *The ground was rather dry before the tornado. It was quite wet after it.* . . . The direction of the storm-path at this point was still east-south-east. . . .

R. Johnston, Union township, section 33: The wind commenced to blow very hard from the *south.* Went into the cellar. Two small buildings were first blown to the north. The kitchen was blown south-east. The barn and other buildings went south. The main building was pushed a few feet to the south-west. It grew so dark that one could not see ten feet. . . .

Mr. Johnston's house stood exactly in the centre of the whirlwind. . . .

Andrew Maholland, Union township, witness: It was near six P. M. when the storm struck us. *Felt the air to be very hot, like steam, before the storm.* The wind at first came strong from the east, and was accompanied by a *driving wet.* The roof of the house was blown to the south-west.

Mr. Maholland's house stands fifty rods to the north of the centre. . . .

D. H. Gorham, Union township, section 34, witness: The tornado arrived at my house at 5.55 P. M. Saw the storm gather in the west-north-west one and a half hours before it came. Saw a little lightning as it approached, but none after it arrived. Saw two clouds, one in the south-west and one in the north-west, with a red streak like sunset between them. Afterward saw only one cloud, rolling forward like a wheel. Heard a roaring a little before the storm arrived. It grew so dark that I could not read—a black darkness. First there came a blow from the south-east. After that there came a slight lull, and hail as large as hen's eggs fell straight. Then there came a harder blow from the north-east. Then for three minutes there fell a perfect torrent of rain. Rode out immediately, and the water on the road reached to the horse's belly. My outbuildings were damaged by the north-east wind. Fences were thrown down a mile wide.

Mr. Gorham's house stands fifty rods north of the centre of the storm. . . .

At D. M. Kline's farm fences were thrown down a mile wide. *They were thrown toward the centre from both sides. The storm at this point had greatly diminished in violence.*

O. Chatterton, Lee township, section 1, witness: Heaıd the roaring only a few minutes before the storm came. The wind blew first from the *south-west*, then from the *north-east*, and then from the north. Saw no lightning. A tremendous rain fell about eighty rods south from the house. . . .

Isaac Sechleider, Deerfield township, section 7, across Spoon River: Mr. Sechleider's house stood near the summit of the bluffs which face the river. It measured 16 by 22 by 12. It was blown south east three rods, and deposited on its roof. The five inmates were not much injured. The storm smashed the timber somewhat on the south-east bank.

About a mile farther on it became impossible to track the storm. Before proceeding to where it next struck, it may be advisable to insert some testimony from Prairie City and the neighborhood. Prairie City is about one and a half miles south from the storm-path.

The editor of the Prairie City *Herald* testified that he thinks the storm was opposite a little before six P. M.

C. H. Hemenover, Prairie City, testified that oak-leaves fell during the storm, and that the wind blew very strongly from the *south*. He keeps a thermometer, but did not look at it that day. Thinks temperature was not over 70°.

L. B. Day, Prairie City, witness : Saw a cloud in the north-west of a funnel shape ; heard a roaring sound for perhaps five minutes. The wind blew strongly from the *south-east* all of a sudden, accompanied with hail about the size of pigeons' eggs. There was an under-current of clouds from the south-east overhead. Just as this south-east wind blew it grew very dark. After the tornado passed, the wind changed to the *north-west*, and a smart shower fell. Then it cleared up, and the sun shone. . . .

A. T. Irvine, station agent, Prairie City: The telegraph was not disturbed by free electricity during the passage of the tornado. It only ceased to work between this and Avon after the wires were broken by the wind. The wind blew from the *south-east* as the storm approached. It rained quite a while from the south-east. Then it changed to the south-west, still raining ; and when the rain somewhat ceased, it came from the *north-east*. . . .

Having learned that the tornado had made another descent at Utica, near the Illinois River, I proceeded thither.

Jacob McCan, Utica, Banner township, Fulton county, witness : Storm came about half past six P. M.; saw lightning and heard thunder in the north-west, where a heavy cloud had long been gathering ; saw two under-clouds, one in the *south-west* and the other in the *north-west*, moving toward each other.* They were wind-clouds. Above them was a dark green cloud. The two clouds were whitish, and were *boiling up*. The sky to the east was clear at this time, the storm coming up as an isolated, solid mass of cloud. The wind commenced to blow hard from the *south-west*. Then there came a *brief lull;* then a second blow from the *north-west*. With the north-west wind there came a *blue smoke*. It came in through the broken window. It came right in the fury of the gale. It was all dark in front of the window with it. This north-west wind was *pretty cool*. It hailed a little before the storm, and it rained very hard after it.

Nearly all the houses in Utica were more or less damaged, and several were blown down. *The village stands on the bottom-lands of a small creek running into Illinois River. High bluffs rise all around.* The tornado was here travelling south-east. It came down about one-half mile to the north-west of Utica. It continued to overthrow trees until it reached Illinois River, which is distant from Utica about one mile. *It then turned abruptly to the north-east, travelling up the stream*, which it then followed for about fifteen or more miles in a straight line, but much farther counting the bends in the river. . . .

* Evidently the commencement of a new tornado.—W. B.

Mapleton, Peoria county; Here there fell hail as large as hazel-nuts, and a very heavy rain, accompanied by thunder and lightning. It occurred after six P. M. William Harrison testified that he saw trees in considerable numbers which had been blown down in the storm of May 22.

Pekin: the ferry man testified that there was a big rain storm with high wind. The smoke-stack of his boat was somewhat damaged by it. Mr. Tazewell stated that the high wind came first, then the hail and rain.

Fred Netz, Washington, Illinois, witness: It blew very hard about 6.15 P. M. There was a heavy rain.

Thomas Handsacker, editor of the Washington *Herald*, Washington, Illinois: The storm came at 6.10 P. M., or very nearly. I watched the cloud. Did not see any funnel appearance or any whirling. There was a very heavy rain, accompanied with thunder and lightning. The wind blew down numbers of trees in different directions, but mostly from the south-west.

*Special despatch to the Chicago Times.*

OTTAWA, ILLINOIS, May 23.

The tornado which passed through central Iowa seemed to have spent its force here last evening. An enormous quantity of rain fell in an incredibly short time, and the trains on both railroads were delayed for hours. Bridges were swept away and much damage done. Ottawa lay directly in the line in which the storm was travelling when I ceased to follow it.

*Special telegram to the Chicago Times.*

SPRINGFIELD, ILLINOIS, May 23.

A very heavy storm of wind, rain and hail passed over this city last night.

*Special telegram to the Chicago Times.*

PEORIA, May 24.

The severe storm of Thursday night did much damage in Princeville, this county. A narrow strip of wind passed through Southern Village, almost literally demolishing the house of Oliver Moody.

Such is a statement of the facts connected with the Iowa and Illinois tornado of May 22, 1873, so far as I have been able to collect them. I spared no pains in order to render it scientifically complete, sometimes travelling miles under a fierce sun, and with a temperature among the nineties, in order to obtain the evidence of one man. The information given by any witness by no means represents the number of questions asked him. These were extensive, and calculated to extract all the knowledge on the subject possessed by those under examination. For instance, the following question was addressed to all and sundry: Did you observe any pointed objects, such as lightning-rods, posts, etc., tipped with flame during the progress of the tornado? But being uniformly answered in the negative has not been formerly inserted in the statement of facts. Also a description of the sound was exacted from all witnesses, but only a few typical ones have been inserted. I regret this at present, because I have learned from experience that very important questions may attach themselves to a description of the sound. While interrogating parties the utmost vigilance was exercised to prevent them from giving conclusions for what they saw and heard. This was a very troublesome point, and caused the interrogator to appear in many cases in the highest degree rude, while it also excluded from these pages the names of persons who observed accurately, but who are unable to distinguish between the *esse* and the *ergo*.

No opportunity was allowed to pass of obtaining information. Whether at home, on the road or in the field, all met were questioned. Of course by far the majority could give no information worth taking.

It will be noticed that the statement of facts for Iowa is much more exhaustive and instructive than that for Illinois. There are several reasons for this:

1. Some weeks had already elapsed since the tornado, and its traces were becoming rapidly obliterated, both in the memories of the witnesses and upon the surface of the earth.

2. It was later in the day when it occurred, thus hiding the light of the sun more completely by the tornado-clouds as they approached, and rendering it more difficult to observe accurately their forms and proportions.

3. The storm in Illinois seems to have been of a somewhat different character from that in Iowa, by its form rendering observation more difficult.

It may perhaps not be deemed irrelevant to mention that the best information was uniformly obtained from those who are not natives of the localities in which they live, but have settled there from other States or other countries. The reason of this may perhaps be that Iowa and Illinois are but recently settled, and that consequently the native-born population have not yet had time to arrive at years of discretion, whereas the original settlers are in the prime of manhood or verging toward old age.

With regard to the angles of elevation given, it must be borne in mind that they are only approximations. Very few indeed of the witnesses have accurate conceptions of angles. I generally made them point in the direction in which an object was seen, and so estimated the angle.

---

# APPENDIX D.

(*From the New York Herald.*)

## ATMOSPHERIC COMETARY INFLUENCES.

*To the Editor of the Herald:* On the 30th of July, 1874, I made an aërial exploration from the city of Philadelphia, under the direction of the meteorological section of the Franklin Institute, with instructions to make such observations as the day and circumstances would invite, keeping in view the marked disturbances of our atmosphere for some time past, and during the proximity of Coggia's comet. The main experiment designed in a series of balloon observations to be made was to ascertain the quantity of solid matter contained in the air in the form of animal and vegetable spores and particles floating over cities, as provided for by A. Purves, Esq., in his contribution to that end, but being deferred until the necessary instruments were prepared by Dr. William H. Wahl, scientist of the institute.

I took with me, as assistants, my niece, Mrs. Ihling, and my grandson, Master John Wise, they being entrusted with the thermometer and barometer. The day was clear and warm, and the sky overhead slightly dotted with cumulus clouds, but these disappeared before we ascended. It occurred to me that Coggia's comet during its perihelion passage would necessarily cast a penumbra over and through the atmosphere of our planet, and that this might be the cause of the extraordinary meteorological disturbances that assailed our earth with "cloud-bursts" and floods. Now, it is an established meteorological law that the temperature of our atmosphere diminishes with the height in regular order. So I have found it in my thirty-nine years' experience in cloudland and in my four hundred and forty-six aërial voyages, with only one exception.

### REMARKABLE INCREASE OF HEAT.

I had no idea that when I should make my 447th ascension—the one in question—I would meet with such decisive meteorological conditions confirmatory of the presence in our atmosphere of a disturbing cause, reasonably to be attributed to the action of Coggia's comet. Before leaving the earth I had the thermometer secured in a paper shade, where, at the moment of leaving the earth, it marked 72 degrees (Fahrenheit). Another thermometer, exposed in the car, marked 81 degrees. This instrument was broken in the ascent. I had intended to have the two noted all the time; but owing to this accident, the sheltered one was the only one used. At one minute past four P. M. we cut loose from the earth, and now, without a detailed narration of sights, sensations and incidents, I will briefly state the results obtained. As we rose we felt much like approaching a vast conflagration, and the first remarks of my assistants were, "Ain't it getting hot up here?" As the aneroid gave the altitude, so did the thermometer register an increase of heat. This seemed so remarkable to me, and so adverse to my long aërial experience, that I very naturally sought for the cause of the phenomenon. The sky was clear of clouds, except on the outer circular horizon that bounded the view. In nine minutes after we cut loose from the earth we rose to an altitude of 5400 feet over the southern portion of the city, and the thermometer marked 81 degrees. From this moment for two hours and fifteen minutes the following observations were made; and in order to be more certain of their correctness, I looked over the instruments in the hands of my assistants. I held the watch; and whenever I called time, they would answer with temperature and height. The aneroid marked the feet of altitude on its vernier.

### VARIATIONS OF HEAT AND ALTITUDE.

| | *Time.* | | | *Altitude.* |
|---|---|---|---|---|
| | *H.* | *M.* | *Thermometer.* | *Feet.* |
| Start, | 4 | 01 | 72 | 0,000 |
| Calm, balloon stationary, | 4 | 09 | 81 | 5,400 |
| Hazy, | 4 | 12 | 81 | 5,500 |
| | 4 | 15 | 82 | 5,600 |
| Balloon slightly agitated, | 4 | 20 | 79 | 5,400 |
| | 4 | 25 | 86 | 5,600 |
| Air hazy and striated, | 4 | 27 | 82 | 5,900 |
| | 4 | 31 | 83 | 5,550 |
| | 4 | 34 | 82 | 5,250 |

| | Time. H. M. | Thermometer. | Altitude. Feet. |
|---|---|---|---|
| Mist, and excessive heat was felt here, | 4 42 | 83 | 5,400 |
| | 4 50 | 85 | 5,000 |
| Out of the mist, | 4 55 | 82 | 4,400 |
| | 5 00 | 82 | 3,450 |
| | 5 02 | 90 | 2,250 |
| | 5 05 | 90 | 1,450 |
| | 5 08 | 85 | 1,230 |
| | 5 15 | 85 | 1,100 |
| | 5 18 | 89 | 1,400 |
| | 5 22 | 83 | 2,050 |
| | 5 24 | 82 | 2,450 |
| | 5 25 | 81 | 3,150 |
| | 5 32 | 70 | 4,350 |
| | 5 35 | 70 | 4,900 |
| Mist, | 5 40 | 70 | 5,750 |
| | 5 45 | 70 | 5,500 |
| Objects very distinctly seen below, | 5 48 | 69 | 5,800 |
| | 5 50 | 70 | 5,300 |
| | 6 00 | 70 | 3,500 |
| | 6 05 | 71 | 1,900 |
| | 6 16 | 73 | 1,400 |

At twenty minutes past six we struck the earth in the town of Vineland, New Jersey, forty miles from the starting-point.

From this place I reascended with the boy, leaving the lady behind, and rose to the height of four thousand five hundred feet. The view was greatly expanded in the twilight, and the ocean shore was well defined when viewed from the greatest altitude and at a distance within fifty miles. Our point of view was a pivot round which the Delaware River and the capes north of its mouth semicircled on our horizon.

As seen by the tabulated notes above, the temperature increased as we rose, and this was sufficient to induce a deep interest to my observations. It will also be seen that the temperatures are very irregular in regard to altitudes, but in this due allowance must be made for the times of fluctuation of perpendicular and horizontal movement of the balloon. When we entered hot strata, it always felt like approaching a conflagration, the heat producing an unpleasant sensation on the hands and face. My assistants were considerably scorched, and I felt its effects myself as forcibly as the application of a mustard plaster.

In addition to the thermometric revelations, so adverse to a normal condition of atmosphere, my attention was drawn to a peculiar shadow that overlaid the city from a north-west to south-east direction. This penumbrous shadow was well defined in its marginal lines, because it was dark, while the town north-east and south-west of it appeared as white as chalk, as did also the neighboring towns within the range of Wilmington to the south and Norristown to the north, both of which were plainly seen. As we receded from the city the shadowed part vanished into a very dark-colored obscurity, while its outer precincts were still visible as habitations. This phenomenon, coupled with the striated appearance of portions of the atmosphere, very naturally led the cogitating mind to Fraunhofer's spectral lines. These appearances were so marked, and the anomalous temperatures experienced so expressive, that nothing could satisfy my conjectures of the cause so well as the idea that

THE ATTENUATED ENVELOPE OF THE COMET

was transmitting beams and rays of sunlight with focal power into our atmosphere, and thus producing positive and negative lines as we find them under the spectroscope. It further induced the thought, May not all the convulsions and extraordinary disturbances of our atmosphere owe their origin to the movement of cometary bodies falling between our planet and the sun in their erratic courses, visible and invisible to our ocular powers?

My conjectures I give simply as such, and as a natural outflow of inductive reasoning.

In my thirty-nine years' experience in the upper air I never found an increase of temperature as I ascended. Once, in the month of October, I found it a little warmer up in a mist, nine thousand feet high, and only once, and then without those widely different conditions of but a few minutes of time apart as experienced in the present instance.

THE STRIATED PORTIONS OF AIR,

as noted, seemed like twitchering beams, such as we see over a heated surface in the sunlight, and these spectra seemed not remarkably strange in themselves, since we often behold phenomena of that kind in appearance in the aurora borealis. The dark beam or brush that stretched out over the city was more remarkable since it was not a cloud shadow, because there were no clouds visible except a bank that skirted the horizon; neither was it smoke, but it was a well defined penumbra or shadow, or a dark spectral brush, or negative ray, and it was persistent in its appearance until distance hid it from view. There was also during the two hours of observation more than ordinary refraction of light through the surrounding portions of air. The Delaware, visible from Trenton to the Capes, could in places be seen looming upon the horizon cloud bank, while at others it seemed submerged under the horizon, and this was reasonably the result of the striated condition of the air. When near the Delaware, and while swinging over it, its bottom was distinctly visible within the space of a few miles each way. Even the river-bottom grasses were clearly discernible, although the Delaware is a turbid stream.

THE CAUSES OF ATMOSPHERIC COMMOTIONS.

As it has ever been my practice to relate things as I see them, and to state the instrumental observations as exhibited by the instruments, I herewith submit for general criticism and analysis the results obtained in my earnest and best efforts to subserve science and human progress. There was considerable electrical action manifested in going up and down, as also in passing through different regions. Having no electroscope, I could only notice it in the attractions and repulsions of the fine sand used for ballast, and in the small tissue-paper cards that were thrown out from the car.

The observing and studious scientist will readily comprehend the effects that would follow if a great lenticular body as translucent as the envelop of a comet is should be placed between a planet and the sun. While we have frequent atmospheric convulsions from causes little understood, we have in the present instance a comet in its perihelion passage going between the earth and the sun as a positive datum, and one that should not be overlooked lightly in its meteorological aspect. A filmy cloud or a field of mist, as is occasionally met with by the observing aëronaut, never fails to remind him of the effects of heat and cold attendant upon these interventions in their radiating and reflecting forces. The cosmosphere is full of these meteors, comets and cometary masses; and if it was not Coggia's comet that produced these results of abnormal floods, temperatures, cloud-bursts, thunderbolts, etc., and the phenomenal anomalies of temperature we experienced, what other cause shall we attribute them to?

JOHN WISE.

PHILADELPHIA, August 13, 1874.

# APPENDIX E.

(*From the Signal Service Report for* 1873.)

## THE NOVA SCOTIA AND NEW JERSEY STORMS OF AUGUST, 1873.

WASHINGTON, D. C., September 30, 1873.

SIR: In accordance with instructions received from Colonel Mallery, I have endeavored in the short time at my disposal to prepare a brief preliminary account of the severe cyclone that visited the shores of Nova Scotia and Newfoundland on the 24th and 25th of August last, where it did immense damage, and have also given some attention to the preliminary storm of August 13 and 14, which was severely felt on the shores of New Jersey.

In preparing the maps which accompany this report, an attempt has been made to gather in, from all possible sources of information, such meteorological observations as, although somewhat crude, may enable us to obtain a better understanding of the extent of these storms. To this end application has been made through Captain Howgate for the logs of a number of vessels that have passed in or near the regions visited by the storms in question. A list of the sources of information will be found in the Appendix No. 1, and it is proper here to state that the office is especially indebted to the kindness of the Hon. Secretary of State; the Hon. Secretary of the Navy; Prof. Joseph Henry, of the Smithsonian Institution; Mr. Lorin Blodget, of Philadelphia; the representatives at Washington of the New York *Herald*, *Times* and *Tribune*, and the Boston *Advertiser* and *Journal;* Dr. Smallwood, of Montreal; Prof. Kingston, of Toronto; the captains of the steamship Sonora, brig Dorothea, steamer E. M. Arndt; Mr. T. C. Hill, of Sydney, Cape Breton; W. Allison, of Chatham, Cape Breton; and Mr. H. Clift, of Harbor-Grace, N. F., for courtesies shown in the supplying of such material as was available for the purpose in hand. In Appendix No. 2 will be found a list of those vessels whose logs were used in connection with the observations made upon shore.

Besides the meteorological features of the hurricane, the great destruction of life and property has rendered it proper that I should prepare a brief statement of such details as have been collected up to this date. In this work I have been especially assisted by Sergeant Pearson, who has prepared a detailed map and the accompanying table, in which is shown the geographical distribution of the damage done to life and property. The sums total given in this final table are evidently far within the probable truth, and I have thought it not improper to make the following slight additions in order to arrive at a more correct idea of the ravages of this terrible storm:

One thousand and thirty-two vessels, of which four hundred and thirty-five were small fishing-schooners, are known to have been destroyed during the 24th and 25th of August in the neighborhood of the Gulf of Saint Lawrence and the Atlantic shores of Nova Scotia, Cape Breton and Newfoundland. On the other hand, over ninety vessels were destroyed by this hurricane in the course of its passage over the ocean before reaching Nova Scotia, making a grand total of at least one thousand one hundred and twenty-three vessels destroyed within a few days by its power. Two hundred and twenty-three lives are definitely reported as lost, and the most moderate estimate of the numerous cases in which whole crews are stated to have been lost swells this number to nearly five hundred, while if to this is added the loss of life on land, and the loss in the earlier history of the cyclone, the grand total amounts to at least six hundred lives. The summary given shows that little less than nine hundred buildings were damaged or destroyed during the 24th and 25th of the month. Any endeavor to estimate the value of the property destroyed is attended with great difficulties, but may be within bounds if to the seven hundred thousand dollars damage done to wharves and crops is added one thousand dollars for each building, two thousand dollars for each of the larger vessels, and one thousand dollars for each of the smaller vessels, which would give a total of three and a half millions of dollars—a sum that, it will be seen, may easily be far below the truth. It is not unimportant to here remark that the ravages of this storm have seriously crippled the interests of the American and Canadian fisheries, and that the loss falls with special severity upon Gloucester and other cities of New England.

The following maps* accompanying this report give a general view of the progress of the storm:

Map No. VII. shows the meteorological conditions at 4.35 P. M., Washington time, August 23.

Map No. VIII. shows the meteorological conditions at 4.35 P. M., August 24.

* See Figs. 13, 14, 15, 16 and 17, page 184 *et seq.*—W. B.

Map No. IX. shows the conditions at eleven P. M., August 24.

Map No. X. shows the conditions at 7.35 A. M., August 25.

Map No. XI. shows the conditions at 4.35 P. M., August 25.

On the latter chart the previous track of the storm, as far as it has been traced, is also given; and in Appendix No. 12 is a table giving the geographical positions of the storm-centre, showing it to have been one of a not very large class of cyclonic storms that, beginning in the West Indies, work westward and northward, up between the Bermudas and the Atlantic coast, and then turn north-eastward toward Newfoundland. It is scarcely to be doubted that such a storm as this must have continued its course for several days longer toward Europe; and it is an interesting fact that the *Bulletin International* of the Paris Observatory shows that a severe storm moved over the northern portion of Great Britain on the 31st of August, reaching Norway on the 2d of September; and although no logs of vessels have yet been received from the eastern half of the Atlantic Ocean sufficiently precise to establish the details of the connection between this European storm and that of the preceding days in Nova Scotia, yet the interval of three and a half days is so short as to leave no reasonable doubt but that they were identical.

It has frequently been stated that while no doubt could exist as to the identity in general of the great American and European storms, yet that no single instance of the kind has as yet been well established. It is to be hoped that the present contribution to this subject may be considered as removing all doubt on this matter, although no pains will be spared to secure further testimony.

The principal features of the weather in the Middle and Eastern States during the period embracing the present study may be briefly summarized as follows:

On the morning of the 12th an area of slight barometric depression existed west of the Alleghanies. The temperature throughout that region was of about the normal value; the wind light and variable. The influence of this depression was, however, already perceptible on the Middle Atlantic coast, where easterly winds with clouds and light rain were reported, while over New England and Nova Scotia the barometer stood somewhat about the average value, with northerly winds and clear weather. Vessels off the coast reported north-easterly winds, and those over a hundred miles distant designated these as gales. By the morning of the 13th the barometer had fallen decidedly on the Middle Atlantic coast, and north-easterly winds increasing about to high with rain prevailing throughout these States, while in New England the pressure had slightly risen, it being apparently highest at that time over Maine and New Brunswick. The indraft of air from the ocean continued during the 13th and until the 14th, producing, as has been quite frequently noticed on other occasions, a continued increase of the disturbance that had been initiated the previous day along the Atlantic coast; very heavy rains fell during the night, and a secondary barometric depression appears on that morning to have been central over the peninsula lying between the Chesapeake and Delaware Bays. It is, perhaps, impossible to say whether this depression originated in Virginia or off the Atlantic coast, and whether it had moved north-eastward or merely northward.

This delicate point could have been settled, probably, had we been able to obtain any accurate meteorological reports from the peninsula in question; as it is, the depression passing through Delaware on the nights of the 13th and 14th was apparently accompanied by two, if not three or four, smaller storm-centres, which, being of the nature of tornadoes, seemed to have done considerable damage, both by wind and rain, in Eastern Pennsylvania and in Maryland. The most severe winds were, as is always the case, reported from the New Jersey coast; and destructive as these north-easterly gales were to property on the land, it is satisfactory to be able to refer to the letter of Captain Felber, of the steamship E. M. Arndt, who testifies that, being on his way to New York with a disabled propelling-screw, and relying entirely upon the winds, he was fortunate enough to obtain a copy of the New York *Herald* on the 10th of August, of the preceding day, containing the prediction of continued north-easterly winds along the New England coast, and relying upon this made a speedy and safe passage to the harbor of New York, which he entered at six P. M., August 13.* The storm which on the morning of August 14 was probably central near Long Branch, New Jersey, appears to have increased somewhat in size and severity during the day, producing brisk and high north-easterly winds in Southern New England, which increase was, however, quite in accordance with our previous knowledge of the diurnal growth and subsidence of these phenomena. Owing to the presence of a large body of cold, dry air to the northward, the meteor could advance but very little in that direction; it appears rather to have moved directly eastward, or possibly east-north-eastward, and on the morning of the 15th to have been about

* Capt. Felber doubtless travelled with the polar current in a return oscillation of a preceding north-east storm.—W. B.

one hundred miles south of Cape Cod, while north-easterly winds, diminishing in force and backing to north, prevailed, with clouds and light rains, in New England.

During the 15th easterly winds with rain prevailed at Halifax, and the disturbance seems to have almost completely died away. It is important to notice that, while this comparatively insignificant storm was thus passing north-eastward over New Jersey toward Nova Scotia, the barometer had steadily risen at the Bermudas, with light winds and pleasant weather on the 16th, but with somewhat stronger south-westerly winds and rain on the 13th, 14th and 15th. The highest pressure of the month was attained at the Bermudas on the 18th of August, and rainless weather continned in these islands from the 16th to the 21st of the month; indeed, the drought of August and September has been much complained of by the residents of those islands. During the former interval the cyclone, which has been frequently termed the great Nova Scotia cyclone, was steadily developing some five hundred miles to the southward. The first report that has reached us concerning this hurricane is probably that of the 13th of August, when the bark Crest of the Wave reported a heavy gale veering from north-east to south-east, in latitude 13° and longitude 27°; as, however, our next definite information concerning the hurricane is dated on the 18th of the month, it would be too much to assume more than that the weather experienced by the bark Crest of the Wave was intimately associated with the early history of the Nova Scotia cyclone. The observation, however, deserves to be recorded, inasmuch as several of these storms are already known to have originated not far from the region in which the Crest of the Wave then was, and it is far from impossible but that we shall, by further diligent collocation of ships' reports, be able to carry back the history of the Nova Scotia cyclone from the 18th to the 13th of August, and possibly still further, and to show that this belongs to the class of cyclones that originate near the coast of Senegambia, and distinguished from those that originate further to the west. Be this as it may, the history of the Nova Scotia cyclone since the 18th of August seems to be sufficiently clear. It was at noon of that date in about latitude 22° and longitude 60°, with light north-east winds and falling barometer at the Bermudas; at noon of August 19th it was in latitude 22°, longitude 63°; at noon of August 20th, in latitude 27°, longitude 66°; at noon of August 21st, in latitude 30°, longitude 67.5°, with falling barometer and strong north-easterly winds veering to south-east at the Bermudas; at noon, August 22d, in latitude 33.5°, and longitude 68.5°; at noon of August 23d, in latitude 37° and longitude 67°, with south-westerly gales at the Bermudas. At this time the barometric depression attending the cyclone seems to have extended to a distance of at least five hundred miles north-west and northward of its centre, with falling barometer and cloudy weather reported in New England and Canada, while the report from Mount Washington shows continued north-westerly winds.

In the multiplicity of conflicting accounts concerning the position of vessels and the weather experienced by them on the 23d, 24th and 25th of the month, it is difficult to satisfy that desire for the exact truth which should guide the study of Nature; and in stating as my conclusion that the centre of the cyclone and its most terrific manifestation of power did not pass directly over Nova Scotia, but kept perhaps two hundred miles off its coast, I am aware that discrepant observations may be adduced conflicting with this conclusion. It is my belief, however, that at midnight of the 24th–25th the centre of the storm must have been in latitude 44° and longitude 56°. It was about this time that the lowest barometers were experienced in Halifax, Sidney, Charlotte Town, and also on board several vessels at that time near the coast of Nova Scotia. Between sunset and sunrise of this night occurred the greatest destruction of life and property in this region, due to a terrific easterly wind, which within twenty-four hours backed from south-east to north-west. On the 25th at noon the storm was apparently central in latitude 44.5° and longitude 54.5°. It was at this time that the lowest barometer was reported on the Magdalen Islands, Gulf of St. Lawrence. It is to be remarked, however, that the lowest reading of the barometers in Nova Scotia and the Gulf of St. Lawrence when reduced to the sea-level do not fall below 28.90, while the occasional reports of barometric readings made by vessels at sea, incorrect though they may be, owing to our ignorance of the errors of the instruments, yet uniformly point to a pressure at least as low as 28.30 inches near the centre of the cyclone. On the 25th at midnight it is impossible to locate the region of lowest barometer nearer than is indicated by the winds at Harbor-Grace, Newfoundland, and Cape Breton, which point to the centre as being in latitude 46° and longitude 52°. At noon of the 26th the centre must have been about latitude 47.5° and longitude 50°. At this same rate of progress the centre would at noon of the 27th be in latitude 49.5°, longitude 54.5°. The accompanying table, Appendix No. XII., gives in addition to the preceding positions, which are comparatively well established, also the positions of the barometric depressions that reached the shores of Great Britain a few days subsequently, as shown by the *Bulletin International;* this disturbance was apparently far less severe than that of Nova Scotia, which is in accordance with the well-recognized general rule that these storms gradually extend over a large circular area, and, after diminishing in force, completely break up on encountering large continental masses of dry air.

In connection with this brief sketch of the progress of the Nova Scotia cyclone, I would respectfully direct your attention to the fact that whenever we have telegraphic communication with the Bermudas it will become possible to greatly extend the scope of the storm predictions, and by the co-operation of the fast-sailing European steamers to forewarn vessels leaving the ports of the United States of the existence of any cyclone that may be in progress some distance off the coast. It is indeed evident that, as any portion of the territory covered by the Signal Service stations is liable to storms approaching from the south-east, south-west or north-west, it should be equally protected, if possible, on all sides. The advantages of an extended correspondence with navigators have been very strongly felt in the prosecution of this work, and a very considerable extension in this direction of the work of the Signal Service would seem to be justifiable.

I have the honor to remain, very respectfully, yours,

CLEVELAND ABBE,
*Assistant, Office Chief Signal Officer.*

Brig. Gen. A. J. MYER,
*Chief Signal Officer, United States Army.*

---

## APPENDIX F.

(*From the Signal Service Report for* 1874.)

### MONTHLY WEATHER REVIEW, JULY, 1874.

* * * * * * * * * *

THE influence of the land upon atmospheric pressure has been unusually well marked. Upon Chart No. II. is represented the general distribution of this pressure for the month. A comparison of the months of June and May shows that the area of mean low barometer has moved slowly to the north-eastward, and that it now extends over the centre of the continent; in the mean time, the barometric pressure has increased in the southern and south-eastern portions of the country which is now within the limits of the increased area of high barometer, extending over the Atlantic between the twenty-fifth and fortieth degrees of latitude. During the past three months there has been a gradual increase of pressure in the region last named, the direction of increase being westward from the Atlantic, while during the same time there has been but little change in the mean barometric readings of the central depression. Compared with July, 1873, there has been but little change, both years showing an excess of the mean pressure previously calculated. On the Pacific coast there has been no marked variation from the monthly mean, the pressure being greatest at Portland, Oregon, and least at San Diego, California, thus indicating that the mean pressure on this coast increases with the latitude within the limits of the United States, while the reverse obtains on the Atlantic coast. The barometric range is shown to be greatest in the northern districts near the forty-fifth parallel of latitude, and from this region southward it is gradually diminished, finally becoming least in Florida.

*Areas of high barometer.*—These areas are not traced on the charts, but their general direction of progression has been from the north-west to the south-east; they have moved with less rapidity after reaching the Atlantic, becoming more extended in longitude, conforming to the general contour of the coast, and in some cases extending to the westward, in the direction of the gulf coast. They have also been uniformly attended by fair weather, falling temperature, and less relative humidity, and followed by rain, especially in the Atlantic and Gulf States, after the winds had shifted to easterly.

No. I. The first area observed was central off the South Atlantic coast on the 4th, and gradually extended to the westward, apparently following and displacing the depression which existed in the Gulf during the 2d, 3d and 4th.

No. II. was central in Manitoba on the 10th, passed thence almost due east to the Atlantic by the afternoon of the 12th, after which the pressure increased in the Atlantic and Southern States, and on the 15th it was still traced in the south-eastern portion of the country.

No. III., observed in the Missouri valley on the 15th, had passed from the Pacific coast south-eastward to this position, after which it extended over the southern portions of the country, and disappeared on the 26th.

No. IV. During the 28th, 29th, 30th and 31st this area moved from the north-west to the South Atlantic coast, succeeding the depression which was attended by unusual rains in the Eastern and Middle States. . . .

*Areas of low barometer.*—Eleven areas of atmospheric depression have been observed.

No. I. was apparent in Manitoba on June 30, and moved rapidly toward the Atlantic coast during July 1 and 2, following the general course of the great lakes, and moving with less progressive velocity as it approached the coast.

No. II. was attended by the unusual rains near the gulf coast during the 2d, 3d and 4th, and is interesting from the fact that it is the first barometric depression of the season which originated in the tropics having a progressive movement to the westward. This storm had its parallel in July of last year, but usually they are not observed within the limits of the United States until the season is more advanced. Its westerly course, with a velocity of twelve miles an hour, carried the centre of the depression slowly toward the dry and sandy plains of Texas, where it disappeared, and was followed by the succeeding high barometer from the Atlantic coast, which now moved to the westward and became central in the Lower Missouri valley on the morning of July 6. The same cause which produced the shifting of the mean tracks of barometric depressions in the temperate zone may be equally effective in changing the mean latitude of tropical storms.

No. III. The approach of this depression from the extreme North-west was indicated by the reports from that region on the 2d of July, while No. 1 continued within the limits of the eastern station and No. 2 in an undeveloped condition in the gulf. It passed from its initial position to the eastward as far as Lake Huron without marked results, except that on the morning of the 3d it had almost lost its identity as a defined area of low barometer, the centre of depression having increased thirty-five hundredths of an inch, and the gradient diminished from 0.1 inch in eighty miles to 0.1 inch in two hundred miles. On the morning of the 4th this depression had taken the form of a slightly eccentric ellipse, the transverse axis of which coincided with the forty-fourth degree of north latitude, and was four hundred miles in length.

The area of high barometer which had previously extended over the districts on the Atlantic coast, and which by its southerly wind had accumulated a supply of vapor in these districts, now moved to the south and westward, apparently drawing the depression toward the coast in the most direct line. In this, as in other storms, there has been a deviation to the south of the direct course as the depression approached the coast.

Severe local storms occurred in the southern half of this depression, while its centre was near the eastern portion of Lake Erie, the region of greatest severity being near the Atlantic coast, and including New Jersey, Delaware, Maryland and the eastern portions of Pennsylvania and Virginia.

Nos. IV. and V. No decided change occurred in the atmospheric condition within the United States until the 7th, although there seems to have been some disturbance in the Lower St. Lawrence valley, which caused local storms in the northern portions of New York. The general barometric depression in the north-west now contracted as an area of low barometer, central in the western portions of Kansas, and moving slowly to the eastward during the succeeding twenty-four hours, completely lost its cyclonic appearance in the Upper Mississippi valley. This was succeeded by No. V., an extensive depression central in the Upper Ohio valley, indicating an unstable condition of the atmosphere throughout the country east of the Mississippi River. After the barometric gradient had increased, this storm passed to the north-east to the Lower Lake region, where it seems to have been retarded, the easterly movement of its centre during thirty-six hours being less than two hundred and fifty miles, while its movements in latitude were much greater.

No. VI. This disturbance was indicated by the appearance of an extended trough of barometric depression on the afternoon of July 11. It had taken the form of a circular depression, central in the Upper Ohio valley on the succeeding morning, when a small central area could be distinctly traced. A general rain prevailed at this time in the districts of the Atlantic coast and in the Lower Lake region, the course of the storm being directly to the east, with a mean velocity of twenty-five miles per hour, and a greater barometric gradient of 0.1 inch in fifty miles.

No. VII. Observed in the North-west on the morning of the 14th, while an area of decidedly high barometer extended over that portion of the United States south of the Lake region. These general conditions continued while this depression moved almost directly east toward the Lower St. Lawrence valley without producing any serious disturbance within the limits of the United States. Generally it has been observed that the relative positions of the areas of high and low barometer materially affect the course of the latter, and that the former seem to deflect the latter from their mean tracks.

Nos. VIII. and IX. were only partially developed areas of low barometer, central in the North-west near the boundary of the United States on the 18th and 22d. They produced no disturbance, but caused a rise of temperature in the Mississippi valley.

From the 21st until the 25th the barometer continued low in the Western Territories, with but slight changes of pressure within the States until the development of storm marked No. X., which can be traced to the west of the Rocky Mountains by a reference to the barometric readings taken at the stations in the Far West. This storm moved with quite a uniform velocity of about forty miles per hour, producing heavy rains over a belt of country seven hundred miles in width, extending from the Upper Mississippi valley to the Atlantic coast. The midnight reports of July 26 show that the depression divided, leaving a small elliptical area in the Ohio valley to the south-west of Lake Erie, while the principal area was to the north-east of this position. Such a distribution of pressure would necessarily give a continuous supply of warm moist air flowing from the south-east over Ohio and Pennsylvania, while a supply of cold currents flowing from the north and west in the rear of the more advanced depression would be forced over the same region. It was the sudden interference of these currents which produced the heavy rains which occurred in Western Pennsylvania on the night of the 26th. On the morning of the 27th the depressions had again united, forming an extended but narrow trough nearly parallel to the coast, where southerly winds continued, while in the Lower Lake region and the St. Lawrence valley the winds had backed to north and west. This depression did not pass directly to the Atlantic, but apparently extended over the entire country south of the Lake region, and continued until the 29th, when it was replaced by an equally extensive area of high barometer.

No. XI. The afternoon report of the 29th from the north-west indicated the approach of this depression, but at no succeeding report could its centre be more than approximately located; it passed to the north of the lakes, and was only attended by light local rains in the regions north of the Ohio valley.

*Local Storms.*—These storms have been particularly marked for their severity during the past month. Their occurrence seems to depend upon the relative distribution of barometric pressure considered in relation to the topography of the country. The region of greatest frequency has been in the vicinity of the Appalachian chain, where the vapor from the gulf and the Atlantic was forced over the ascending plains by the prevailing southerly and south-westerly winds. Those producing the greatest destruction of life and property occurred on the 4th, 7th, 24th and 26th of the month. On the afternoon of July 4 the depression already referred to as No. 3 was central near the eastern portion of Lake Erie; at midnight this depression was located near the eastern boundary of New York, south of its previous position. The sudden veering of the winds in the south and west quadrants of this area was attended by violent storms during the afternoon and evening in the States of Maryland, Virginia, Delaware, New Jersey and Pennsylvania. From an examination of a large number of reports referring to these storms, it is shown that the regions of severity were limited in area, and that the storms uniformly approached from the north-west. The storm of the 24th occurred at Eureka, Nevada, and was very destructive; but no official report has been received concerning it. . . .

---

## MONTHLY WEATHER REVIEW, AUGUST, 1874.

* * * * * * * * * *

*Areas of low barometer* accompanying Chart No. I. show that the paths of the centres of eleven have, approximately, been traced. Their centres have been located for each synchronous observation (three times daily), and these connected. In case of doubt as to their position they were united by broken lines. Such are observed during every month, as many pass to the north of the Lower Lake region and the St. Lawrence valley on their way eastward. Frequently they leave minor depressions within the limit of the stations. In detail they are as follows:

No. I. properly belongs to July, having moved from Dakota eastward over the Upper Lake region to the St. Lawrence valley on the 29th, 30th and 31st ultimo. On the 1st and 2d instant it disappeared to the eastward, having been accompanied by generally light thunder-storms from the lower lakes, Ohio valley, Tennessee and the south Atlantic States eastward. A hurricane prevailed on Mount Washington on the 1st, and a tornado at Troy, N. Y., on the 2d.

No. II. was first felt on the 3d at the Rocky Mountain stations by cloudy, threatening or rainy weather and brisk southerly winds.

Very heavy hail fell on the "divide" between Denver and Colorado Springs, Col. At the latter place a bank of water passed down the creek at seven P. M., sweeping everything, and supposed to have been caused by the hail-storm. On the 4th the barometer fell quite rapidly from the Upper Mississippi valley westward, with increasing east to south winds. At St. Paul violent high winds prevailed during the evening. The centre passed within the limit of the stations on the 4th, and down the Missouri Valley on the 5th, with threatening or rainy weather from thence to the upper lakes. On the 6th it separated into two, one gradually disappearing over the Indian Territory, the other following the course shown on the chart. Cloudy or rainy weather accompanied it, except in the Gulf States. Remarkably heavy rains fell on the Middle Atlantic and New England coasts, with brisk and high easterly winds. Violent thunder-storms are reported as having occurred in Ohio, Indiana, New York, Pennsylvania and North Carolina.

No. III. passed to the south and east of Nova Scotia on the 6th, producing rain and brisk east to north winds in that section. It was evidently a cyclone, and most severe at some distance off the coast. A sailing-vessel reported having experienced a hurricane for eight hours upon this date in that vicinity, the wind backing from east to north.

No. IV. was first observed by the falling barometer and high temperature on the 8th and 9th, at the stations in the Rocky Mountains and the Lower Missouri valley. From Nebraska and Iowa southward to the Gulf States the temperature continued rising, and thermometer readings varying from 100° to 106° were reported for several days. On the 10th the centre moved within the limit of the stations; on the 11th north-eastward over Lake Superior into Canada; on the 12th to the north of the St. Lawrence Valley, leaving depressions in the Lower Missouri valley and New England. Occasional rain fell during its progress over the North-west and the Lake region, but became quite general, with severe thunder-storms in New England and the Middle States. A destructive tornado prevailed at Dixon, Ill., and a gale at St. Paul, during the night of the 10th; violent north-west winds at Davenport, Iowa, on the night of the 11th; hurricane on Mount Washington and severe thunder-storm at Berlin Heights, Ohio, on the night of the 12th.

No. V. moved eastward from Dakota on the 15th, 16th, and 17th over the Upper Lake region into Canada, accompanied by occasional rain, with high winds at St. Paul on the evening of the 16th and a hurricane on Mount Washington during the night of the 18th.

No. VI. During the day the barometer fell very rapidly over the North-west, with brisk south and east winds, and during the night of the 18th the central depression passed from Dakota to Minnesota, and thence, on the 19th, over Lake Superior into Canada. Rain fell in the North-west and Lake region, and at places high winds prevailed.

No. VII. advanced from Dakota on the 20th. The peculiarity of this consists in that it sent out in advance a secondary depression over the middle Atlantic coast, producing at places severe thunder-storms. In the States east of the Rocky Mountains rainy weather accompanied them, with also severe thunder-storms in the Southern States.

No. VIII., appearing from Dakota, moved down the Missouri valley and disappeared over the South-west without producing any serious disturbance.

Nos. IX. and X. The low barometric readings at the Rocky Mountain stations on the 26th and 27th indicated the presence of a serious disturbance. On the 27th the pressure rapidly diminished from the Upper Mississippi valley westward, and on the 28th there appeared an extensive trough of low barometer, extending from Indian Territory northward over Minnesota and Manitoba, but being lowest over the latter and the Lower Missouri valley. Previous to this time it is probable there was one low barometer, which gradually developed into the two. From the chart. it will be seen that No. IX., after separating into three distinct areas, finally disappeared in the Southern States and Ohio valley. In their movements across the country cloudy or rainy weather became quite general, except in the west Gulf States, Lower Lake region, Middle States and New England, with very serious and destructive storms. Heavy rains and high winds are reported from Iowa, Tennessee, Georgia, Louisiana, and no doubt occurred in all the Southern States.

No. XI. was of minor importance, producing rain in Maine and the eastern British Provinces. It apparently united with No. X. over the mouth of the St. Lawrence River.

*Areas of high barometer.*—Of the most marked, the *first* apparently extended itself south-eastward, on the 2d and 3d, from Manitoba over the Lake region, and on the 4th and 5th over the Atlantic States. The *second*, following low barometer No. IV., first appeared over the Lake region from Manitoba on the 12th and 13th, where it remained nearly stationary until the 15th, and .extended itself over the Middle States and to the east Atlantic coast on the 16th and 17th. On the 18th and 19th the *third* gradually appeared over the

Lower Lake region, Middle and South Atlantic States, which extended over the South Atlantic and East Gulf States on the 19th and 20th, and then slowly disappeared. The *fourth*, following low barometer No. VII., was felt over the Lake region on the 24th, moved over New England and the Middle States on the 25th, and disappeared on the 28th in advance of depressions Nos. IX., X. and XI. On the 31st the *fifth* moved south-eastward over the Lake region, succeeding low barometers Nos. IX. and X. The movement of these areas has been confined principally to the Lake region and the Atlantic States. They have been more prominent than heretofore for August, and have failed to reach the Southern and Western States, especially the South-west and West, over which sections the barometer has continued low for longer periods than usual.

---

## MONTHLY WEATHER REVIEW, SEPTEMBER, 1874.

* * * * * * * * * *

*Areas of low barometer.*—The tracks pursued by the areas of low pressure are given on Map No. I.; further details are found in the following paragraphs. It will be seen that these have, as in previous years, been frequently pushed far to the west and north, but that the better-developed, severe cyclones Nos. I., III., IV., V. and XIII. have pursued tracks differing but little from their normal courses.

Storm No. I. This small but well-marked cyclonic depression became first apparent on the 1st, near Nova Scotia, but kept to the eastward of that province, and passed beyond Cape Breton, without being accompanied by high winds on the land as far as reported. In its earlier course during the latter part of August, this storm may have passed near and to the north-east of the Bermudas.

No. II. This depression moved eastward over Lake Superior to the Gulf of St. Lawrence, followed by an area of high barometer, and generally accompanied by rain in the Lower Lake region and St. Lawrence Valley. While this disturbance was central over the Gulf of St. Lawrence, on the 3d, a belt of notable contrasts of temperature extended from Iowa to New England, and severe gales were reported in Eastern Massachusetts, followed by rapidly-falling temperatures.

No. III. The brisk and high north-east winds that prevailed on the 3d on the western coast of Texas appear to have been connected with the presence of a barometric depression in Northern Mexico, and which may originally have entered that country from the Pacific coast, as the barometer was below the average in Southern California during the preceding day. If a definite central area of depression existed on the 2d and 3d in Mexico and Texas, its location must have been approximately as given on the chart. The cyclonic character of the disturbance on the 4th is not well shown by our observations, but may reasonably be inferred from the severity of the gale which raged on the 4th and 5th from Galveston southward, and which resulted in a large destruction of property along that coast. The barometric disturbance undoubtedly spent itself, in great part, in Central Texas, where, however, the depression continued during the 7th, and on the 8th the existence of a storm-centre in the interior of Kansas became evident. This depression then continued its course northward to Manitoba, which it passed on the 10th.

No. IV. While the severe storm mentioned in the previous paragraph was moving northward into Texas, a similar and better developed cyclone was pursuing an almost parallel course about one thousand five hundred miles to the eastward. The published weather-maps of the morning of the 7th show the existence of this storm a short distance south-east of Nova Scotia. Its previous history has been traced by means of the published logs of ocean-vessels, from which it appears that during the 5th the storm-centre passed a short distance south-west of the Bermudas, where the gale was quite severe, and on the 6th recurved on its northward track, and that as early as the 2d instant its force was felt by a vessel in latitude 28° 10′ and longitude 55° 38′. The track given on Chart No. 1 may be regarded as a first approximate determination of its course, which, on the afternoon of the 7th, passed over Cape Breton Island. The lowest depression observed at Cape Breton was 28.75, which corresponds with the figures reported from ocean vessels, by many of which the hurricane wind was described as being one of the most severe ever experienced.

No. V. The cyclone No. IV. was immediately followed by No. V., which passed nearly midway between Cape Hatteras and the Bermudas on the 9th, producing high winds on the North Carolina coast. The path of this depression remained persistently some distance east of the Atlantic coast, but its centre must have passed quite near Cape Breton on the morning of the 11th.

No. VI. This depression was preceded by rain and low barometer, with southerly winds in Oregon on the 10th. It was itself first well defined on the afternoon of the 11th, when it was central in Minnesota. The cold north-westerly winds that followed in its rear gave rise to numerous rain-areas from Missouri to the Upper Lake region while the barometric depression moved rapidly north-eastward over Lake Superior and beyond our station.

No. VII. The origin of this depression during the 13th appears to have been similar to that of area No. III., the barometer having been reported quite low during the 11th in Southern California, and the existence of a depression in Northern Mexico and Western Texas, on the 12th and 13th, may be inferred from the prevailing winds. This depression was, however, but very feebly marked, as it moved eastward, and became more or less marked by the influence of depression No. VIII. to the northward. On the afternoon of the 15th, however, No. VII. became distinctly separate from No. VIII., and on the morning of the 16th was central in North Carolina, while north-east winds and heavy rains extended from that State north-eastward to New England. The further history of this disturbance becomes very interesting, from the fact that an unexpectedly large area of high barometer moved into the Gulf of St. Lawrence, whence a stream of air flowed steadily for over three days from the north-east along the Middle and East Atlantic coasts, bringing cloud and rain to all that region, and causing the barometric depression to dwindle away and disappear as it moved *north-westward* into Central New York. The rains of the 15th, 16th and 17th ended the drought which had prevailed for six weeks on the Middle and East Atlantic coasts.

No. VIII. This depression, of which but slight and uncertain traces are visible previous to the afternoon of the 13th, moved eastward into Upper Canada, where it was lost sight of on the 15th.

No. IX. The low barometric pressure that prevailed on the 14th and 15th from California to Texas was probably the initiative of a disturbance that was central on that day in Montana, and on the 16th in Dakota, whence it slowly moved into Manitoba, and thence apparently eastward.

No. X. This depression developed slowly in Kansas and Northern Texas on the 16th and 17th, and was well defined on the 18th, as it passed eastward over the Lower Missouri valley into Illinois. On this day occurred the lowest barometer during the month in Kansas, New Mexico, Colorado, etc. In the south-eastern portion of Iowa and the adjacent portions of Illinois and Missouri the wind and rain on the 18th were exceedingly severe, and much damage was reported. The course of this storm-centre then turned northward over Upper

Michigan into Canada, producing high south-west wind on lakes Michigan, Erie and Huron on the 19th.

No. XI. This disturbance was preceded by a low barometer in Southern California, and probably southward over Mexico, but itself apparently had an origin on the border of Texas and Mexico on the 22d, in a manner similar to that of No. X., since it would appear that during the previous two days dry, cold currents of air flowing south-eastward from the extreme north-western part of Texas underran and uplifted the warm air of the plains. On the 24th this area of low barometer passed northward over Indian Territory, and on the 25th united with No. XII., which had rapidly developed in Montana.

No. XII. The trough of low pressure that stretched during the 25th from Kansas to Manitoba had, by midnight of that day, contracted to a small area in Minnesota, which moved slowly eastward into Canada, developing a quite low central pressure, and accompanied by southerly winds and rain over the lower lakes on the 26th and 27th.

No. XIII. While No. XII. threatened on the 26th to give rise to a very severe storm on the lakes, a notable cyclonic disturbance moved north-eastward over the Gulf of Mexico for whose early history no data have as yet been received. Its existence was first rendered evident by strong north-east winds on the Texas coast on the afternoon of the 25th, at which time the central depression must have been south of Louisiana, and possibly near Yucatan or Mexico. During the nights of the 27th and 28th the centre passed north-eastwardly over Upper Florida to the coast of Georgia, pursuing a track medial between those followed by storms Nos. VI. and VII. of September, 1873. As the present cyclone passed along the Carolina coast on the 28th, it developed a force that has been very generally compared to the hurricane of 1854. The centre of this storm passed a short distance east of Charleston and west of Wilmington and Norfolk, crossing Chesapeake Bay on the morning of the 29th; here the violence of the winds sensibly diminished, while the barometric depression spread irregularly in various directions. After passing east of the New Jersey coast the storm seems to have turned northward through New England, and is lost sight of on the afternoon of the 30th at the mouth of the St. Lawrence. . . .

*Areas of high barometer.*—Of these areas the most notable has been No. V., which obtained its greatest development on the 18th, when it was probably central on the Gulf of St. Lawrence.

No. I. This passed from British America on the 1st, south-eastward over the lakes to the Carolina coast on the 2d, followed by storm No. II. on its north-eastern boundary, and by the still higher pressure of the next paragraph.

No. II. is first reported in Oregon and British Columbia on the 2d. It moved south-eastward over Dakota on the 3d, to South Carolina and Georgia on the 8th. Clear, dry weather accompanied it over the greater part of the country, except the Texas coast, during that period.

No. III. began to press southward over the St. Lawrence valley on the 12th, and after passing over New England disappeared east of Cape Cod on the 15th.

No. IV. was, apparently, a western division of the same area of cold, dry air, and moved south-eastward on the 12th over Dakota, disappearing on the 14th over the Lake region.

No. V. appears on the 14th as a continuation of No. IV., and extended on the morning of that day over the Upper Missouri valley. It passed thence eastward to the Upper Lake region on the 16th, where it appears to have been reinforced by further contributions from Hudson Bay and Labrador, forming an unusually extensive area of high pressure, whose centre was over the Gulf of St. Lawrence on the 18th and 19th, where the barometric readings averaged 30.70 on the morning of the former day. The influence of this high barometer in producing continued easterly winds and rain on the New England and New Jersey coasts from the 15th to the 20th has already been alluded to.

No. VI. The extensive area of low pressure prevailing over the Lake region on the 18th and 19th seems not only to have drawn from the northward and eastward the air that produced the high barometer of the preceding section, but also induced a flow from the south and west that gave rise to No. VI., whose existence may be traced from the Ohio valley on the morning of the 21st, backward to Indian Territory on the 19th, and forward over Maryland on the 22d to the Middle Atlantic coast, where traces of it still remained on the 26th.

No. VII. This area began, like the preceding one, in or near Texas, and, like it, its origin is attributable to the presence of an area of low pressure (No. XIII.) which existed on the 27th in the Gulf of Mexico. Like it, also, the highest barometer at centre moved eastward, and was not remarkably conspicuous.

www.ingramcontent.com/pod-product-compliance
Lightning Source LLC
LaVergne TN
LVHW010149110826
845151LV00002B/465

* 9 7 8 1 4 2 5 5 3 7 1 9 7 *